Martial Arts
Instructor's
Desk Reference

Martial Arts
Instructor's
Desk Reference

Sang H. Kim, Ph.D.

Turtle Press   Hartford

To contact the author or to order additional copies of this book:
Turtle Press, P. O. Box 290206, Wethersfield, CT 06129-0206. (800) 778-8785

LCCN 2002008281
ISBN 1-880336-71-5
Printed in USA
9 8 7 6 5 4 3

DISCLAIMER

Exercises described in this book may be strenuous and may result in injury to the practitioner. Readers should understand the potential dangers of an exercise before performing or teaching it. This book is intended to provide information about the subject matter covered. It is sold with the understanding that publisher and author are not rendering legal, accounting or other professional services. Neither the author nor the publisher assumes any responsibility for the use or misuse of information contained in this book.

Library of Congress Cataloguing in Publication Data

Kim, Sang H.
    Martial arts instructor's desk reference : a complete guide to martial arts administration / by Sang H. Kim.
        p. cm.
Includes index.
    ISBN 1-880336-71-5 (pbk.)
    1. Martial arts—Study and teaching—Handbooks, manuals, etc. 2. Martial arts schools—Administration—Handbooks, manuals, etc. I. Title.
    GV1102.7.S85 K56 2002
    796.8—dc21
                                    2002008281

Contents

Drills, Drills, Drills **10**

  Safety 11
     Competition 11
  Conditioning 13
  Basic Movements 20
     Basic Movements: Individual 20
     Basic Movements: Partner 22
     Basic Movements: Group 26
  Self-defense 31
  Forms 34
  Sparring 36
  Mental Training 39
  40 Ways to Disguise Repetition 41

Nuts and Bolts **44**

  Conditioning Exercises 45
     Flexibility 45
     Strength 46
     Endurance 46
     Agility 47
  Interval Training 48
     Sample Interval Training 49
  Art and Science of Timing 50
     Time Factors 50
     Space Factors 51
     X Factors 52
  Injury Prevention Essentials 53
  Preventing Overuse Injuries 56
     Warning Signs 56
  Teaching Self-defense 57
     Basic Skills 57
     Safety Cautions 58
  Sparring Without Fear 59
     Source of Fear 59
     Application 59
     Contact 60
  Sparring: Why Teach It? 61
  Summer Training Safety 64
     5 Ways to Reduce Heat Related Risk 65
     Avoiding Dehydration 65
  Realistic Form Applications 66
  Introducing Weapon Training 69
     Choosing a Weapon 69
     Introducing the Weapon 69
     Teaching the Basics 70

Teaching Children **72**
   Methods of Learning 74
      Reinforcement 74
      Association 74
      Insight 75
   Factors Affecting Learning 76
      Asking vs. Telling 76
   Short Attention Spans 79
   Attention Deficit Disorder 81
      Four Symptoms in Detail 82
      Other Personality Traits 83
      Myths about ADD: 85
      ADD Facts: 86
      Strategies for Improving Behavior 87
      Handling Non-Compliant Children 91
   Reinforcement or Punishment 92
      Using Positive Reinforcement 92
      Giving Directions 92
      Strategies for Long-Term Change 93
      Using Negative Reinforcement 94
      Using Negative Consequences 96
      Promoting Self-discipline 97
   Improving Attention Spans 98
   Learning Disabilities 102
   Dealing with Aggression 105
   Separation Anxiety 108
   Shyness 113
   Developmental Stages 116
      Ages 4-6 116
      Ages 7-9 118
      Ages 10-12 119

Class Management **120**
   The Ideal Schedule 121
   Setting Objectives 125
   Class Intensity 126
   Class Structure 128
   Teaching New Skills 129
      Introducing Skills 129
      Observational Learning 129
      Shaping 130
   Teaching Complex Skills 132
      Motivation 132
      Rewards 132
   Roll Tape 134
   Educational Goals 136
   Evaluation 140
      Testing Objectives 141
   Effective Promotion Testing 142

Student Retention **144**
  15 Retention Strategies 145
    Preventing Dropouts 145
    Instructor Related Reasons 145
    Staying in Touch 147
    Student Related Reasons 147
    External Factors 149
  Retaining Female Students 151
  Black Belt Retention 154
    Adult Motivation 154
  Analyzing Student Retention 156
    Identifying Causes 157
    Analyzing Trends 159
    Taking Action 159
  Managing Parents 160

Public Relations **166**
  The Value of Publicity 167
  Types of Publicity 170
  The Press Release 173
    Format 174
    The Headline 176
    The Body of the Release 176
    Supporting Materials 177
    Presentation 178
    Follow-up 178
  Targeting the Right Media 180
    Newspapers 180
    Magazines 186
    Radio 190
    Television 191
  Professional Phone Tips 194
  Power of the Internet 197
    Promotion 197
    Communication 198
    Maintenance 199
  Creating a Professional Image 200
    Atmosphere 200

Marketing **202**
  Low Cost Marketing 203
  Marketing Strategy 217
    Price and Place 219
    Promotion 220
  Myths of Advertising 223
  Setting Tuition Rates 228
  Summer Survival Tips 231
  Economic Cycles 234
    Anatomy of a Decline 234

Growth 237
Saturation 240

Hosting a Tournament 242
Attributes of Success 243
Selecting the Right Size 247
    Tournament Size Worksheet 251
Budgeting 253
    Budget Worksheet 253
Staffing 258
Master Timeline 262
Purchasing Supplies 265
The Entry Package 268
Post Event Reporting 270

Instructor Survival 272
Motivation 273
Managing Change 275
Defusing Anger 277
Preventing Burnout 280
Limited Training Time 283
Controlling Nervousness 285
Instructor Assessment 287

Building Leadership 290
Building Leadership 291
Staffing 293
    Why Hire? 293
    Staff Retention 293
    Staff Positions 294
    Communication 297
Selecting Instructors 298
    Evaluation Scale 298
    Instructor Competence 300
Outreach Programs 302
    The Benefits 302
    Getting Started 304
    Program Structure 305
    Negotiating 305
    Staff Conflicts 307
    Making it a Success 307
Branch Schools 309
Solutions 309
Pros and Cons 310
Choosing a Location 311
The Teaching Staff 312

Drills, Drills, Drills

Over 300 ways to make classes fun and exciting

In this section . . .

11   Safety
13   Conditioning
20   Basic Movements
31   Self-defense
34   Forms
36   Sparring
39   Mental Training
41   40 Ways to Disguise Repetition

Competition

Friendly competition is a healthy way to pump up the energy of a class.

Many games and drills can be modified into simple competitions, especially for children's classes. As long as you keep the competition fun and fair by teaming or pairing strong performers with weaker performers, kids look forward to this segment of class.

Give everyone a chance to win by varying the nature of the competition.

In addition to the more traditional games of strength and skill, try easy contests to see who can:

• name everyone in class
• count to ten in Japanese
• name 5 kicks in Korean
• stand on one leg longest
• do the slowest push-up
• recite the meaning of their belt

"Teaching classes every day, year after year can quickly become monotonous."

Drills, Drills, Drills

Over 300 ways to make classes fun and exciting

Boredom—your students' boredom and your own—is your biggest enemy as a martial arts instructor. Teaching classes every day, year after year quickly become monotonous if you are not constantly searching for new teaching ideas, drills, games, exercises and techniques. Not only do your students get bored doing the same old drills, you get bored teaching them over and over. To maintain an excited, active student body and keep yourself excited about teaching, you need a ready source of ideas and brain ticklers.

This section is meant to be just that: a resource that you can turn to while you are developing your lesson plans or just before you head out of the office to start a class, a quick reference guide packed with new ideas as well ideas you have long forgotten or that lead you to create your own games and drills. Before we look at the drills, let's cover a few basics about how to use this section and how to safely implement new ideas in your classes.

Safety

A major concern in teaching is safety. Introducing a new skill or drill increases the chance of an injury occurring. There are several reasons for this:

1. New skills can cause confusion if directions are not given clearly or students are allowed to practice them unsupervised. **Walk through each new skill and demonstrate it** before letting students try it out. Supervise practice carefully. Correct or stop students who are not executing skills correctly.

2. New skills often use previously unused muscles or actions. **Introduce new skills only after preliminary conditioning** for the skill has been completed. For example, if you plan to introduce a jumping spinning kick in three weeks, lead up to it by doing plenty of stretching and strengthening of the leg and torso muscles that power the kick.

3. New skills may be harmful to students of certain ages, weights, skill levels or ability levels. Thoroughly **test each new skill** for potential problems before introducing it to the class.

4. Students may not understand the risk associated with new skills. **Explain what students should or should not do** to limit the risk of a new skill.

5. Equipment used in the skill may be faulty, dangerous or difficult to use. **Inspect all equipment** to be used prior to each class and instruct students in its proper use.

Using this Section

Drills, Drills, Drills is divided into six categories to make it easy for you to quickly find the type of drill, game or idea you are looking for. Many ideas can be adapted to fit other categories with small modifications, but each is listed only once in the category where it best fits.

1. **Conditioning**: Fun ways to strengthen, stretch and condition the body

2. **Basic Movements**: New ideas to take the repetition out of practice

3. **Self-Defense**: Exciting drills to make self-defense practice more realistic

4. **Forms**: Unique ways to reduce boredom on the road to perfection

5. **Sparring**: Exciting tips to pump up sparring practice

6. **Mental Training**: Unique suggestions for training the mind with the body

Animal Conditioning Drills

Put some fun in warm-ups for kids by imitating animals. Use your imagination and get the kids using their large muscle groups for strengthening and endurance.

- **Frog jumping** (squat down and bounce up high)
- **Snake crawling** (slither along with lots of wiggle in the midsection)
- **Monkey hopping** (bound across the room in quick succession)
- **Kangaroo leaping** (go for height or distance)
- **Crab walking** (great for upper and lower body coordination)
- **King Kong stomping** (get those knees up really high)
- **Tiger running** (speed running on all fours)
- **Alligator walking** (get in push-up position and walk forward on all fours moving right arm/leg together then left arm/leg together)
- **Chicken walking** (flap those wings and strut around)
- **Bird take-offs** (arms up over the head, then down to sides as they jump up)
- **Seal walking** (lie on the belly, hands in push-up position and legs flat, use the hands to walk forward while the legs drag behind like a seal's back flippers)
- **Duck walking** (squat and walk low)
- **Inchworm crawling** (in push-up position, walk the legs forward so the hips come up high, then move the hands forward so the body lowers back to push-up position)

Races

Kids love races and races are a fun way to burn off some energy. Use them to pump up a class at the start, tire out the kids for a more serious drill or reward a good class.

- **Animal races**: let the kids choose what animal they will imitate
- **Relay races**: make teams and race across the floor and back
- **Disciplined relays**: the winning team is first one to finish racing *and* be sitting in a straight, quiet line
- **Hopping races**: each kid has to hop (skip, jump) across the floor; for more challenge, hop holding a ball between the knees
- **Hoop race**: place a series of hula hoops on the floor, kids hop from one to the next across the floor
- **Elimination races**: have a single elimination contest to crown a grand champion
- **Three legged races**: partner similar size kids and have them make a three legged team using one of their belts to tie their legs together
- **Wheelbarrow races**: one kid holds the other's feet while he races across the floor on his hands
- **Shuttle run racing**: each kid races across the floor, touches a target and races back
- **Technique races**: do movements (punching, front kicking, footwork) quickly across the floor
- **Theme races**: kids imitate running in mud, against the wind, up hill, over hot coals, like their favorite cartoon/video game character
- **Leap frog races**: two person teams alternate between squatting and leaping over the squatting partner.

Obstacle courses

Making an obstacle course on the mat is a great class starter for children's classes. Don't let anyone stand around waiting in line. Assign an exercise like jumping jacks or running place between turns at a station. Some ideas for stations to keep everyone moving:

- Jump over a pile of kicking shields
- Crawl through a tunnel of kicking shields without touching them
- Jump over a series of heavy bags laid about two feet apart
- Kick or strike a hanging target, hanging bag or stand up heavy bag
- Weave around a line of hand targets
- Duck walk under a hanging heavy bag
- Look in the mirror and yell (kihap/kiai) loudly five times
- Roll between two kicking shields without touching them
- Block an "attack" by a blocker or foam wand
- Kick a paper cup off of the top of a standing bag
- Crawl under a stick balanced on two chairs
- Walk on a line on the floor (masking tape works well & removes easily after use)
- Hop over a belt laid on the floor to form a zigzag course
  Some stations may require an adult to reset or facilitate.

10/100

If you do a lot of routine conditioning exercises, go around the room and have each student count off ten of an exercise while the whole class does them.

Example: Start with each of 10 students counting out 10 jumping jacks for a total of 100, then have 10 students each count off ten push-ups for a total of 100. The next ten students each count off 10 sit-ups for a total of 100.

Counting for the class also helps develop confidence and leadership skills.

Group Warm-up

Make three to four small groups, each led by a black belt or advanced student. Each leader has a specific task like stretching, lower body strengthening or ab/back strengthening.

Give five minutes for the leaders to take their groups through a series of appropriate exercises. Then have the groups change leaders, so each leader takes a new group through his set of assigned exercises. Keep rotating until every leader has worked out every group.

Tag

This is another classic game that kids can instantly relate to. It gets them excited, makes them move quickly and gets their brains thinking about strategy.

- **Classic tag.** One child is *it* and he has to tag the other players. When he tags someone, that player becomes *it*. Players can be tagged anywhere in the room, except when they are on *home base*, a designated safe spot. No player can stay on home base for more than fifteen seconds at a time.

- **Freeze tag.** When a player is tagged by *it*, they become frozen in place until they are tagged and freed by another player (not *it*). The first person to be tagged three times becomes *it*.

Balance Games

Develop balance and leg strength with these one-legged balance games:

- **Gombae paree:** Partners stand about two feet apart, each standing on one leg and holding the other foot in both hands in front of him just below his belt. On your signal, partners hop towards one another and try to knock each other down. Players must hold their foot with both hands at all times and use only their body weight (no knees or elbows) to unbalance each other. The first to touch any part of his body other than his hopping foot to the ground is the loser.

- **Gombae paree with shields:** Instead of using the body to knock down the opponent, give each student a kicking shield. Both students hop on one foot holding the kicking shield at belt height. On your cue, they try to unbalance each other as in gombae paree. Contact with the other person can be made only using the blocking shield.

Back-to-Back Standing

- Pair off students of similar size. Each pair sits back-to-back on the floor with their legs bent and their arms interlocked with their partner's at the elbow. On cue, they try to stand up together. Variations:

- Partners sit back-to-back, but do not lock arms. On your cue, they lean into each other and try to stand.

- Three or four students sit in a circle with their backs to the center of the circle (touching each other) and lock arms. On your cue, they stand as a group.

Push-ups

Variations on the traditional push-up:
- Hands next to each other (beneath the sternum).
- Hands spread out wide to the sides.
- Hands above the head.
- Do push-ups on the fingertips, on all ten or just a few fingers if possible.
- Do push-ups on the knuckles or the backs of the hands
- Push off the ground and clap hands together before landing.
- Put the feet on an object or have a partner hold them about twelve inches off the ground.
- Do push-ups on just one hand or just one foot.
- Do them slowly, counting to ten on the way up and ten again on the way down.
- Do them with a partner. Both partners begin in ready position (with the arms extended) for push-ups. Partner A does one push-up while Partner B maintains the ready position. Partner B then does one push-up as Partner A maintains the ready position. Each partner continues to add one push-up on his turn until both have done ten successive push-ups. For advanced students, let them continue by counting backwards from ten to one.
- Do push-ups from a handstand while a partner supports the feet.
- Double push-ups. Partner A lies on his back with his knees bent, feet flat on the floor and arms extended straight in front of himself. Partner B stands above A's head then leans forward and places his hands on his partner's knees for support. A then takes B's ankles in his hands, so B is balanced on A's knees and hands. Once B stabilizes his balance, he begins doing push-ups while A holds supports his ankles. For very fit students, A can lower and raise B's ankles in time with his push-ups.

Sit-ups

Variations on the traditional sit-up:
- Crunches with the feet and head off the floor.
- Alternate twists to the right and left with each sit-up.
- Side sit-ups (lie on the side while a partner holds the legs at the ankles and knees)
- V-ups (legs up with feet pointing toward the ceiling, touch hands to feet)
- Pair off and have one partner hold the other's ankles for support. Partner A does as many sit-ups as he can in sixty seconds, with Partner B encouraging him as the sit-ups become difficult. Partners then switch positions.
- For evenly matched students, pair off and make a contest of who can do more sit-ups in sixty seconds.
- A partner sits at the feet of the student doing the sit-ups and holds both palms out as targets. With each sit-up, the student executes a cross punch to each palm.
- Partners lock ankles and do sit-ups at the same time. The first time up, Partner A passes an object (a target or ball) to Partner B, the next time up, Partner B passes it back and so on.

Jumping

Variations on jumping to develop leg strength:
- Split jump, touching feet to hands outstretched to the sides
- Pike jump, touching feet to hands outstretched to front
- Jump and touch knees to chest
- Jump and touch feet to buttocks
- Jump and touch the soles of the feet together
- Be a jack in the box, squat down and pop up on the instructor's signal
- Jump and spin 360° or more in the air
- Jump and touch an object hanging from ceiling
- Jump over a stack of shields or heavy bags
- Jump up and extend the arms and legs (like an X)
- Jump over a stick held by instructor
- Jump onto and off of a low step or bench
- Jump off of a step, land and quickly execute a jump kick to a target
- Have students make a circle around instructor, instructor rotates in place and swings a jump rope or belt around and students jump over it when it approaches them

Line Drills

Form two lines with higher ranking students in the front of each line. Have the lines move all the way to one side of the practice area. At your signal or at preset intervals, the two people at the heads of the line begin moving across the floor doing the assigned movement. When they reach the other side they form a new line there or go to the end of the line they came from. Some skills for line drills:

- Sprinting
- Single leg hopping
- Zigzag running
- Sliding
- Bounding
- Ski jumps (two feet together, jumping side to side like a skier)
- Twists (feet together, twisting the upper and lower body in opposite directions while hopping forward)
- Pendulum jumps (the right foot touches the left foot, sending it out to the left and then back to touch the right foot, sending it out to the right - looks like a clock pendulum)
- Scooping (bend and touch the hand to the floor near the foot, in a scooping motion)
- Skating (like a speed skater)
- Knee to chest bounding
- Running backwards
- Backwards knee to chest bounding
- Jumping jacks (moving sideways across the floor)
- Continuous punching while running
- Free combinations with footwork

Partner Stretches

Stretching with a partner can be fun when done correctly. Each student should be paired with a partner similar in size/skill level and partners should never push each other beyond their personal comfort level.

- Partner A stands with her back to the wall and extends her leg into a front, side or round kick. Partner B holds A's ankle and raises her leg slowly to a comfortable height. Hold for about thirty seconds then switch places.

- Partner A sits on the floor in a butterfly stretch (knees bent, soles of the feet touching) and Partner B slowly presses down on A's lower back or knees.

- Partner A lies on the floor and raises his leg to the ceiling. Partner B holds A's ankle and slowly pushes toward A's chest.

- Partner A lies on the floor and raises his knee toward his chest. Partner B holds A's ankle or shin and slowly pushes toward A's chest.

- Partner A sits with her legs extended straight in front of her. Partner B slowly pushes down on A's lower back.

- Both partners sit on the floor with their legs split apart, and their feet touching (or one person's feet touching the other's ankles). They grasp hands and Partner A leans back slowly and pulls Partner B forward. After thirty seconds, they switch and Partner B pulls Partner A forward.

- Both partners sit on the floor with their legs extended straight out in front of them and the soles of their feet touching. They grasp hands and Partner A leans back slowly, pulling Partner B forward. After thirty seconds, they switch and Partner B pulls Partner A forward.

- Both partners stand back-to-back and link arms at the elbow. Partner A leans forward and slowly takes Partner B (who is bending backwards, looking at the ceiling) onto his back. Students with knee or back injuries should not do this exercise.

- Both partners face each other and place their hands on the other person's shoulders. At your signal, they step backward until they are bent over ninety degrees at the waist and their upper bodies are parallel to the floor. For advanced students, ask them to take one step backward every fifteen seconds until they can no longer hold the stretch.

- Partner A stands in a low front stance. Partner B places his foot on A's shoulder (facing to front like front kick or to side like side kick) and A supports B by holding his hand or arm. If B is flexible, A can stand up slowly to extend the stretch.

Worst Skill Training

Students tend to practice the skills they are good at or enjoy and neglect those they find difficult. To improve weak skills, have everyone practice his or her "worst" kick, combination, form or self-defense technique.

During the practice, walk around and give pointers on how to improve or explain what the student is doing wrong. For a large class, have assistant instructors or senior ranks assist in correcting problems.

In addition to improving their skills, students are relieved to see that everyone has a "worst" skill. Just knowing that they are not the only ones who are struggling with a technique is a big relief.

Basic Movements: Individual

Individual drills and games

See also . . .
Basic Movements: Partner . . . . page 22
Basic Movements: Group . . . . page 26

One Skill/Many Targets

Sometimes there is a kick or strike that needs additional practice before the class can move on to a more advanced skill. To get in the required repetition without boredom, try varying the targets used. Spend five minutes each on:

- Kicking in the air
- Kicking facing a partner (no contact)
- Kicking a hand target
- Kicking the heavy bag
- Kicking a hanging ball
- Kicking a paper
- Kicking a shield
- Kicking a partner with chest gear on (light contact)

Whether you have the entire class go through each drill in order as a group or divide up into small group stations, each student will have spent forty minutes working on one kick in a variety of situations.

Dynamic Tension Practice

Practice a single movement as slowly as possible, putting full concentration into maintaining muscle tension throughout the movement. Variations:

- Less skilled students may need to hold a stretching bar to practice dynamic tension kicks.

- Once students get the hang of it, see who can do the slowest push-up or hold their kick extended the longest.

- Add a breathing exercise to the movement, extending a single exhalation from the beginning to the completion of the movement.

Video Training

Use videotapes in class to provide excitement and feedback:

- Tape each student performing a movement then have the class compare/critique (constructively) the movements.

- Tape sparring matches and watch them to identify bad habits, new combinations and defensive openings.

- Conduct half hour video lessons in which you tape a student for ten to fifteen minutes then play back the tape and critique their movements.

- Watch an instructional tape and then practice movements from it, especially if the movements are very complex and can be watched in slow motion.

- Watch a scene from a martial arts movie then put on a skit imitating the fight scenes.

- Watch a scene from a martial arts movie then rearrange the scene so the loser of the fight in the movie ends up winning.

- Watch a competition video to get pumped up for a sparring class.

- Watch a competition video and ask students to identify points scored, pick the winner before it's revealed on the tape or identify new skills they can practice.

Resistance Training

Resistance training is a common traditional exercise to strengthen many types of basic movements.

Have one partner begin a punch (extended 25%) and the other partner place his palm against the punching surface of the fist. On your signal, each person puts full power into punching/resisting until the punch is fully extended.

If the resisting person is stronger, he should take a little off his resistance so his partner is challenged, but not defeated. This exercise can be varied for just about any movement.

• For kicking, use a bungee type cord with one end tied around the ankle and the other end held by the partner.

• For throwing, have one partner grasp one end of a belt or bungee cord and the other partner grasp the other end. As one person executes the throwing motion with his end of the belt, the other provides resistance.

• Without a partner, a wall can be used for hand strikes by beginning close to the wall and pushing away as the strike extends.

Basic Movements: Partner

Partner drills and games

See also . . .
Basic Movements: Individual . . . . page 20
Basic Movements: Group . . . . page 26

Stronger Stance

There are many games to develop stronger stances:

• **Front stance palm push**. In front stance, partners place their right or left palms together and push.

• **Horse stance palm push.** Partners face each other in horse riding stance about arm's length apart. They place their palms together and begin pushing. The first to push the other off balance wins.

• **Front stance shoulder push.** In front stance, partners place their right or left shoulders up against each other and their hands on the other person's shoulders. The first to push the other off balance wins.

• **Front stance straight-arm push.** In front stance, partners bend at the waist and place their outstretched hands on the other person's shoulders. The first to push the other off balance wins.

• **Push the donkey.** Both partners assume front stance, with one standing directly behind the other. The partner in the rear places his hands on the other person's lower back and attempts to push him forward. If he moves, the pushing partner wins, if he resists for one minute (or whatever time limit you set) the resisting partner wins.

- **Back stance single hand tug.** In back stance, partners grasp hands (arm wrestling grip) and try to pull each other off balance.

- **Back stance cross hand tug.** In back stance, partners cross their arms (like a low X block) and grasp hands (handshake grip). The first to pull the other off balance wins.

- **A frame.** Partners stand at least two arms' width apart, facing each other. They lean toward each other, arms extended over their heads and bring their palms to meet against each other. Once they are both leaning into each other, they simultaneously push off and return to their place. The father apart they stand, the more difficult it is to return to the starting position.

- **Team tug.** Two students (Students A and B) assume the back stance single hand tug starting position (see above). Two more students (C and D) stand behind A and B. C places his hands on A's waist and D places his hands on B's waist. At your signal, A and B try to unbalance each other, helped by C and D who pull them backwards by the waist. Additional students can be added to form larger teams.

- **Line tug.** Form a single file line of students in which the first student faces the front wall and the second faces the back wall, the third faces the front wall and so on. Have each student assume a front stance and link hands with the people on each side of him. At your command, the students facing the front wall pull toward the front wall and the students facing the back wall pull toward to back wall. The team to move the line in their direction (toward the front or back wall) wins.

Target Variety

Many schools use hand held paddles or mitts for practice. Hitting the same old target every class can get boring so try some substitutes:
- **X-ray paper** or a thin sheet of plastic (to create a big noise when struck)
- **A partner's hand**: practice accuracy and a light touch
- **A foam pool noodle:** strike the tip or the side for accuracy in striking
- A water filled **heavy bag**
- A human shaped stuffed or rubber target
- A **pillow case** with targets drawn on it and pulled over a heavy bag
- A **chest protector** or **head gear** held by a partner to simulate a sparring situation
- A **piece of paper**: see how many hits it takes to tear the paper (speed is essential)

Grappling Drills

Whether you practice grappling or not, these drills be a fun test of skills:

- **Turn around wrestling**. Partners sit back to back and on your signal, turn around to kneel facing each other. Each person puts his hands the other's shoulders and immediately tries to unbalance him. The first person to touch any part of his body above the knees to the ground is the loser.

- **Arm wrestling.** Pair off students for games of arm wrestling using both right and left hands. Modified arm wrestling can also be done standing or kneeling on one knee (place your elbow on your other knee) or standing on one leg with the other leg extended to the back.

- **Shoulder wrestling.** Partners kneel and place their right shoulders up against one another and their arms behind their back. Using their body weight and not losing contact with their shoulders, they attempt to force the other person to the ground.

Ball or Balloon Games

For these games, you need balloons or very light, inflatable balls (like beach balls).

- **Balloon hit.** One partner tosses the balloon and the other hits, kicks or blocks it.

- **Balloon dodge.** One partner tosses the ball and the other dodges it.

- **Stomach crunchers.** Partners lie on their stomachs, facing each other. They take turns passing the balloon back and forth over a short distance. During the game, neither person can touch their hands or feet to the ground. This one shouldn't be done for more than a few minutes at a time.

- **Drop kicks.** One partner lies on her back and the other stands near her feet. The standing partner drops the balloon over the lying partner's feet. The lying partner must kick the balloon before it hits the ground.

- **Over/under pass.** Partners stand back-to-back. The first passes the ball through his legs to the other person. This person then passes the ball up over his head back to the first. After a few passes, change directions. The first person passes over the head, the second under the legs.

- **Line pass.** Form a single-file line and pass the ball down the line varying passes to the right and left sides, over the head and through the legs. When the ball reaches the end, have everyone turn around 180° and pass it back the way it came.

Belt Tug of War

Line students up on opposite teams, holding a belt like a tug of war rope. Tape off two lines on the floor, one at the head of each team. On your command, the teams assume front stance or back stance and begin pulling. The side to pull the others over their line wins. Variations:

- **Circle tug.** Tie the ends of an old belt together so it forms a circle. Have four people grasp the belt at different points around the circle (equal distances from each other) and at your signal, begin pulling. Anyone who can pull the group in his direction wins.

- **Two hand tug.** Partners face each other and take off their belts. They each grasp one end of a belt in their right hand and one end of a belt in their left hand. At your signal, they begin tugging with both hands. The first to pull the other over a designated mark on the floor (use tape or a target placed between them on the floor) wins.

- **Back-to-back, two hand tug.** Like two hand tug, but partners stand with their backs to each other and grasp the belts with their hands extended above their heads.

- **Crab tug.** Two students get in the crab walk position (from a seated position, place the palms on the floor behind the buttocks and lift buttocks off the floor). Each student uses one hand to grasp the end of a belt. At your signal, they begin tugging. The first to pull the other off balance wins. To develop leg strength, make a loop in each end of the belt and have each student hook one foot into the loop on their end. At your signal, they tug with their feet and try to unbalance each other.

25

Fun House

Create a fun house with hanging or standing heavy bags. Hang or place the bags around the room and have the highest rank student start moving through them, striking or kicking each bag.

As soon as the first student moves away from the first bag, the next student follows the first through the course. Let the bags swing or move freely, creating the need to dodge the bags, think quickly and strike according to the moment.

Caution: Juniors who are small enough to get knocked down or injured by a swinging bag should sit out.

Add One Drill

Students form a line or circle so they can see each other. The first student performs a kick or strike. The student next to him repeats the movement, then adds her own. The next student performs the first two skills, then adds his own.

Continue until someone goofs up, then have the next student start a new sequence. Keep track of how many skills are performed in the longest sequence then challenge the next class to break the "class record."

Basic Movements: Group

Group drills and games

See also . . .
Basic Movements: Individual . . . . page 20
Basic Movements: Partner . . . . . . page 22

Drill Circle

Students form a circle around the instructor who holds a target pad in each hand. The instructor goes around the circle presenting the target to each student in order for a prearranged kick or strike. Variations:

- The student executes one of a number of predetermined strikes depending on the target position (i.e. flat for punching, facing downward for front kick, angled for roundhouse kick)

- The instructor randomly moves around the circle quickly presenting and removing targets for students to strike. Give each student only a second or two to respond then move to the next person.

- The instructor presents two targets for a combination strike or kick.

- The instructor presents the target and the student keeps striking repeatedly until the target is removed.

Group Heavy Bag Drills

If you don't have a lot of heavy bags, use group drills to allow each student to get more bag time per class.

- Have two students face each other on opposite sides of the heavy bag. At your signal, they both begin executing right leg roundhouse kicks until told to stop. They should kick as quickly as possible while trying to maintain a synchronized rhythm

- Two students face each other as above, but this time they use footwork to move 90° to their right after each kick. Partners should stay on opposite sides of the bag as they move around it.

- Three to six students surround the heavy bag. At the signal, all begin throwing combination punches. As the bag begins to swing, each student has to work to hit the moving bag while remembering to dodge it when it swings towards them.

- Two to four students surround the heavy bag. At your signal, they begin the following combination: right punch, left punch, right punch, left punch, right palm strike. The strikes should be done continuously with maximum power until the instructor stops the group.

- One partner faces the bag and the other holds the bag by the sides or bottom. The holder controls the pace by moving the bag in various directions while the other student tries to strike the bag with combinations. The holder should move around the bag while the other student uses footwork to stay opposite him. The holder can also swing the bag at the other student to practice evasion.

Speed Target Hitting

To improve speed in a fun way, have the student move between targets as quickly as possible. Use sets of thirty seconds for intermediate students and one minute or two minutes for advanced students.

- Set-up two target holders about six to ten feet apart, facing each other. Have a student stand between the targets and strike them alternately, using footwork to cover the distance between the two.

- Make two lines with a target holder facing the head of each line. The first student in each line should face the target holder in fighting stance. At your signal, they both kick as fast as they can (with a kick you have specified). The first to hit the target wins and the other student does a few push-ups or jumping jacks before returning to the end of the line. If you make an uneven number of people in the lines (i.e. five in one line and four in the other), each student gets to pair off with a different person on every turn.

- Have students form a single file line facing you. Using two soft paddle targets, randomly present one for striking. As soon as the student hits the target, use the other to lightly swat at an opening in his guard. He should block or evade your "attack." After one attack/defense sequence, he goes to the end of the line.

- For one on one drills, use two hand targets or mitts. One student holds the targets while the other faces him in fighting stance. At your cue, the target holder begins moving around, randomly presenting the targets to his partner for striking or kicking. For advanced students, the holder moves backwards, sideways and forwards. For less experienced students, the holder moves only backwards to avoid injuries.

- To practice combinations, make a line of two to five target holders. The remaining students move down the line quickly kicking and striking the targets, using footwork to move from one to the next.

- Make a circle of four target holders and have the kicker stand in the middle. The kicker should go around the circle, striking each target in quick succession, changing direction using footwork.

- With a single target, have the student strike as many times as possible in one minute. Encourage students to improve on their number each turn or make it a class competition for the most strikes in one minute.

Bubble Blowing

If you have a floor that is easily washable or if you can take the class outside, get a bottle of bubbles and a bubble-blowing wand (most jars come with a wand). Blow the bubbles high in the air and have the kids kick and punch them as they drift to the ground.

To prevent chaos, assign everyone a "territory" and tell them they can only attack the bubbles in their territory.

Hackey Sack

A hackey sack is a small bean bag, usually about two inches square. The object of the game is to keep the sack airborne using only the feet and legs.

It can be played individually, with a partner (pass back and forth) or with a group (pass around the circle). Great for agility, foot-eye coordination and fun!

Reaction Drills

Practice of basic movements can become boring long before a skill is mastered. Reaction drills are a fun way to disguise repetition and improve reflexes. In general, reaction drills involve the instructor activating a cue at random intervals and the students responding as quickly as possible to the cue.

- **Action reaction.** On your action cue, students perform the reaction skill. Your action should be related to the skill being practiced. For example, you step toward the group and they react with a back step and front kick or you throw a punch and they block and counter punch.

- **Light reaction.** In a semi-darkened room, have the students spread out where they can see you. Using a flashlight, randomly turn on the light as a signal for them to perform the designated reaction skill.

- **Sound reaction.** Using your hands or a double target, clap when you want the students to perform the designated reaction skill. You can set a pattern like one clap for right punch, two for left punch and three for front kick.

Group Target Game

Divide the class into two groups, lined up on opposite sides of the room. Every person holds a target, facing the center of the room. At your signal, the person at the head of each line begins moving down his line kicking the targets in quick succession. When he reaches the end of the line, he runs to the other line and takes the place of the target holder at the head of that line. This person then begins kicking through the line and changes lines when he reaches the last target.

Rolling Falls

Once students have mastered rolling falls, test their skills with some fun games. These drills are only for advanced students who are in good shape.

- Rolling falls over a soft shield target
- Rolling falls over a stack of shield targets
- Rolling fall, jump up, kick the heavy bag with a jumping kick
- Rolling falls over a stick balanced on two chairs
- Rolling falls under a stick held by the instructor
- Rolling falls between two sticks (one at knee height and one at shoulder height)
- Rolling falls over a folding chair
- Rolling falls over a person or row of people kneeling down and leaning forward (heads touching the ground)
- Rolling falls over a person standing bent over at the waist
- Rolling falls over a heavy bag (the long way)

Blindfolded

Practicing self-defense skills blindfolded can add an element of uniqueness to class and develop sensitivity.

One student is blindfolded and the other attacks with a hold (not a strike). The blindfolded student reacts quickly with counter. Responding with strikes should be avoided so the attacker does not get hit accidentally. Some students may find this exercise frightening at first, so start easy and work up to more challenging skills.

Creating Variations

Pair off students and have them perform self-defense skills, changing the strikes, locks or finishes slightly to come up with a new technique.

Team Skits

Have a team skit contest. Divide the class into small teams and give them five minutes to create a short self-defense skit with a story line. Then have the teams perform for the class. For juniors, invite their parents in at the end of class to watch.

Self-defense

Realism in practice

Environmental Training

Self-defense practice can get boring and repetitive after the initial fun wears off. To introduce realism and variation try adding environmental elements. Be sure to remove any obvious safety risks and caution students to apply common sense in their use of realism.

- Have everyone bring their winter coats, gloves and hats to class and put them on for practice.

- Practice in shoes, especially heels, heavy boots or dress shoes.

- Ask each student to bring a backpack, purse or brief case to class and practice techniques while carrying their bags as they do on a routine day.

- Practice techniques in a small space, like a corner or hallway. Watch out for the walls!

- Practice techniques surrounded by chairs or other everyday objects encountered in a school or office setting.

- Practice skills sitting in a car.

- Practice outdoors on grass, gravel or dirt.

- Practice in semi-darkness.

Random Attack and Defense

Students love to try out their self-defense skills in a realistic scenario. With a group of intermediate or advanced students, have them form a line (one behind the next) in front of you. As each student comes to the head of the line, quickly throw an attack (for which they have learned a defense) at them. Allow a few seconds to react. Whether they successfully defend or not, their turn ends in less than ten seconds and they return to the end of the line. Keep moving quickly and vary your attacks.

This drill has many variations; some of them can get quite rough if you are not careful. Keep a tight reign on safety rules and have students wear protection gear when necessary.

- **Circle:** Form a circle with one person in the middle as the defender and those forming the circle as attackers. Go around the circle and have each attacker enter the circle and attack the defender with an approved technique. (i.e. one that the defender has learned)

- **Numbered circle:** Form a circle as above and give each person in the circle a number. Call out a number and that person runs into the circle and attacks as above.

- **Advanced numbered circle:** Call out two or three numbers at once so the defender has to cope with multiple attackers.

- **Anything goes circle:** For advanced students, allow any type of attack, within safety precautions. The defender has to defend drawing upon his or her knowledge, but not necessarily using a preformulated defense technique.

- **Timed circle:** Call out a number and that person can play attacker for thirty seconds or one minute, launching a series of attacks against which the defender must defend.

- **Payback circle:** Play any of the circle games above, but allow the defender to attack any one person on the outside of the circle when you call "payback."

- **Weapons circle:** Give some or all of the attackers training weapons: rubber knives or guns, foam sticks, whatever you train with. The defender practices avoidance and disarming skills.

- **Time out circle:** If the defender cannot subdue an attacker in a preset period of time (no more than thirty seconds) he or she is out and the attacker becomes the new defender.

- **Throwing or takedown circle:** One student stands in the middle of the circle and practices a throw or takedown on each person in the circle. Once he completes one rotation, he joins the circle and the first person he threw enters the circle.

Verbal Self-Defense

Give students simulated situations in which they might find themselves (bar fight, playground bully) and ask them to talk themselves out of the situation without using their physical skills. An instructor can play the bad guy to control the course of the scenario or let two students role-play.

Class Rotation

Make two lines down the middle of the room, so each student is facing a partner in the line opposite him. On your signal, each person in Line A throws a random attack at their partner in Line B, who defends. On a second signal, each person in Line B throws a random attack at their partner in Line A. Once both sides have completed their attack and defense techniques, have the class rotate with each person taking a step to their right to face a new partner. Students at the end of the lines rotate over to the other line, instead of stepping to their right. Move through the full line rotation once or twice, giving each student a chance to face many different types of partners. For lower ranking students, limit attacks to those the students have learned. For advanced students, allow them to improvise attacks and defenses within reason.

Brainstorming

Once students have a solid grasp of self-defense basics, pair them off and assign a single attack, such as a grab or lock. Working together, each pair should come up with as many defenses as they can think of in a set period (five minutes maximum).

Variations

There are many ways to vary form practice—some with specific benefits, others just for fun.

- **Blindfolded.** Students practice with their eyes closed or blindfolded. Spread out with plenty of room around each student. Stop students who stray too close to the wall or others.

- **Freeze.** After each movement, students freeze for ten to thirty seconds.

- **Slow motion.** Focus on each movement and break it down.

- **Dynamic Tension.** Use resistance in each movement, taking a ten count to complete a block strike or punch.

- **Change of location.** Face in a different direction, move to a different room, go outside.

- **Noisy forms.** Add a shout to every movement in the form for emphasis (and stress relief).

- **Compounded forms.** Add a movement to each movement. For example add a front kick to every block, a second punch to every punch, a double kick to every kick.

- **Synchronized.** Group students in pairs or small groups to practice in synchronization.

- **Single movement forms.** Do the pattern of the form, but use only one movement, like reverse punch, for every step of the form.

- **Stance only forms.** Drop the techniques from the form and practice only the stances and footwork/transitions.

- **Animal forms.** Ask each student to perform his or her favorite form the way an animal (tiger, monkey, elephant) might do it.

- **Confusion forms.** Do the form backwards or in a mirror image. Give a prize to anyone who gets it right!

- **Multi-direction forms.** At your signal, students stop and turn 90° to the right then continue with the next movement. Give the stop and restart signal several times during the form, forcing the student to rely on internal cues rather than directional markers in the room.

- **Weapons forms.** Practice a simple form using weapons strikes and blocks instead of empty-handed movements.

Change the Count

Frequently change the way you count for forms practice. Some ideas:

- One count for one movement.
- No counting, students go at their own pace from start to finish.
- One count for one segment (predefined group of movements).

Creative Forms

If you don't regularly include creative forms in your class, spend time once a month to let students make up their own form and demonstrate it in class. At the beginning, limit the forms to ten movements. When students are more skilled at making their own forms, lengthen the number of movements.

Applications

Teach the applications of movement sets within each form. Students often find forms more interesting and realistic when they see the connection between the movements and real life applications.

Shadow Sparring

Shadow sparring is a commonly used drill to practice individual combinations and skills. Students simply face forward in a group and begin simulated sparring on the instructor's signal. After a while, this can get boring. Try these variations:

- **Monster sparring.** Students have to defeat a flying monster, a crawling monster, a six-armed monster, or whatever your imagination creates.

- **Musical sparring.** Turn on upbeat music for interval training. Students shadow spar when the music is on and do breathing exercises or stretching when it stops. Vary the length of sparring and resting to create a killer workout.

- **Follow the leader sparring.** A black belt stands in front of the class (facing in the same direction) and students imitate his or her shadow sparring movements. Change black belts several times for a good variety of skills.

- **Defeat the leader sparring.** A black belt faces the class and students shadow spar against his or her movements, as if in a real match.

- **Simon Says sparring.** The instructor calls out directions as in Simon Says, for example "Simon says use only roundhouse kick" or "Simon says practice your jab." If the students respond to a command not preceded by "Simon says" they sit down. Play until one or a few students are left standing then start over.

- **Scenario sparring.** This can be serious or silly. The instructor calls out scenarios for the students to follow like *Your opponent is rushing at you, Your opponent is behind you, Your opponent takes you down on the ground* or *Your opponent is a three eyed flying wildebeest.* Students react accordingly.

Sparring matches

Most schools have students face each other for practice sparring. However, sparring with feedback can be more fun, not to mention helpful in improving competition skills. Some fun ways to stage matches in class:

- **First point.** Select two evenly matched students to face each other. At your signal, they begin sparring. The first student to score a point continues on against another opponent and the loser sits down.

- **Challenge sparring.** Two students face off for a short match in any format you choose. After the match, the loser sits down and the winner "challenges" a student of their choice.

- **Rotating matches.** This drill is more suited to children than adults. Have a group of about ten kids face off in pairs and begin non-contact sparring on your command. Watch the group and call any points you see ("Jimmy, one point") as they are scored. You won't see everyone score every point, but try to catch each kid at least once. The kids will really work to get your attention. After a couple of minutes, have the group sit down to rest and call a new group.

- **Point tag.** To practice speed and concentration rather than techniques, have a game of point tag. Give the students a goal like tagging the other person's left shoulder or belt knot. Each student has to protect his own target while trying to tag the other student's target area. Once a student is tagged, the match is over.

- **Counter sparring.** Give points only for counterattacks. Each partner takes turns initiating an attack for the other to counter. Only successfully countered attacks score points.

- **Initiative sparring.** To develop aggressiveness in sparring, give points for initiative attacks (when the attacking student is the first to move), but not for counters or follow-ups.

- **Combination sparring.** To develop combinations, give points only for the second, third or fourth technique in a combination.

- **Limited weapons sparring.** Allow students to only use one limb or side of the body to score with.

- **Limited techniques sparring.** Limit sparring to the techniques you designate, to force students to practice only those skills.

- **Target sparring.** Give each student a soft foam target and let them bop each other lightly. Any hit that touches the opponent's body without being blocked scores a point.

- **Confined space sparring.** Tape off a small square on the floor (about one quarter the size of a normal ring). Students must stay within the square to score.

- **Total point sparring.** A match is limited to the amount of time it takes to score a total of 2, 3 or 4 points. Whether the score is 2 to 0 or 1 to 1, a 2-point match is over as soon as the second point is scored.

- **Defense sparring.** One partner is on offense and the other on defense. For every successfully landed strike, the offense partner scores a point. If the strike is blocked or avoided, defense scores one point. Each exchange is scored for one partner or the other.

Simon Says

Play the traditional game of Simon says (or Sabumnim says, Sifu says, Sensei says) using punches and kicks. The leader calls out techniques and students should perform only those preceded by "Simon Says." Anyone who does a technique not preceded by "Simon Says" or does the wrong technique has to sit down.

Whistle Drill

A more advanced variation of Simon Says is the whistle drill. The students spread out on the floor and you give a command like "jumping jacks" then blow a whistle. The students do jumping jacks until you blow the whistle again. They then freeze until you give another command and blow the whistle to signal them to begin.

Any student who moves between whistles is out and has to sit down. You may also try to trick students into moving by calling a technique, but not blowing the whistle. Any student who does the technique is out. For really tough students, talk to them, approach them, ask questions and try to distract them into to moving.

Mental Training

Brain games

Statue

Develop student's discipline by practicing being a statue in attention stance or front stance or whatever movement you choose. For young children keep the time short (no more than one minute) but practice five or six times throughout a class. When the kids find the game too easy, try to distract them with noises or motions.

Orchestra of Techniques

Bring a few noisemakers to class (whistle, tambourine, small drum, gong, bell, etc.). Assign a technique to each sound, like whistle=jab, gong=reverse punch, clap=front kick, tambourine=forward roll. Randomly make the sounds and give students a few seconds to respond. For added challenge, make combinations of sounds or add more sounds/techniques.

Active Visualization

Asking students to sit and visualize their newly learned skills is a great tool for solidifying new concepts, but they may drift off if they are not guided. One method of insuring their concentration is to walk around during the visualization time and randomly select students to stand up and perform what they are visualizing. Everyone else should remain seated with their eyes closed. Because they may have to perform at any time, everyone stays focused on visualizing.

Spatial Perception

Pair off students by size (and possibly gender to avoid embarrassments). One partner closes his eyes and the other lightly taps him on the head or shoulder. As soon as he is tapped, the "blind" partner tries to tap back. Partners can try to confuse each other with footwork and deceptive body positioning.

Sound Perception

Have students spread out and close their eyes. Move around the room and make a sound by tapping an object or clapping. Ask students to turn toward the sound or take one step in the direction of the sound. Then have them open their eyes to see who was correct (correct students will be facing you). Vary your distance from the group and the volume of your sounds.

Discussion Topics

Class discussions can be used to get kids involved and break up the monotony of continuous physical activity. Try simple discussion topics when class is lagging or students are distracted. Some suggestions:

- How to be safe traveling to and from school
- What to do if someone bullies you at school
- What to do if you are home alone or with siblings
- How to avoid conflicts without fighting
- When it is okay to use martial arts to defend yourself
- Why martial arts should not be used to bully or hurt others
- Why martial arts should not be played with or taught to friend
- How to set and achieve short term goals
- How short term goals relate to long term goals
- What is concentration, how to concentrate
- How to finish what you start
- The importance of practice and preparation
- Who to talk to when you have a problem
- A topic suggested by the children or that concerns a problem being experienced by a child in class

Martial arts, by its very nature, requires repetition of techniques for improvement and mastery. Many students never make it past the beginning stages of learning because they find the repetition involved in learning skills boring, especially compared to more exciting competitive sports. Here is a summary of forty ways to disguise repetition in every area of instruction:

Change the Skills

- change the strike in a self-defense sequence
- change the kicks in a form
- add or subtract movements in a form
- substitute low strikes and blocks for middle section movements in a form
- do one-step sparring skills from the opposite side (i.e. left handed)
- do a mirror image of a form by starting in the opposite direction
- use only one skill for sparring
- allow only one hand or foot to be used during sparring
- do self-defense skills with the eyes closed or the lights out (exercise caution)

Change the Count

- have students do a kick with each count
- a set (i.e. 10 kicks) with each count
- as many kicks as they can do in 30 seconds
- as many kicks as they can do before a song ends
- ten kicks with the right then with the left at their own pace
- a sequence of different kicks with each count

Change Locations

- take the class outside
- to the park
- to the beach
- to another part of the school (warm-up room, waiting room)

Add an Element

- practice self-defense with a wood, foam or plastic weapon
- give students chalk to use to score in mock knife sparring bouts
- practice kicks over a chair
- bop students with a blocker if they drop their hands during target kicks
- spar against two or three or four people instead of one
- give students bags to carry or other hindrances during self-defense practice
- let everyone wear coats, hats and winter gloves during self-defense practice
- practice forms using a weapon strike to replace punches

Add Creativity

- give everyone five minutes to create a ten movement form
- make teams and have a self-defense skit competition
- have students create their own kicking combinations
- ask each child to perform his favorite form the way an animal (a tiger or monkey) would do it
- have each student create a five minute warm-up or cool-down routine

Add Competition

See who can:
- do the most kicks in thirty seconds
- do the most push-ups
- do the slowest push-up
- stand on one leg the longest
- jump kick the highest
- jump over the highest stack of kicking shields
- recite the meaning of a form or belt perfectly
- name everyone in the class
- name ten blocks (or kicks or strikes) in English or in the language of your art
- defeat the most sparring opponents consecutively

Nuts and Bolts

The Building Blocks of Class Development

In this section . . .

45   Conditioning Exercises

48   Interval Training

50   Art and Science of Timing

53   Injury Prevention Essentials

56   Preventing Overuse Injuries

57   Teaching Self-defense

59   Sparring Without Fear

61   Sparring: Why Teach It?

64   Summer Training Safety

66   Realistic Form Applications

69   Introducing Weapon Training

Conditioning Exercises

Balance without Boredom

See also . . .
Conditioning . . . . page 13
Interval Training . . . . page 48

Conditioning exercises are the foundation on which martial art skills are built. Yet many instructors treat them like a necessary evil to be done and forgotten as quickly as possible. In a successful curriculum conditioning exercises directly relate to the core curriculum and provide a sense of challenge, accomplishment and fun.

Conditioning exercises are grouped into five major categories: warm-up, flexibility, strength, endurance and agility. Each category must be covered in a class, either as a target activity or as part of a training exercise.

Warm-up

A warm-up period is the first stage of every class. For beginners the warm-up lasts fifteen to twenty minutes. For more advanced students who arrive early and begin warming-up on their own, five to ten minutes is adequate.

A warm-up begins with gross motor exercises like jogging in place, bouncing or jumping jacks to raise the body temperature and increase circulation in preparation for more strenuous work. Once everyone begins to sweat lightly, move to major muscle and joint loosening exercises, such as joint rotations and dynamic stretches. Upon the completion of these exercises, students are ready to begin the core class activities.

Flexibility

"Research shows that stretching done in the middle or at the end of a workout has better results than stretching done at the beginning of the workout."

Many instructors include flexibility exercises as part of the warm-up. This is the traditional style of teaching, although not the most effective. Research shows that stretching done in the middle of the workout or at the end has better results than stretching done at the beginning of the workout.

The best approach is to include light dynamic stretching such as back and side leg swings, raising kicks, arm swings and trunk twists after the warm-up. Toward the middle or end of the class, progress to more intensive static stretches like the straddle split, hamstring stretch, groin stretch and trunk twist. This strategy results in greater flexibility and fewer injuries.

Strength

Up to this point, about one third of the class has been spent on warm-up and flexibility exercises and the students are probably getting anxious for some more intensive skill building activities. Strength training is an excellent activity to incorporate directly into the learning portion of the class. It does not have to consist of endless sit-ups and push-ups.

Take a look at your curriculum to find ways to create strength-building exercises from your core activities. For example, when teaching front kick, begin with twenty knee lifts for each leg. Knee lifts build strength in the legs and stomach and are directly related to the performance of a good front kick. Knee lifts, also called chambering, can be applied to every type of kick.

For exercises that cannot be related to the curriculum, have a "self-challenge" between activities. Time the students for one minute and let them count how many sit-ups they can complete. Take a one-minute rest then do another one-minute set of sit-ups. Challenge everyone to improve on their previous number.

Another way to take the boredom out of strength training exercises is to let students work in pairs or teams to encourage each other when the exercises get tough.

Endurance

Endurance training takes place throughout the class period. After the warm-up, keep the level of intensity high for at least twenty minutes for beginners and longer for advanced students. Obviously high intensity is relative. For beginners, high intensity may mean light activity for twenty minutes while for advanced students, high intensity may mean ten rounds of sparring with different partners.

Avoid endurance exercises as a stand-alone activity. Endurance exercises by nature are lengthy, difficult and boring. Twenty minutes of varied target kicking is much more fun for students than twenty minutes of jogging or stair climbing. This is the key to training for some students. They find the variety and challenge of martial arts much more interesting than an hour of stationary bike riding or running on the treadmill.

Agility

For simplicity, consider agility to encompass the remaining conditioning attributes necessary for martial arts. Agility exercises improve balance, coordination, timing, accuracy and speed. This sounds like too much to lump into one category, but many exercises develop all or most of these attributes at one time.

For example, target kicking develops timing, speed, coordination, and accuracy. It is also directly related to the student's skill development and has endless variations, making it fun and challenging. Another example is sparring, which improves coordination, timing, accuracy, speed and reflexes, as well as applying the skills learned in class.

Conditioning is an integral part of every martial arts class. When planning your classes, look carefully for creative ways to implement conditioning drills. In general students prefer learning new skills and perfecting basics to rote conditioning exercises.

By blending conditioning drills into the core curriculum, your students will see improvement in their fundamental physical condition without the boredom usually associated with basic conditioning.

Interval Training

Improving Speed Power and Stamina

See also . . .
Conditioning Exercises . . . . page 45

Many athletes train for endurance by running or exercising at moderate levels over long periods of time. This is effective only if the target activity also involves prolonged activity. For most martial artists, interval training is a more efficient method of building speed and endurance than sustained aerobic activity.

Interval training consists of a series of short, high intensity exercises focused on a specific area of the body. For example, alternately sprinting for one minute then walking for thirty seconds is more effective than running at a slower continual pace over the same distance. Jumping rope for five rounds of three minutes each with a short rest between rounds is more effective than continuous stationary biking for the same time.

The ultimate goal of interval training is to increase the percentage of fast twitch muscle fibers in the target muscles. It has been shown that long distance runners have eighty to ninety percent slow twitch fibers. Conversely, sprinters have a comparable percentage of fast twitch fibers.

Because martial arts are so often a test of skills between two opponents, explosive speed like that of sprinters is necessary for success. The combatant who strikes first and fastest is likely to be the victor. And since most confrontations, whether sport or defense, are decided in a few minutes or less, short-term (anaerobic) endurance must be developed.

To improve explosive speed and short-term endurance, training must focus on the consistent overload of the muscles targeted for development. An excellent system

"For most martial artists, interval training is a more efficient method of building speed and endurance than sustained aerobic activity."

for progressively stressing muscle groups is interval training.

Interval training can take many forms including sprinting, weight lifting, swimming, or any other activity that can be performed in short, explosive bursts of two minutes or less.

Because interval training must directly work the muscles for which the athlete desires to develop explosive power, you will have to adapt your training to your goals. Listed at right are examples of interval drills that fit well in a martial arts class.

Sample Interval Training

Target kicking. Each student does as many of a kick or strike as possible in twenty or thirty seconds. Limit to simple skills and work in sets of three.

Pair off students and have them **spar intensively** for one minute. After thirty seconds rest, rotate partners and repeat.

Run **sprints** across the training hall in sets of five or ten per class.

Spar one minute with the **heavy bag**, then rest thirty seconds. Repeat for three rounds.

Do short intensive sets of **calisthenics**, such as push-ups, sit-ups and squats with a focus on overloading the target muscles.

Pair up students for contests of **isometric strength** such as arm-wrestling, tug of war and attempting to push/pull the partner out of a front or back stance.

Of all the attributes that determine the outcome of a conflict on the street or in the ring, timing is one of the most critical. When faced with an opponent who is bigger, stronger, more flexible or faster, the best weapon is perfect timing. Consider bullfighting. Compare the size, strength, speed and power of a man and a bull. The bull would seem to have a considerable advantage, however the bull rarely wins. Why? The matador knows how long to wait before moving out of the bull's line of attack and he understands the precise moment at which he must strike the bull to win. If he miscalculates by even a split second, the bull will emerge victorious.

Martial arts are much the same. Many people enroll to learn self-defense, to discover the secrets of survival against a bigger, stronger or more aggressive opponent. In the early stages of learning, the practice of physical skills is essential to developing the ability to protect yourself. However, there comes a point in every student's training when something more is needed. Something beyond powerful kicks and speedy punches. This is the point in training to teach a sense of timing.

There are three factors that affect the development of timing in the martial arts: Time Factors, Space Factors and X Factors.

Time Factors

Time Factors determine the **speed and timeliness of the response**. Keep in mind that speed in timing does not mean being fast, but being on time. Time Factors are:

• **Reflexes:** Many people confuse timing with reflexes. Good reflexes are the ability to perceive an action, make a judgment about the action and respond accordingly. Reflexes can be developed through response-oriented drills with a partner and reaction target drills. The goal in reflex training is for the student to respond to every action his partner makes with an appropriate reaction.

• **Speed:** The speed needed for good timing is not the speed of a sprinter; it is the speed of the matador. Being fast is not good enough; **you have to be fast at a precise moment**

50

in time. Speed in timing can best be improved through free sparring or random self-defense practice with a partner.

• **Agility:** Agility gives the student the ability to respond to an opponent with any technique he chooses. It is essential to successful timing, because knowing what to do is not enough. The student must be able to physically execute his response without hindrance. Agility is developed through running drills, footwork, shadow sparring and knee pitching.

• **Synchronization:** In responding to an attack, the body obeys the commands of the mind. The mind must be able to direct the body instantaneously and accurately. This is the most difficult Time Factor to develop because it requires many years of practice. In martial arts, the achievement of mind and body synchronization is often called *Mushin* or "No Mind, Spontaneity." It is a goal not only in the enhancement of timing, but of all martial arts training.

Space Factors

Space Factors take into consideration **where you are and where your target is,** as well as the movement of both you and your opponent. Space Factors are important in successfully hitting the correct target with the correct weapon. Space Factors are:

• **Accuracy in Motion:** The opponent presents a moving target and to hit a moving target, you have to anticipate where the target will be when you want to hit it, not where it is now. To develop accuracy in motion, teach step sparring drills or prearranged self-defense. Through prearranged practice, students instinctively discover their own ways of anticipating their opponent's movements.

• **Linear Distance:** The distance from you to your target determines what type of response is required. If your opponent is close to you, a short and explosive technique is appropriate. If your opponent is far away, a step might be needed before striking.

• **Relative Distance:** Because timing is a dynamic trait, it involves not only the linear distance to the target, but also the relative distance to the target. Is your opponent directly in front of you, off to the side, behind you, above you? Adapt your response accordingly. Both linear and relative distance can be improved through target drills, partner drills, prearranged practice and free sparring.

X Factors

X Factors are the final piece in the timing puzzle. They are **confidence and relaxation**. Winning through timing paradoxically requires toughness and softness. You have to be tough enough to resist the instinct to retreat in the face of your opponent's attack and soft enough to relax until the moment of action. If students are too tense, they miss the chance to respond to their opponent's attack and get hit. If they are too nervous, they shrink away from their objective and respond haphazardly, missing the intended target.

When you are teaching or supervising the practice of timing drills, watch carefully for these two important negative reactions in students. Less experienced students are often too tense or timid in most drills. Point out these mistakes early in their training, so they do not become habits.

Overly timid students need more time to practice arranged drills with a partner to build their confidence and lessen their fear of partner interactions. Overly tense students need to practice more sensitivity and agility drills to shift their focus from the end result of the technique (hitting power) to the flow of the technique itself. Through guided practice, all students can develop accurate timing instincts.

"You have to be tough enough to resist the instinct to retreat in the face of your opponent's attack and soft enough to relax until the moment of action."

One of the leading causes of dropouts among martial arts students is injuries sustained during training. As an instructor, one of your primary responsibilities is to prevent injuries.

Although some injuries occur no matter how many precautions you take, there are many injuries that should never happen in the care of an experienced instructor.

In the Classroom

1. Make your practice area safe by ensuring that it is well lit, free of obstacles and sharp objects, well ventilated, climate controlled, and large enough to comfortably accommodate your largest class.

2. Spectators (especially young children) and students who are not involved in class should not be on the mat. Have separate warm-up and waiting areas.

3. Teach hazardous or impact skills on mats or a padded floor.

4. If you have mirrors or picture frames in the training area, use only nonbreakable safety glass or plastic. Secure them tightly to the wall.

5. Anything hanging on the wall should be free from sharp edges or projecting parts.

6. Weapons should be stored securely and accessed only by those who have the instructor's permission.

7. Keep a well-stocked first aid kit on hand.

8. Learn CPR and first aid. Require all of your assistants to do the same.

9. Keep equipment in good repair and check it before every use.

10. Avoid physically intense activities in extremely hot weather.

11. In very cold weather, avoid activities that require a large range of motion or great flexibility.

Before Class

1. Conduct a thorough warm-up of at least ten to fifteen minutes for beginners and five to ten minutes for advanced classes.

2. Do not let students practice when they are ill or fatigued. Suggest they sit and observe if they are not feeling one hundred percent.

3. Implement a conditioning regimen for stretching and strengthening appropriate muscles before teaching difficult skills.

4. Require students to have a physical exam before enrolling.

5. Request that students disclose pre-existing conditions in writing when enrolling.

During Class

1. Set and enforce safety rules for potentially hazardous activities.

2. Children should be supervised by an adult at all times.

3. Begin new exercises and skills cautiously and monitor the students' response.

4. Never teach skills that are beyond a student's range of ability.

5. Teach new skills in stages. Rather than teaching a jumping spinning kick in one lesson, start with the jump and spin movement, then add the kick as students improve their balance and coordination in the air.

6. Increase the speed and power of new skills gradually as students' skill and comfort level increase.

7. Require students to use proper protection gear for contact activities and for every type of sparring, including non-contact sparring.

8. Strictly enforce contact rules. If a student violates those rules, even by accident, have sit out for a few minutes and cool down.

9. Prohibit techniques like eye gouges, knee breaks, ear slaps, chokes and others that cannot be practiced safely or applied safely in sparring.

10. Teach the correct use of equipment like kicking shields, targets and heavy bags for both the students striking the equipment and those holding it.

11. Teach students to breath properly during exercises. Deep breathing supplies the muscles and brain with oxygen and enhances performance.

12. Pair students who are similar in size, age and ability level for partner activities and sparring. If you see a mismatch, stop class and rearrange the pairing.

13. Spend five to ten minutes at the end of class for cool down exercises.

14. Provide immediate care for injuries when they occur.

15. Don't encourage the "no pain, no gain tough guy mentality." Students should not train through or walk off a potentially serious injury.

16. Do not allow students to resume training until they have fully recovered from an injury suffered in class. Students who suffer a concussion should not return to contact activities for thirty days.

17. Allow students to excuse themselves from drills and exercises if they have an injury or condition that would make participating hazardous.

Most importantly, stress safety first and foremost in every class.

Warning Signs

Be on the lookout for students who might fall victim to an overuse injury. **Common causes** of overuse injuries include:

1. The student is too heavily involved in the arts.

2. The student is working at a level above his ability.

3. The student uses the same workout routine every day.

4. The student comes to class when tired, ill, etc.

5. The student's conditioning level is poor, resulting in him "cheating" to perform difficult skills.

Recovery

Suggestions for **resuming a normal training program**:

1. Take time off to rest and recuperate.

2. Train on alternate days or limit training to twice a week.

3. Vary the training routine to include new/different skills.

4. Change the objectives of training to focus on self-fulfillment.

Preventing Overuse Injuries

The dangers of overtraining

See also . . .
Injury Prevention Essentials . . . . page 53
Preventing Burnout . . . . page 280

Overuse injuries are some of the most common injuries found in adult martial artists. Particularly susceptible parts of the body include the knees, back and shoulders, but an overuse injury can occur in any area that is used repetitively. Overuse injuries are not sudden occurrences. They creep up slowly and return frequently. If left untreated, they become chronic and can put an end to the enjoyment of martial arts for many adult students.

Overuse injuries can be lessened or prevented by detecting the **early signs of overtraining** and counseling the student.

Some warning signs are:
1. Pain or stiffness in the area during exercise
2. Pain or stiffness in the area during normal activities
3. General fatigue or malaise
4. Poor overall performance, feeling of being in a slump
5. Frequent illness
6. Obsession with martial arts
7. Desire to be the best or win at any cost
8. Lack of identity outside of the arts
9. Poor concentration, feeling distracted and restless

If you identify more than three of these characteristics in a student, it may be sign that he is **overtraining** and headed for an overuse injury. Frequently, an overuse injury is a precursor to **burnout**, which leads the student to discontinue martial arts training. Before these consequences occur, counsel the student on techniques for getting back on track.

Basic Skills

Before beginning partner drills, novice students learn and practice the basic skills needed for self-defense.

Basic **skills to be mastered before beginning partner drills** include:

1. Blocking/Evading
2. Striking
   Punching
   Elbow Striking
   Knee striking
   Kicking
   Butting
3. Immobilization
4. Escape skills
5. Locks
6. Throws
7. Takedowns.

When students are proficient at basic movements, begin partner drills. Suggested **defenses for partner drills**:

- Front Choke
- Front Bear Hug
- Shoulder Grab
- Wrist Grab
- Pinning
- Rear Headlock
- Collar Grab
- Rear Choke
- Side Headlock
- Rear Bear Hug

Teaching Self-Defense

Using partner drills effectively

Teaching effective self-defense skills is an excellent way to create excitement and enthusiasm. Self-defense practice demonstrates the relationship between the skills practiced in class and their application in real life. Seeing this relationship creates a sense of urgency in learning. Students see the potential for crime all around them and urgently feel the need to learn to defend themselves effectively.

Self-defense practice also creates constructive interaction among students. Through working with partners and simulating self-defense situations, they get to know and trust each other, creating a positive atmosphere in the school. At the same time, partner drills add variety and challenge to the curriculum by forcing students to make their skills work against an attacker.

1. Controlled Partner Drills

The first type of drill introduced is the controlled partner drill. Line up the students so they are facing a partner of similar size and skill level. Demonstrate the drill several times while explaining key points to be practiced. Next, lead the class through the drill slowly while explaining it. Do this twice, once for each partner to practice. Allow the teams to practice slowly while you circulate around the room and make corrections or provide clarification. When it appears that most teams are performing the drill accurately, ask them to alternate attacking and defending more realistically for thirty to sixty seconds. Emphasize control and safety.

To prevent unnecessary injuries in partner drills, observe the following:

1. No contact with striking or kicking skills unless both partners are wearing safety gear.

2. Begin the drill at walk through speed until both partners are comfortable with the skill.

3. Emphasize control and respect between partners.

4. All students should listen for and immediately obey the start and end signals given by the instructor.

5. Pair students according to size and ability.

6. Watch for the development of personal rivalries that may lead an escalation of force.

"Seeing the relationship between practice and real life creates a sense of urgency in learning."

2. Semi-controlled Drills

At the intermediate stage, the student should understand the methods of practicing self-defense well enough to allow more freedom in practice. Semi-controlled drills give the teams more options to create a better sense of realism.

Using new skills, introduce two or three options for defense against the same attack. Allow the students to practice the options at their own pace, freely alternating among them as they progress. Set a time limit of sixty seconds in which to finish a specific number of attack/defense scenarios to encourage quick thinking and reflexes.

The semi-controlled drill can also be used to reduce the boredom of reviewing skills. Set a time limit of sixty seconds and give the students a few techniques to review. One partner attacks randomly using the designated skills while the other partner defends using a variety of options. At the end of the time limit, the partners switch roles.

Semi-controlled drills improve reflexes and imprint the techniques in the subconscious mind. This is a critical phase in moving from learning a skill at the beginner stage to automatic execution of the skill in the advanced stage.

3. Free Combat Drills

Free combat drills are for advanced students who have a large repertoire of skills and a good fundamental understanding of the principles of self-defense. Drills may be done with complete control or with light contact to protected areas covered by safety gear.

In free combat, partners attack and defend at random, with either or both partners free to attack depending on the skill level of the participants. For the first few trials, allowing only one partner to attack is recommended. Once the students are comfortable with this type of drill, give both partners permission to attack at will.

To maintain safety and control, limit the drills to thirty seconds at a time and rotate partners frequently.

Source of Fear

For most advanced students sparring is a fun, challenging and rewarding part of martial arts training. For beginners, however, it can be a source of fear and intimidation. Fear of sparring can take many forms:

- Fear of getting hit
- Fear of getting hurt
- Fear of not being in control
- Fear of embarrassment
- Fear of being powerless
- Fear of looking foolish
- Fear of failure or losing

Fortunately, most of these fears can be overcome through a plan of progressive training. If students are introduced to sparring gradually and in "safe" situations, they can face their fears and learn to enjoy sparring.

"The best weapon for fighting fear is knowledge."

Sparring Without Fear

Reducing student anxiety

See also . . .
Sparring . . . . page 36
Sparring: Why Teach It? . . . . page 61

The best weapon for fighting fear is knowledge. People are naturally afraid of the unknown. When students understand the fundamentals of sparring, they are able to apply this knowledge systematically, lessening their fear. Begin by introducing the concepts of offense and defense:

- Simple one or two technique attacks.

- Footwork for avoidance.

- Basic blocking

- Combinations of footwork and basic kicks

These skills can be practiced in the air or on a target but not with a partner at this stage. You want the students thinking about how the skills are used but focusing on developing control and refining their technique at this stage.

Application

When students begin to grasp these ideas, move on to teaching applications in arranged sparring. Pair off students of equal skill and size. One partner performs a designated kick and the other partner responds with the defense or counterattack you designate. Some tips for successful arranged sparring:

- Students practice only the designated skills

- All activities are noncontact, with kicks and strikes kept about a foot from the partner's body

59

- Students wear light protection gear to become accustomed to the feel of moving while wearing it

- Skills are done at walk through speed first then gradually increase in speed

- Students who do not exercise control are asked to sit out or practice without a partner

Once students are comfortable with the idea of working with a partner, begin intensifying the difficulty of the arranged sparring. From arranged sparring, progress to semi-free sparring. Semi-free sparring allows students some freedom of skill selection while maintaining a framework of expectations. Semi-free sparring drills include:

- The attacking student can only use roundhouse kick (or any kick you designate) and the defending student can only evade and block.

- The attacking student can only use roundhouse kick and the defending student counters with footwork and roundhouse kick.

- The attacking student must use a combination of two techniques with the defender blocking the first and countering the second.

- Both students may use any techniques they like, but only to the body.

- Students "exchange" attacks, alternating single techniques while the other simply avoids the attack.

By defining limits, students not only feel safe in knowing what to expect, they are able to focus on developing specific areas of offense and defense. One of the most challenging aspects of learning to spar is the vast number of choices available and the short amount of time in which decisions must be made.

Contact

The level of contact in sparring can present a special hurdle. If your style practices non-contact point sparring, you do not need to address this issue. If you practice a light or full contact style, students need to graduate from non-contact to contact practice, usually beginning at the intermediate level. Some instructors choose to make contact optional while others make it a requirement.

If you require contact, there may be some dropouts when students reach this stage. To ease the transition, begin again with arranged sparring drills, allowing students to make light contact while wearing a full set of protection gear. From arranged drills, progress to contact semi-free sparring, again wearing full gear and emphasizing technique over brawling. For full contact, additional instruction time should be spent on how to absorb a full contact hit and effective methods of defense. Whatever level of sparring you choose, your students will benefit from the confidence and knowledge gained through testing their skills on the mat.

Sparring: Why Teach It?

Real life applications of sport style sparring

See also...
Sparring Drills .... page 36
Sparring without Fear .... page 59

One of the most controversial debates in the martial arts is the place of sport style sparring. Many traditional and street oriented practitioners believe that it is a useless part of the martial arts when it comes to defending yourself. What do you say to a student who says sparring is fake or a waste of time? Does sparring contribute to self-defense or should it be taught separately for only those students who want to compete?

Full contact sparring, like that of Olympic style taekwondo, traditional karate and kickboxing has more to offer the self-defense practitioner than initially meets the eye. Consider the following benefits of full contact sparring:

1. The ability to perform under pressure.

By practicing continuous (without stopping for points) full contact sparring, students learn to deal with the unrelenting attacks of an opponent. They must respond to the opponent's attacks by defending accurately and forcefully or risk getting injured by a full contact strike. Although participants wear protection gear, a full contact kick to the head still results in a knockout.

2. The ability to quickly adapt to the opponent's actions.

Because free sparring is not prearranged, an opponent can use any type of attack (within the rules) that he chooses. The student must be prepared to counter a variety of movements, adapting to an ever changing situation. Although the street fighter has a much broader choice of weapons to use, the experienced competitor is prepared to respond quickly and calmly to unknown situations through sparring practice.

3. The ability to protect yourself when injured.

In almost every sparring match, as in almost every self-defense situation, participants get hit and possibly hurt. Whether it is a bruised foot, banged shin, black eye or something more serious, students learn how to continue in spite of minor pain. If you watch competitors leave the arena after a day's competition, most are sporting some sort of bandage or ice pack.

Injuries, and the pain associated with them, cause the human body to instinctively shut down. If a student is not prepared for the mental and physical shock of an injury, he may be unable to continue to defend himself when injured.

4. The ability to withstand the opponent's blows and respond calmly.

Novice students often imagine themselves stepping onto the mat and taking on opponents with the calm of the black belts they have watched spar. When they face their first opponent reality sets in. When you get hit, a natural response is anger—a quick instinctive flash that urges you to exact revenge on your attacker, even if it is your classmate.

Learning to overcome this feeling is essential to both competition and self-defense. With experience, competitors learn to take their opponent's blows in stride and respond calmly with appropriate counterattacks.

5. The ability to think clearly under duress.

In other words, don't panic. The first time anyone faces someone who wants to hurt them, even in a competitive match, there is a tendency to suddenly forget everything and resort to hopelessly fending off a reign of blows. To overcome the instinctive fear when confronted with a physical threat, students must face the fear and practice controlling it in a secure environment. Skills are useless if they cannot be put to use in a stressful situation.

6. The need for mental and physical endurance.

Regular sparring builds endurance physically and mentally. Physical endurance is important in confrontations when an assailant is larger or more experienced in fighting. Mental endurance is necessary to concentrate fully on the attacker's actions and read his intentions as well as in formulating strategy.

7. The ability to strike with power and accuracy.

Hitting the heavy bag is useful, but as the saying goes, heavy bags don't hit back. Nor do they move around and avoid attacks. If students want to learn to apply skills realistically, encourage them to practice against a live opponent, simulating a real situation. Of course, applying deadly skills (like eye gouges) is impossible but sparring creates a forum for applying a limited number of skills against active resistance from an opponent. Students learn what works and what doesn't when the pressure is on.

8. The ability to move quickly.

Practicing skills in training drills improves form, but only the pressure of a realistic confrontation can create the speed necessary to attack and defend successfully. Through sparring, students develop speed in evasion, defense, strategy, footwork and counterattacking.

9. The ability to spot your opponent's vulnerabilities and exploit them.

Through practice students learn to spot weaknesses in the opponent's defense, read his next move, detect bad habits and intercept telegraphed movements. This is something that can be learned only from experience and it is essential to defeating an assailant who is bigger and stronger.

Although full contact sparring is certainly no substitute for practical self-defense skills, it can enhance your students' ability to defend themselves. By giving them a chance to put themselves at physical risk, sparring creates a realistic threat and gives them the opportunity and the tools to learn to control that threat and their response to it. In this sense, self-defense and full contact sparring are one in spirit.

"Sparring creates a realistic threat and the opportunity and the tools to learn to control that threat."

Summer Training Safety

Beat the heat

See also . . .
Injury Prevention Essentials . . . . page 53

Summer training brings with it a unique set of teaching concerns. In most places summer means hot humid weather which makes exercise more taxing and potentially dangerous, if the proper precautions are not observed. The following are some general guidelines for a safe and healthy summer in your school:

1. **Heat related ailments** are more likely to occur when:

   • the weather turns suddenly warm

   • students are in an air conditioned environment all day then workout in a warm school/gym

   • students are overweight

   • rest breaks are not given

   • the body's water supply is not replenished

   • students become fatigued or are in generally poor health.

2. **Heat cramps** may result from a loss of salt due to excessive sweating during exercise. Marked by painful cramps in the arms legs and abdomen heat cramps are best treated by having the student rest in a cool area and drinking plenty of water. If the cramps persist or worsen the student should seek medical assistance.

3. **Heat exhaustion,** also the result of excessive sweating and water loss, is marked by profuse sweating, faint rapid pulse, cold moist skin and a normal to slightly elevated body temperature. The student should move to a cool area, loosen clothing, elevate the legs and drink plenty of cool water until medical help can be provided.

5 Ways to Reduce Heat Related Risks:

1. Encourage students to **drink enough fluids** during the day, up until one hour before class begins.

2. **Give water breaks** during class. If you do not have a water fountain, recommend that everyone bring a water bottle.

3. Recommend that students **drink only water during exercise**. Water is absorbed most quickly by the body. Sports drinks should be saved until after class because the sugars they contain slow absorption of liquids.

4. **Reduce the intensity** of class and provide down time for stretching or meditation.

5. **Do not push students** beyond their comfort level. Allow anyone who becomes overheated to sit out for a break. Pay special attention to students who are older, overweight, have respiratory/cardiac problems or out of shape.

Avoiding Dehydration

Dehydration can be a threat during the warmer months or during prolonged workouts. Some steps you can take to **prevent dehydration**:

- If your school is not air-conditioned or is poorly ventilated, give regular water breaks and tone down workouts on very hot days.

- If your school is air-conditioned, caution is still warranted because people are generally more fatigued and may have spent the day working outdoors. By the end of the day, they are in danger of becoming dehydrated, even in a climate-controlled environment.

- During long intensive workouts, give water breaks at least every thirty minutes.

Some steps your students can take to **stay properly hydrated** during training:

- **Drink before** a workout. Feeling thirsty is a sign of impending dehydration. On average, most people need eight ounces of fluid for every twenty minutes of exercise.

- Avoid drinks with **caffeine, alcohol, or carbonation**.

- **Cool fluids** are absorbed more rapidly than warm fluids.

- For workouts of one hour or less, water is adequate for replacing lost fluids after exercise. For longer workouts, sports drinks may be appropriate.

One of the most common questions presented by students of all levels is: What is the purpose of practicing forms? Whether your students know them as kata, poomse, hyung, patterns, forms or some other name, the question always implies the same doubt. How does this dance-like performance relate to sparring or self-defense? How can I apply what I practice in real life?

Many instructors have never learned realistic applications for the forms in their system and teach forms to improve balance, coordination, power and other aspects of conditioning. While this is a valid approach, each form also has a more realistic purpose: the application of techniques against an opponent.

Teaching the application of each movement of a form (or at least some of the most important movements) gives the student a deeper understanding of what he is learning and lends purpose to form practice. When the student visualizes how each technique is intended to be used, he can create a more realistic rendering of the form.

Assessing your Resources

Many styles teach applications for each form from the beginner level. They may be taught as applications, self-defense techniques or step-sparring sets. If you have learned the applications for each form in your style, you are in a good position to pass them along to your students.

"What is the purpose of practicing forms?"

"How does this dance-like performance relate to sparring or self-defense?"

"How can I apply what I practice in real life?"

If you have not learned a formal system of applications as part of your training, you have two choices: seek out a knowledgeable instructor from whom to learn the applications or create your own.

Learning Applications

Each style of martial arts has at least one instructor who has taken the time to systematize and preserve the applications found in that style's forms. There are many videotapes and books available that detail these teachings. If you find a suitable set of applications for your style, study and practice them from the most basic form. Once you are satisfied with your ability to execute and understand each technique, begin introducing them to your students.

Creating Applications

If you do not have access to a system of applications for your style, you have to create your own. You may also want to create your own applications if you cannot find a system that works well with your curriculum. The applications should enhance, but not duplicate the skills you teach as part of your self-defense and sparring curriculum.

To create your own applications, begin with most basic form of your style. Break the form down into logical sets of movements. The most common sets involve one or two defensive movements followed by a number of offensive movements.

Once you have created logical groupings, interpret the actions for use against a partner. If the first movements of the form are low block and step forward punch, then obviously your partner has to throw an attack for you to block, then retreat when you punch. With basic forms, the applications should be obvious.

As you progress in difficulty level, the applications may become subtler or even hidden. If you cannot directly interpret a movement, create a variation that works with a partner. Form applications do not have to be literal copies of each movement. They should, however, preserve the spirit of the form and the intention of the movement.

In time, you may be teaching an application and suddenly realize that there is a better or easier way to apply a particular technique. When you reach this level, you can create variations and teach them to your advanced students to maintain their interest and increase the depth of their form practice. Applications encourage advanced students to continue practicing even the most basic forms to discover their hidden mysteries.

Introducing New Applications

As with any new curriculum, introduce the applications gradually. For beginner level students, the introduction of new curriculum elements comes naturally because beginner students are not set in their ways and have few expectations in terms of curriculum requirements. They view the change as they would the introduction of any other new skills.

With advanced students, however, reactions vary. Many students are intrigued by the introduction of a new way of practicing. They immediately begin incorporating the new skills into their practice routines and are eager to learn as much as possible about the application of each technique. Nurturing of these students fosters a successful introduction of application training as a curriculum requirement.

On the other hand, there are students who resist the introduction of such a large body of new knowledge. They may believe that they were getting along just fine without learning applications and they don't want to be bothered memorizing many new techniques. To make these students comfortable with the new curriculum, proceed progressively, introducing one new skill at a time and giving adequate practice time in class.

To prevent advanced students from feeling overwhelmed, begin introducing the applications to them first. Once they feel comfortable with the skills, begin teaching the lower belts. By using this system, advanced students have the knowledge to help the lower belts learn and are not embarrassed at learning the same skills as the lower ranks. You help them preserve their status as senior students while teaching them valuable new skills.

Choosing a Weapon

Questions to ask when choosing a weapon to teach:

1. Is it legal to buy, use and carry?

Local laws vary on the legality of purchasing and carrying various weapons. It is your responsibility to fully understand those laws before introducing a weapon into your curriculum.

2. Do I understand the weapon?

Before you teach a weapon, you must be knowledgeable about its use. If you do not have an instructor, videos and DVDs are a good source of supplementary instruction.

3. Does it complement the skills I already teach?

Choose a weapon that is similar in style and content to the skills you are teaching in class. It is easier to learn a weapon that is similar to current movement patterns than to start from scratch with a foreign concept.

4. Will I teach it to children?

Some parents are concerned about weapons. A safe weapon to start mature children with is the short stick. It is non-threatening and easy to manipulate for their smaller body structures.

Introducing Weapon Training

Supplement empty hand skills

Training with weapons has long been a part of many martial arts systems' curriculum. But in light of the increasing violence in our society, many instructors have decreased or even dropped their weapon instruction. Students and parents perceive empty handed martial arts training to be defensive, but they object to the offensive nature of weapon training.

This attitude has left many instructors hesitant to introduce or pursue a program of weapon training in their school. However, learning to skillfully control a weapon can be a valuable lesson for serious martial artists and provide a challenging addition to the advanced curriculum. And a weapon curriculum can give advanced student an incentive to continue their studies as they begin to master the basics of empty hand training.

Introducing the Weapon

If your students have never practiced with a weapon before, they will be very curious about its use and anxious to begin training immediately. Before you begin the physical portion of the training, a few preliminary steps will help your teaching go smoothly.

1. Introduce the purpose of the weapon.

Discuss briefly how the weapon is used offensively and defensively. If you know the history of the weapon, give a brief overview.

2. Demonstrate the etiquette of using the weapon.

All traditional weapons have a correct method for handling, for exchanging the weapon between partners and for carrying it outside the training area.

3. List the safety rules.

When you introduce a weapon into the training hall, there is always an increased safety risk. Make the safety rules clear to all students and demonstrate safety procedures. Clearly state behaviors that will not be tolerated in the class such as dropping or throwing the weapon or using the weapon during horseplay.

4. Emphasize each student's personal responsibility.

If each student purchases their own weapon, explain their responsibility for taking care of the weapon, including whether it should be carried in a carrying case.

5. Special cautions for children.

If children are participating in the class, ask them to get their parent's permission before beginning training. You should also emphasize the seriousness of the use of a weapon and it's potential to harm others if used irresponsibly.

Teaching the Basics

After you have reviewed the introductory steps, begin the physical training. As an example, we will use the short stick. The first skill taught is the grip. Each student is taught how to hold the stick and how to correctly transfer the stick from one hand to another while bowing.

Once the proper grip and bowing are taught, the ready stance is introduced. From the ready stance, students are taught to move forward, backward and sideways. Although grip, stance and footwork practice may seem monotonous, they should be practiced thoroughly before beginning the blocking and striking instruction. Once the students have a firm foundation, begin teaching the use of the stick as a combat weapon.

First teach the simple upward and downward blocks and the straight strike. Next introduce the inward and outward blocks as well as the thrust. Teach more complicated blocks and strikes as they progress.

Once everyone has a basic understanding of the fundamental blocks and strikes, introduce the first pattern to reinforce the movements learned and to practice footwork and turning.

You can also begin teaching arranged partner drills to realistically practice the blocks and strikes learned earlier. From these partner drills, students learn realistic free combat skills to apply later in their training.

A weapon curriculum, and the short stick in particular, is developed much like the empty handed curriculum. You begin by teaching fundamentals, progress to arranged partner drills and patterns and eventually reach the stage where students can successfully apply their skills in free combat.

Teaching Children

Proven Strategies and Approaches

In this section ...

74 Methods of Learning
76 Factors Affecting Learning
79 Short Attention Spans
81 Attention Deficit Disorder
92 Reinforcement or Punishment
98 Improving Attention Spans
102 Learning Disabilities
105 Dealing with Aggression
108 Separation Anxiety
113 Shyness
116 Developmental Stages

Giving Directions

Children are much more likely to follow concrete than abstract directions:

Abstract direction: Everyone behave during testing.

Concrete direction: While you wait for your turn during the test, sit up straight and don't talk.

Abstract direction: Be nice to your Mom and Dad at home.

Concrete direction: Tonight I want everyone to help out with one chore without being asked. When you come to class on Friday, be ready to tell me which chore you did.

Abstract direction: It's important to pay attention in school.

Concrete direction: This week, try to raise your hand and answer a question at least once in every class at school.

Teaching Children

Proven strategies and approaches

Teaching martial arts to children can be both one of the most rewarding and one of the most frustrating experiences you can have as an instructor. Children are the future of martial arts, eager to learn and excited about their lessons. They are far more impressionable than adults and therefore more likely to absorb the full benefits that martial arts can offer them as a person.

However, children can be much more difficult to teach than adults. If you accept children under the age of nine, you will spend a great deal of time explaining and re-explaining the rules of the school and the way to do techniques. You will also find yourself dealing with more serious issues like children who have attention deficit disorder, learning disabilities, separation anxiety and aggression problems, all issues rarely faced in adult classes.

The goal of this section is to help you successfully teach these difficult children by providing specific strategies and approaches that have been proven to work in a martial arts class setting. Before discussing specific problem areas, let's take a closer look at how children learn and what an instructor can do in general to promote learning in all age students.

There are three methods of learning: reinforcement, formation of associations, and insight.

Reinforcement

Reinforcement may be direct or indirect. **Direct reinforcement** occurs when a student performs a skill and receives immediate confirmation that the skill was performed correctly. Direct reinforcement can be verbal (an instructor's feedback) or tangible (scoring a point in sparring or throwing an opponent during a self-defense drill). All of these outcomes point to success and the students learns that this action was correct and desirable. If the student missed the point or was unable to throw his partner, he would learn that the movement was executed improperly and try a different approach or strategy.

Indirect reinforcement is also called observational learning. A student observes another person then imitates or does not imitate her behavior, depending on whether or not reinforcement is received. For example, a student is asked to demonstrate a kick then praised by the instructor. The other students in class learn from observing her behavior and the instructor's praise that her performance was correct and they attempt to imitate it, subconsciously associating the praise received by the demonstrating student with their own performance.

Direct reinforcement often works better for children than for adults, while indirect reinforcement works well for all ages.

Association

Attitudes and feelings about situations, people, places or things are learned through association. Learning through association can often be unplanned and have unforeseen negative consequences. Association means that a previously neutral situation or subject becomes associated with a distinct emotional response or characteristic.

Consider a common occurrence in martial arts classes. A student is struggling with his side kick, so the instructor stops the class and has him demonstrate the kick. The instructor then shows the class what is wrong with the kick and corrects him. This works well for the instructor because what the student is doing wrong is often the same thing that several other people of the same rank are struggling with.

Correcting one student in front of the group indirectly corrects the others as well. For the student who is corrected in front of his classmates, however, the side kick may take on a new unpleasantness. Where before he felt his side kick wasn't that great, he didn't feel it was any worse than others of his peer group. Now, he feels he has been singled out as an example of a bad side kick and may avoid practicing the kick. Through that one experience, his feelings about the side kick and his own competence at it have markedly changed.

Of course, association could also turn a neutral situation into a positive outcome. If the instructor selects a student whose side kick is a good model for others and explains why his kick is outstanding, the student would see his side kick as better than his other kicks where before he never gave it much thought.

Be aware of opportunities to use learning by association positively and make a conscious effort to avoid negative learning by association situations.

Insight

Insight is characterized by a sudden enlightenment with regard to a principle or underlying concept. Learning by insight often occurs suddenly after a period of study or practice. For example, you have explained the timing of a complex jumping kick to a black belt several times, but he still doesn't seem to get exactly what you mean. One day, as he practices on his own, something suddenly "clicks" and he is executing the kick with ease.

Learning by insight often involves the grasping of a broad concept or principle that can be applied to other areas. Once the student understands how to do a particular jumping kick, he improves his other jumping kicks by applying this knowledge.

Types of Learning Summary

1. Reinforcement
    a. Direct reinforcement
    b. Indirect reinforcement

2. Association

3. Insight

Asking vs. Telling

Asking a child to do a task is not as effective as instructing him to do it.

Examples:

Weak asking phrase: How about if we all quiet down so we can hear about the game we're going to play next?

Strong instructing phrase: When you're quiet, I'll explain the rules of the game.

Weak asking phrase: How many times do I have to tell you not to chew gum in class, Tommy?

Strong instructing phrase: Tommy, go to the bathroom and throw away your gum.

Weak asking phrase: I wish you would stop fidgeting and stay in line?

Strong instructing phrase: Stand right behind Megan in a good fighting stance.

Factors Affecting Learning

Coping with interference

See also . . .
Short Attention Spans . . . . page 79
Developmental Stages . . . page 116

There are a number of factors that affect the scope and quantity of information that a child is able to learn.

1. The Learner

Children's motor, sensory-perceptual, linguistic and academic skills develop in a well-established sequence, with some variation for timing in each individual. A child of four has a very different capacity for learning than an eight year old. A successful curriculum for children takes into account the children's developmental stage. If a large number of children are having difficulty with a portion of the curriculum, it may be too difficult for the children's developmental level. A more detailed discussion of what can be expected at each level of development can be found beginning on page 116.

2. The Environment

The physical environment of the school must be conducive to learning. There should be adequate space for each child to safely move around, adequate heating and cooling amenities, a sufficient amount of age-appropriate equipment that is well maintained, and a set of rules that are consistently enforced to create a well-ordered atmosphere.

Younger children require a more structured atmosphere while preteens and teens should be given the opportunity to develop their growing independence through the use of extended individual practice times and home practice assignments. Ideally, there should be at least two different children's classes based on age.

Beyond the physical environment, the students and teacher(s) have a profound impact on the learning environment, particularly when teaching children who have short attention spans or are easily distracted. The gender of the teacher can have an impact on the child's desire to learn. Older children prefer a teacher of the same gender as themselves, while preschool children respond well to female teachers who they identify with as a mother figure.

The structure of a child's family also affects her ability to learn. If she is used to a rigid family routine, she will respond well to an atmosphere of discipline. If her home life is unstructured, she may seek out the security of structure in the martial arts class atmosphere or she may rebel against it.

Spending time talking with a child's parents may give you clues about her home life and the way she interacts with her parents. You can then structure your interactions with the child accordingly. Watch how the child responds to her parents: is she clinging, dependent, rebellious, tuned out? Some children tune out their parents as soon as the lecturing starts and will do the same to you. Others are so used to getting yelled at, that anyone who addresses them with a raised voice gets ignored or railed against. Some children know they can get their way with their parents by crying, whining or throwing a tantrum. It's up to you to recognize these patterns and break the cycle that the child has fallen into at home.

Which brings us to the effect that expectations have on learning. If you walk through the halls of the average elementary school, you will notice that some classrooms are quiet and orderly while others are chaotic, with children talking out, fidgeting and being disruptive. The difference in the classes is very closely related to the teacher's expectations.

Think back to your days in elementary school. Was there a teacher that everyone was afraid of? Was there a class in which you wouldn't be caught dead passing a note to a

Factors Affecting Learning

1. The learner

2. The environment
   a. physical environment
   b. teacher
   c. child's habits
   d. teacher's expectations
   e. class rules
   f. other students

3. The information
   a. repeated often
   b. relevant

friend? Was there a class that you knew you could get away with anything? Teachers develop these reputations because of their expectations.

Some teachers have high expectations and go to great lengths to communicate and enforce them. They do not tolerate misbehavior because they expect the children to behave at a certain level for their age. Children are adept at sensing a teacher's expectations and react differently from class to class, behaving well for one teacher and misbehaving for another.

Finally, the children in the class have a strong impact on learning, particularly with groups of older children. If children are allowed to giggle when a classmate makes a mistake or to shout out answers or form small, elite groups, the atmosphere of the class is not conducive to learning. On the other hand, if children cheer on their classmates, respect each other, take turns and are supportive, the class atmosphere encourages learning and growth.

When setting class rules, choose rules that create a good learning environment. For example:

    a. Raise your hand to ask a question.
    b. Treat others, as you would like to be treated.
    c. Higher belts should help lower belts with new skills.
    d. Stay in line/no "cutting."
    e. No touching/hitting other students.

Always enforce the rules consistently and patiently so the students clearly know what your expectations are.

3. The Information

The information to be learned and its method of presentation affect whether and how well it is processed and absorbed by students. Material is more likely to be learned if it is:

- **Repeated often.** Skills that are practiced more frequently are more likely to be learned well. For younger students, a curriculum that emphasizes frequent but varied repetition of a small group of skills is more likely to be successful than a curriculum of a diverse body of skills.

- **Relevant.** If a student feels that material is important, she is more likely to have a higher interest level and therefore more success in learning. Try to relate skills to real life wherever possible. For example, show children how a self-defense skill might be used against a playground bully or how a jumping drill will help them learn an exciting jump kick later.

See also . . .
Attention Deficit Disorder . . . . page 81
Improving Attention Span . . . . page 98

Before we look at the needs of ADD/ADHD children, let's consider some strategies for handling an issue that affects all children: the short attention span. The martial arts are inherently designed for adults. Many of the required skills are complex and demand long hours of practice to master. And the forms of most styles are long, complicated and sometimes difficult to remember. How can an instructor adapt the curriculum for the short attention span and limited cognitive abilities of the average child? And what about for children with short attention spans, learning difficulties or behavioral problems?

There are a few simple steps that can be taken to create a style of teaching and curriculum that appeals to children without losing the spirit of the art.

1. Break down complex skills.

Some skills are too difficult for even the most adept junior student. Skills that pose problems include forms/patterns, step sparring, combination skills, complex footwork and spinning kicks. A skill that an adult remembers and practices independently after viewing once may seem impossible to a child. To teach a complex skill, break it down into simpler steps. Teach long forms in sets of a few movements. Practice combination skills one movement at a time, adding a new step only when the student can confidently perform the ones that come before it. Use visual or physical cues like "turn to face the front wall" rather than "turn to your left."

2. Pair more experienced students with students who need extra help.

Children often learn best from other children. When you are having difficulty getting a child to understand a new concept, try pairing him up with a child who can perform the technique well. Ask the more advanced child to *practice* the skill together or to *help* the other child with the skill. Avoid using the word *teach*. The child will attempt to teach the skill just like you were teaching it, with much the same results.

3. Speak and think like a child.

To teach children effectively, you have to speak their language. Many four and five year olds do not know right from left, back leg from front leg or slide from step. Using the same language you use for older children will leave them confused. Instead, rely on visual cues like "Now we're going to use this leg to kick" while demonstrating. You can also compare techniques to simple actions like, "Imagine you are trying to squash a bug with the bottom of your foot" instead of "Put more power into your side kicks."

4. Give specific instructions.

If you ask an adult class to pair off by size, they accomplish it in about thirty seconds. If you give the same instruction to a group of six year olds, you have complete chaos. Children need very specific instructions. Establish a few simple classroom instructions like: make a line for target kicking, face a partner for self-defense, line up, sit down in the back of the room.

Always use the same terms and always wait until they complete the task before giving another. If they have difficulty, demonstrate with a small group then practice a half dozen times, rewarding them when they get it right. Or divide the class in half and see which half can "make a straighter line for target kicking" or "line up the quickest." Practicing basic class instructions might seem like a nuisance, but it makes the class run more smoothly in the long run. By using just a few instructions, the children know what you expect and accomplish it quickly, saving valuable instruction time.

5. Allow for variations.

Children of the same age can have significantly different capacities for learning. Make allowances in your curriculum for those children who learn slower or faster than average. In time, most of these variations even out. If you demand that every child fit into the curriculum, especially when it comes to promotion requirements, you will lose quite a few potentially good students. If you accommodate the fast and slow learners in the beginning stages, in most cases by the time the students become black belts, it is no longer evident who the fast and slow learners were.

Variations of many of the above techniques are repeated in the section on attention deficit disorder. In some cases, ADD/ADHD children require a slightly different approach, but in general implementing the strategies for short attention spans benefit all of the children in class.

Attention Deficit Disorder

Understanding the challenge

See also . . .
Short Attention Spans . . . . page 79
Improving Attention Span . . . . page 98

Attention Deficit Disorder, or ADD, is the most commonly diagnosed of all childhood psychiatric disorders and one of the most common sources of frustration for martial arts instructors who teach children. ADD is believed to afflict three to five percent of all children (around two million children in the United States), with boys making up the majority of those diagnosed. ADD is a behavioral disorder with four major symptoms:

1. Selective attention
2. Impulsivity
3. Distractibility
4. Hyperactivity (in some cases)

It can be mild, moderate or severe, with children who range from somewhat fidgety to completely out of control. Some children with ADD are more distracted in group settings but do well with one-on-one attention while others are affected in all settings.

Although signs of ADD are often present when a child is a toddler, most children are first diagnosed after they begin school. While toddlers are often demanding, destructive, and distracted, school age children are expected to conform to certain behavioral standards that ADD children cannot meet successfully. What was tolerated as rambunctious at home is no longer acceptable in the classroom and the child is referred to a school counselor or behavioral specialist by his teacher.

"Contrary to common usage, not all children with ADD are hyperactive."

The difference between the symptoms of ADD and the inattention, impulsivity and hyperactivity that are a normal part of childhood is that children with ADD exhibit these symptoms all of the time. The symptoms do not come and go depending on the situation or the environment. While the average five year old may go on a tear through the playground with his friends at recess, he is able to settle down to his work when school begins again. An ADD child is as wild in the classroom and on the bus as he is on the playground.

ADD also does not make a sudden appearance when a major life change occurs, such as a parents' divorce. A child who begins acting out after a major change at home most likely has a short-term behavioral problem, not ADD.

Four Symptoms in Detail

1. Selective Attention

Children with ADD do not entirely lack the ability to pay attention to an activity; they tend to the extremes of brief spurts of attention or long periods of intense concentration. Most people operate somewhere in the middle, between the inattention and hyperfocus that ADD kids are drawn to.

Children with ADD may be able to concentrate intensely for long periods of time on activities they find very interesting like playing video games or building with clay, but jump randomly from one task to another in class. Their inability to modulate their attention is often frustrating and confusing to parents and instructors. Problems with attention span become obvious when children enter a structured program like elementary school or karate lessons and are expected to pay attention for extended periods of time. While most children drift off occasionally in class, children with ADD show selective attention most of the time and to an extreme degree, differentiating themselves from other children their age.

2. Distractibility

Children with Attention Deficit Disorder are easily distracted by seemingly unimportant things. They frequently start tasks without finishing any of them. Children with ADD are distracted by both internal and external stimuli, so contrary to logic, isolating them from the class does not solve their distractibility.

Often being completely alone can worsen their ability to concentrate, making them more prone to drift off into their internal world. The best ways to minimize distractibility are to keep the child close to the instructor and to limit potential visual distractions.

3. Impulsivity

Children with ADD tend to do things without thinking through the consequences. They may pull the ponytail of the girl in front of them without considering that it will hurt her or that they will get into trouble. Or they might decide to parachute off the garage roof using a bed sheet because they saw a cartoon character do the same thing on television.

This differs markedly from children with emotional or behavioral problems who engage in destructive behavior out of anger while understanding the consequences. Children with ADD are more likely than other children to have multiple accidents and or injuries, to lose or break things frequently, to lie about their actions and to act inappropriately in class.

4. Hyperactivity

Contrary to common usage, not all children with ADD are hyperactive. Attention Deficit/ Hyperactivity Disorder (ADHD) is the term used when children exhibit hyperactivity in addition to other symptoms. There are three types of ADHD:

    a. Attention-Deficit/Hyperactivity Disorder, Predominantly Inattentive Type

    b. Attention-Deficit/Hyperactivity Disorder, Predominantly Impulsive Type

    c. Attention-Deficit/Hyperactivity Disorder, Combined Type

In fact, children with hyperactivity are not necessarily more active than other children their age, but they are more often active at inappropriate times, particularly in ways that bother others when they should be paying attention to the task at hand. It is the inappropriateness of their behavior that becomes disruptive and gets them into trouble.

Other Personality Traits

In addition to the four major symptoms, children with ADD or ADHD often have other distinct personality traits including:

1. Intensity

Children with ADD are often intense emotionally. They may seem overly emotional and stubborn. They may react to interruptions or frustrations with outbursts of anger or get fixated on one thing, like making a kick perfect, long after the rest of the class has moved on.

2. Overreaction

ADD children are prone to overreaction, getting overly excited when things go well, overly depressed or angry when things go badly. This can be frustrating to instructors whose goal is to encourage children to learn from their mistakes without getting overly disappointed by them.

3. Living in the moment

Children with ADD are governed by the here and now. They tend to easily forget lessons learned in the past and don't look into the future to predict the consequences of their actions. This can also lead to lying to get out of trouble, quickly moving from one activity to the next, and wandering off during an activity to satisfy a more "urgent" need like getting a drink at the water fountain. When teaching children with ADD, bear in mind that their priorities seem unreasonable to adults, yet are very real to themselves.

4. Need for frequent rewards

A reward system is difficult to use to manage the behavior of ADD children because they often forget what reward they are working toward or cannot wait until the goal is completed and lose interest. Consequently, you may find yourself rewarding these children more often for doing less than others in the same class. Try working toward decreasing the frequency of rewards over time or use small, non-material interim rewards such as a star chart or verbal praise.

5. Easily bored

Boredom is a pervasive problem for children with ADD. They seem to career from one activity to another, quickly losing interest in each. Parents and instructors become exhausted trying to keep up with their shifting attentions. Even more frustrating, their boredom is often unrelated to how interesting a subject is. They find a subject interesting one day then be completely unable to focus on it another day.

6. Inconsistency

Children with ADD often have wide swings in their level of performance. One day they may be an outstanding student while the next, they seem to have forgotten everything. Be prepared for good days and bad days. Don't expect that great performance one day to be followed by an even better performance the next day as you would with other children.

7. Egocentricity

When dealing with children with ADD, expect them to frequently complain that they have been treated unfairly, which from their point of view means the other child or adult did not see things their way. They have trouble understanding why others do not see the world from their point of view and this affects their relationships with their peers and their ability to make friends. Similarly, they frequently have trouble seeing things from other people's point of view, making it difficult to explain why their behavior is wrong or distracting.

Although much of the discussion of children with Attention Deficit Disorder centers on their negative personality traits, there are some potentially good side effects of ADD. Children, and adults, with ADD are often more creative, more spontaneous, more focused, more tenacious and more likely to "think outside the box" than other people. You will often find that you are drawn to the students in your class with ADD because they have such magnetic personalities and many endearing qualities. Encourage and nurture this side of their personalities.

Myths about ADD:

1. The child will outgrow ADD.

Some children may show markedly fewer symptoms of ADD after the onset of puberty, but the disorder does not go away. In fact, fifty percent of all children with ADD continue to suffer the side effects of ADD, including inattention, impulsivity, poor social skills, learning difficulties and low self-esteem, long after puberty. Even if a child does outgrow the disorder, he must be treated until that time. If ADD is left untreated, the symptoms often worsen as the child gets older, causing a slightly aggressive three year old to blossom into a destructive, out of control six year old.

2. All children with ADD are hyperactive.
3. ADD and ADHD are the same disorder.

Many children with ADD are mistakenly labeled as lazy or careless. Because not all children with ADD have hyperactivity as is commonly believed, children who are inattentive, but not disruptive or hyperactive, can be overlooked by teachers and parents. Children with ADHD are often diagnosed and treated early because their disruptive behavior demands attention from parents and teachers. Without treatment they upset the entire class. However, children with ADD who are not disruptive, but who go through their days in a world of their own, are easily labeled lazy, unmotivated, or underachievers. It is important to keep in mind that these children need the same treatment as children with ADHD.

Medication

Many parents and doctors choose to use the prescription medication Ritalin (or a number of other medications) to treat the symptoms of children with ADD. Used in conjunction with a behavioral modification program, this can be very effective.

If you have children in your class who are taking medication for ADD/ADHD, you will know if they show up for class without having taken their medication. You should also know that there may be side-effects to these drugs including sleep problems, anxiousness, irritability, depression, verbal/physical tics, headache, stomachache and what might be called the "zombie effect" where the child tends to stare off into space like a zombie. In extreme cases, a child may experience hallucinations or psychosis.

As the medication begins to wear off, the symptoms of ADD or ADHD return. If class is just prior to child's next dose of medication, you may find this occurring. If you have concerns that a child's medication is affecting his ability to participate fully in class, speak to his parents about it.

A different class schedule relative to his medication schedule may help solve the problem. Also bear in mind that some children are embarrassed by having to take medication daily, so keep your concerns confidential. Any discussion of a child's medical situation should be kept between you, other instructors involved in his class and his parents.

ADD Facts:

1. Around two million children (3-5% of the US population) have ADD or ADHD.

2. Boys diagnosed with ADHD outnumber girls by 3 to 1. Boys and girls are almost equally diagnosed with ADD. Boys are more frequently diagnosed with ADD or ADHD at a younger age than girls.

3. ADD is most often formally diagnosed at around age six or seven when a child enters school.

4. The diagnosis of ADD is based on observations by parents, teachers and professionals.

5. Unrecognized and untreated ADD leads to a high incidence of school problems (30 to 50 percent) and a high incidence of problems with the law (20 to 30 percent) in older children.

6. Children diagnosed with ADD should never be treated with drugs only. Behavioral management techniques and learning skills must be included in a successful treatment plan.

7. If recognized and managed, most children with ADD can be taught to use their differences (creativity, spontaneity, tenacity, hyperfocus) to their advantage.

Strategies for Improving Behavior in ADD and ADHD Children

The behavior problems associated with ADD and ADHD tend to lead to other problems. Children who are disruptive in school are quickly labeled troublemakers, ruffians, bullies or just plain dumb. Children at the other end of the ADD spectrum are labeled lazy, stupid, underachieving or spaced out. To make things worse, these children often have trouble understanding why their behavior is wrong. This explains the ADD child's tendency to look genuinely shocked when he gets in trouble. One of the biggest challenges to improving the behavior of the ADD child is teaching him to recognize the consequences of his actions and to see things from other peoples' point of view.

There are some steps you can take to help manage the behavior of students in your class with ADD or ADHD including:

1. Identify problem behaviors.

Objectively identify what problems are the biggest impediments to the child's learning. These may not be the most annoying behaviors or the ones you would most like to correct, so take an unemotional inventory, perhaps involving other instructors or the child's parents. Making a chart can help. For each item, list the behavior, when it most frequently occurs, what triggers it and how disruptive it is on a scale of one to ten. Try to be as specific as possible. For each problem, write down at least one strategy from this report for eliminating or changing the behavior.

2. Identify problems in the class environment.

Look at the way you and other instructors treat the child. Are you overly harsh? Do you "expect" the child to misbehave and punish him more quickly than others? Have you eliminated as many distractions as possible? Is class active and upbeat with lots of short periods of activity and little inactivity? Are the children closely supervised, especially when working in pairs or groups? By looking at the way you teach and the class environment, you may be able to quickly eliminate some undesirable behaviors.

3. Model Healthy Behavior.

Demonstrate behaviors that you want the child to follow like not speaking when others are speaking, putting equipment away after using it, talking in a polite quiet voice and not being overly critical.

4. Partner for difficult tasks.

If a child is struggling with learning or remembering a skill, partnering him with a responsible older child or an assistant instructor can be very helpful. Remind the older child that his job is to be a role model and a helper so he will be a bit more understanding.

5. Count your feedback.

Try keeping track of the amount of positive and negative feedback you are giving an ADD child in class. Although much of the feedback is negative, actively look for areas to praise so you don't come across as mean or nagging.

6. Be specific.

Give an ADD child specific action messages and instructions. He does not grasp the subtlety of a statement like "Hanging on the stretching bar is dangerous." He also does not translate "Pay attention" into "Stop hanging on the stretching bar and get back in line."

You have to spell out, word for word, what you want him to do in the exact way you want it done. If you want him get off the stretching bar, tell him exactly that. If you want him to stop playing with his toes and look at you when you talk, tell him to look at you. By giving instructions that include specific actions, you remove any room for misunderstanding and misinterpretation.

7. Use rewards correctly.

There is a temptation to "bribe" children with ADD into good behavior by lavishing them with material rewards for every good behavior. While material rewards are often appropriate, look for other options first.

Rewards can include praise in front of the class or the child's parents, a simple "thank you" or "good job" that is well timed or the opportunity to hold a special position in class, like line leader. Rewards are also more effective when the child has a say in what he gets for good behavior. And you might be surprised at what he asks for. Some children are just as happy with a sticker to wear on their shirt as they would be with a much more expensive reward.

If a child is set on a material reward, stretch it out with interim rewards of stars or tickets, of which the child has to earn a certain number to get the larger material reward. In doing this, each star or ticket becomes a mini-reward.

8. Use a "when…then" sentence.

If a child is not performing a specific behavior like sitting still or practicing quietly, try using a "when…then" sentence like "When you sit down and stop talking, then I'll explain the rules of the game we're going to play" or "When you are doing that kick well, then we'll kick the heavy bag."

Obviously, the "then" portion of the statement should sound rewarding and hopefully be directly related to the child's good behavior, a positive natural outcome of his behavior. Always use *when*, not *if*, because *when* implies that child will do something and *if* implies that he has a choice.

9. Don't use ADD as an excuse.

Resist the urge to use ADD as an excuse for the child's behavior. If you exempt a child from punishment, responsibilities and expectations because he has ADD, you are doing him a disservice. It may be easier to use ADD as an excuse than to enforce the rules with an ADD child, but that is tantamount to giving up on him. Taking the time and effort needed to help the child is time consuming at first, but pays big dividends in the long run.

10. Speak pleasantly.

If you want an ADD child to listen to you, try speaking slowly, quietly and briefly. Children who are used to getting yelled at tune out the yelling just like instructors tune out children who whine and complain all the time. It also helps to make eye contact before beginning to speak so you know you have the child's attention.

11. Use positive language.

When possible, give directions that tell the child what to do rather than what not to do. "Don't make noise with the target" is not as effective as "Put the target down until I finish talking."

Negative Language	Positive Language
No yelling out.	Raise your hand if you know the answer.
Stop fidgeting.	Sit up straight and tall.
Wrong hand.	Other hand, please.
Don't hit your partner.	Show me good control.
Don't talk while others are talking	Listen carefully to what Tim is saying.
No drinks during class.	As soon as we all line up quietly, we'll get a drink

12. Give advance warnings.

When an ADD child is concentrating on something, changing tasks can cause an angry outburst and deter future efforts. If you see a child working hard on something when it is time to move on to a new activity, give a warning like "Everyone finish up what you are practicing because in sixty seconds we're going to do some sparring." This gives the child time to wrap up his activity at his own pace and is less disruptive.

13. Make a feedback sandwich.

If you have negative feedback, occasionally try sandwiching it between two positive comments like, "You did a great job at getting ready for your test, you just need a little more practice on your side kick. I'm sure you'll practice as well at home as you did in class today." Sweeten the criticism with two compliments when the child's behavior is otherwise very good.

14. Structure the class environment.

Many therapists recommend that parents enroll children for martial arts lessons because they teach self-discipline. One of the ways martial arts teaches self-discipline is through structure, which is well suited to the needs of ADD children.

- Have ADD children stand at the front of the class so they are focused on the instructor and not the children in front of them. If the child's rank prevents him from standing near the front of the class, change the way the ranks line up in children's classes. Instead of lining up all of the higher ranks in the front row with the lower ranks in the back row, make a line for each rank. With this format, all of the black belts stand in rank order from front to back in the line at the right side of the classroom. The next is all of the red belts, then all of the blue belts, etc. If you have a yellow belt who needs to stand at the front of the class, just put him at the head of the yellow belt line. (See the diagram at left.)

Sample class structure

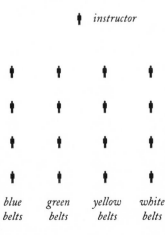

90

- Keep ADD children away from each other and away from children with other behavior problems. Pair them with or stand them near children who follow the rules and set good examples.

- When working with targets or other equipment, supervise ADD children closely, placing them near an instructor who can step in quickly if they begin using it inappropriately.

- Minimize auditory distractions such as noise in the waiting room or the sound of the front door opening and closing.

- If the classroom opens to the waiting room, have the class face away from the waiting room.

- Keep equipment out of reach of curious hands.

Handling Non-Compliant Children

Although defiance, procrastination, forgetfulness, and dawdling are not ADD symptoms, they are often present in children with ADD. There are basically two types of non-compliant children, those who say "no" and mean it and those who say "yes" but don't do what they agreed to do. Some children alternate between both behaviors. Because children with ADD are often frustrated with their behavior and the way they are treated (or perceive they are treated) they tend to exhibit non-compliant behaviors more than other children.

The best weapon for handling non-compliance is consistency. Once a child realizes that you are consistently firm with him, that you won't discipline him one day and look the other way the next, he will begin to bring his behavior in line. He may test you severely first, but if you maintain a consistently firm response, you will soon see changes.

Another helpful strategy is to give the child some responsibility so he can take charge of his world. Allowing him to show that he is "grown up" gives the child more control and reduces his need to try to control his environment through negative behaviors like procrastinating or defying you.

Giving Directions

Giving a child directions requires a formula. Try these five steps:

1. Make sure the child **hears you** and remembers the instruction.

2. Give the child a clear **sequence of actions** to be taken.

3. If necessary, **make a reminder** (such as a pictorial chart) to help the child remember the sequence of steps to be carried out.

4. Set a clear and reasonable **time limit** for completing the task.

5. **Follow up** after the child finishes to praise or correct.

"Punishment does not offer an option for choosing a more desirable behavior in the future."

Reinforcement or Punishment

Choosing the right response

See also . . .
Attention Deficit Disorder . . . . page 81
Dealing with Aggression . . . . page 105

Using Positive Reinforcement

In addition to giving clear directions and using the strategies discussed in the previous sections, one of the best ways to motivate a difficult child, such as a child with ADD, to change his behavioral habits is to reinforce good habits and use them to replace undesirable behaviors. This strategy is challenging and can take a long time to show results, but it produces the long-term changes that parents associate with martial arts training.

While it is easier to simply punish a child for undesirable behavior, the punishment does not give the child an option for choosing a more desirable behavior when faced with the same situation in the future. He learns "what not to do" rather than "what to do." For example, you come into the classroom and find Joey and John running wildly around the room kicking the heavy bags. If you choose to punish them, by making them sit out of class or doing push-ups, you have only taught them that running around is bad. You may well come into class the next day and find them play-fighting or throwing targets at each other or playing with the weapons display.

While you extinguished one behavior, you did not give them a replacement behavior. If you instead call them over and reminded them that school rule number three says that everyone should practice quietly before class, you have not only extinguished an undesirable behavior, you have given them a behavior for which they can be praised in the future. If you come into class the next day and find them practicing, praise their good behavior to reinforce it.

Strategies for Long-Term Change

There are several keys to motivating lasting changes in children's behavior:

1. Pick one behavior at a time to work on.

Think small and focus on the interim steps toward success. By picking a specific behavior instead of trying to randomly target many problem behaviors, you and the child can measure success in concrete terms. When one behavior has been improved, set new goals and move on to another. Sometimes, improving one area has the effect of improving other related areas at the same time. When you teach a child not to impulsively hit others in anger, he may learn at the same time how to make friends more easily or how to control his temper in other situations.

2. Notice the way you are speaking to the child in class.

How much of your communication is praise? How much is criticism or correction? Try to frame your interactions with the child so he is getting at least twice as much praise for things he does right than criticism for problem behaviors.

3. Be specific in your positive feedback.

Saying, "John, you really did a good job concentrating when we were doing target kicking today" is much more effective than "John, you did a good job in class today." By telling the child exactly what he did right, you give him the chance to repeat the behavior in the future.

4. Share good news with parents.

Children with behavior problems often find that teachers only talk to their parents when there is bad news to report. Make it a point to find opportunities to praise the child in front of his parents. This has the added benefit of reminding his parents that you are actively working to improve his behavior, which is probably one of the main reasons they signed him up for lessons.

5. Consider using a reward system.

A reward system, like a star chart, is a program where the child earns a reward for good behavior. The reward should be easy to earn at first then increasingly difficult as the child gains control over his behavior. Rewards don't have to be elaborate or expensive. Most kids are thrilled to earn a sticker, a washable tattoo, a small patch or a cookie if you put the right amount of enthusiasm into rewarding it.

If you prefer not to use material rewards, make things like standing at the head of the line, counting out exercises, being first to get a drink at the water fountain, or using the heavy bag into rewards that students can earn with good behavior.

6. Use reward systems only to establish new behaviors.

If you use a star chart or other reward system, try to discontinue it soon after a child is consistently demonstrating the desired behavior. One way to discontinue a reward system without discouraging the good behavior is to tell the child he is now "too big" for a reward system and you are confident he can keep up his behavior just like all of the other big boys in class. Another method of weaning a child off rewards is to show him the positive consequences of his behavior. If a child learns to practice quietly before class on his own, teach him something new to practice. If he learns to hold a target without being disruptive, let him hold the target for a group of kids to kick.

Using Negative Reinforcement

For some students, positive reinforcement alone is often not enough to change certain behaviors. In these cases, negative reinforcement can be used to supplement praise. Negative reinforcement is most effective when it is used sparingly. Frequent negative reinforcement causes the child to tune you out and quickly lose its effect. Additionally, negative reinforcement should not be used as a threat. Never say "if you don't _____ I'm going to _____" unless you intend to carry out the consequences. Children learn to flaunt your threats if they sense you are not going to follow through with negative consequences.

There are several effective strategies you can try when positive reinforcement alone is not working:

1. Ignore the behavior.

This strategy works for attention getting behaviors like making nonsense sounds or throwing tantrums. However, in a group setting, it can be difficult to successfully ignore a behavior because even if you do not give the child attention, other children might.

Having a few of his friends join him in being disruptive is enough reinforcement for the child to continue acting out. To combat this, change the focus of the class. If the child is making disruptive sounds, try having the class do something very loud, like kihaping, which drowns out his noise and makes it easier to ignore. If he throws a tantrum, ask an assistant instructor to take him to another room to calm down while you lead the class in a fun, and noisy, game.

2. Use the time-out system.

While time-outs seem to have come into fashion in the past decade, it is actually just the name that is new. You can bet mothers everywhere were sending children to sit in the corner long before the word time-out ever entered the English language. To make a time-out effective:

- Identify the time-out area. This can be a corner of the room, a chair or a spot taped off on the mat.

- Make the time out area a spot that is safe (out of the way of the action going on in class) and boring. The child should be able to see or hear that she is missing out on the fun, but not be able to interact with other children or draw attention to herself.

- The length of a time-out is one minute for each year of the child's age. A five year old gets a five-minute time out. Having a timer that rings when time is up can be helpful for both you (you don't want to forget) and the child (she can watch it tick down).

- If the child resists the time-out by standing up or acting out, add an additional minute by turning the timer back one minute. Some children who are very easily distracted may need an assistant instructor to stand nearby so they do not get up and wander off.

- Do not get emotionally involved. Administer the time-out calmly by telling the child what she did wrong and why she should go to the time-out chair. If necessary, have an assistant take her there and keep track of the time. When the time-out is over, matter-of-factly tell her she can rejoin the class. Resist the urge to lecture.

- Administer the time-out as close to the start of the behavior as possible. The longer the child is allowed to continue the behavior, the more potential there is for him to feel that he's successfully gotten away with something.

3. Overcorrection.

Overcorrection refers to making the child suffer negative consequences that make the behavior especially unpleasant.

Reinforcement

Positive:

1. Pick one behavior.
2. Speak softly & briefly.
3. Be specific.
4. Share good news.
5. Use rewards.
6. Transfer rewards.

Negative:

1. Ignore the behavior.
2. Use time-outs.
3. Use overcorrection.

95

For example, if a student impulsively runs out into the parking lot to greet his parents, he puts himself in immediate and serious danger. To impress upon him the correct way to behave after class, have him get his coat and shoes on and sit quietly on a chair in the waiting room. Then have him take off his coat and shoes, put them away and start all over again. Practice five or ten times and you can be sure he will remember to follow this routine after class in the future.

Another example is a child who takes all of the targets down off the wall and scatters them on the floor. Have him pick up and neatly hang the targets back up. Then find some more targets or other gear that needs to be rearranged and supervise him in making the gear neat and organized. Impress upon him the importance of keeping equipment in order.

Using Negative Consequences

To be effective, negative consequences or punishment must be used sparingly and only when you are certain you intend to follow through. Consider the following when punishing a child:

1. Don't take away constructive activities.

Don't take away educational activities, including the learning portion of the class. Take away fun activities like game time, competitions, sleepover night or the school picnic.

2. Punish a child for a reasonable amount of time.

Unreasonably long punishments can make a child more rebellious and reduce his eagerness to comply with the rules once the punishment is over.

3. Take away one thing at a time.

If you take away all of the activities a child enjoys at one time, you not only significantly discourage him, you lose leverage when it comes to future punishment.

4. Never apply a major punishment on the spot.

If a child commits a serious rule violation, remove him from the situation and talk over the appropriate actions with another instructor and/or his parents. Major punishment decisions, such as suspending a child or taking away his belt, should never be made in anger or haste.

5. When taking away fun activities, start with the smallest first.

Take away the least valuable activity and add more meaningful consequences if the behavior continues. For example, a child who pushes another student might have to sit out of the game at the end of class. Another violation means missing movie night at the school while further behavior problems result in being suspended from the competition team for one month.

6. Make groups of rules and decide ahead of time what the punishment will be for violating them.

For example, you might have rules that must never be broken, like using martial arts skills to harm others, and carry a severe punishment if violated. Next are rules that are very important like using self-control during sparring and self-defense with a partner. These rules carry a lesser, but still unpleasant negative consequence when broken. Finally, there are rules or routines that make the school run smoothly like putting away equipment when finished with it. When these rules are broken, a reminder is more appropriate than a punishment.

7. Always stay calm when dealing with a child who has misbehaved.

Never punish a student in anger. If necessary, take a time-out for yourself until you are ready to see the situation impartially.

Promoting Self-discipline

One of the reasons parents enroll children for lessons is the belief that martial arts develop self-discipline. But self-discipline is not an inherent characteristic of martial arts. It is something that must be actively promoted by the instructor.

To instill self-discipline in younger students, gradually transfer the responsibility for discipline from yourself to the student. In the early stages of training, you are the primary source for discipline. The first several weeks of learning are dedicated to familiarizing the student with the rules and behavioral expectations of the school. Once these have been established, it is time to start the transfer of responsibility.

When you see a child taking the initiative during class, point out ways he can do the same at home and at school. Make it a point to ask his parents how he is doing at home and to tell them exactly what he is doing in class that demonstrates his growing self-discipline. By making him responsible for his behavior, you are starting him on the road to becoming an independent, responsible person.

Accidents

The accident rate in children peaks at age nine. The peak is due to a developmental trait that causes children in this age group to overestimate their abilities.

Carefully control the activity and difficulty levels of children ten and younger. They do not have the maturity to judge their limitations and may assure you that they can handle tasks, when in reality they cannot.

Improving Attention Span

Strategies that get results

See also . . .
Short Attention Spans . . . . page 79

One of the most frequent questions instructors ask is: *How can I get kids to pay attention better?*

While a short attention span is normal in young children, some children have seemingly no attention span at all. They drift in and out of class on a cloud or wildly careen from one distraction to the next. Playing simple games and modifying the way you communicate with the class can help lengthen the attention span of young students and reinforce basic martial arts skills.

1. Playing statue.

If you find that the kids, especially beginners, are frequently fidgeting when they should be standing still, play a game of statue. Show the class a simple position like fighting stance, ready stance or low block. On your command, everyone imitates your position and freezes for a count of ten or twenty.

If you want to make it a competition, have the kids who move sit down and then try another, more difficult position, eliminating those who move, until one winner is left standing. Some kids are really good at not moving, so you may have to give them a tough position, like standing on one leg, to find the winner.

A variation of this is to start walking through a form and then call out "freeze." Everyone freezes in place and stays that way for a ten count. If you practice being a statue in every class, the students get better and better at controlling the urge to fidget. Then, at the next promotion test, when you tell them to line up and stand like statues, their parents will be amazed at their self-control.

2. Packing your bag.

This game can be played with everyone seated in a circle on the floor. The first person says, "I've got my bag and in it I put my shoes." The next person must repeat that plus add one more item like, "I've got my bag and in it I put my shoes and my Aunt Jane." It doesn't matter how silly the items are that are added, as long as each child correctly recites the list and adds one thing.

When someone goofs, the game starts over. If you want to add a martial arts element, try something like, "I came to the dojo today and I did a side kick." The next student adds a technique and so on. You can even have the kids stand up and act out the techniques or say them in Japanese or Korean or Chinese if you want to add an additional learning element.

3. Thinking before acting.

Role-playing can be fun and educational for young students. Briefly explain what it means to think before acting then ask the kids for examples of times when they acted without thinking.

Use a couple of the examples for role-playing. Have one of the students demonstrate an example of acting without thinking, like talking out suddenly while the instructor is explaining something. Then ask the student to demonstrate the same situation, but have him think first then act, by raising his hand and waiting until being called on to speak.

Then ask the class to stand up and role-play the same situation (correct behavior) with a partner. Other examples of impulsive behavior might be cutting in line, running out of the training area (instead of walking) when class is over, kicking the targets/bags out of turn, and forgetting to take off their shoes before going on the mat. Some children never give any thought to alternative behaviors, so role-playing serves to illustrate and practice their choices. Remember to praise children who demonstrate the role-played behaviors in class.

4. Rewind.

If a child forgets something, such as a movement or rule, give her a chance to "rewind" and get it right. Once you explain the concept of rewinding (most kids understand this from their VCR) and trying again, all you have to say is "rewind" when you see a mistake. Tell the child where to start over from and give him a second chance.

For example, if a child runs out of class without bowing to the flag at the front of the room like they are supposed to, call out "Jennifer, rewind that." and have her go back to the door and try again. This is a lot more fun than just saying "That was wrong, do it again." Most kids consider it a game rather than a correction.

5. Make one rule at a time.

If you think about the children who present the biggest challenges in class, they are probably breaking quite a few rules on a regular basis. Attempting to fix everything at once will frustrate you both.

While it would be nice to get everyone to follow directions, sit still, stay in line and not talk out of order, in reality, this is the equivalent of spinning plates on sticks. No sooner do you get one spinning than another crashes to the floor. Instead, focus on one rule at a time, perhaps sitting still or not talking out of turn. Make it your rule for the day or week. To insure success, choose a rule that the child or class can reasonably master in a fairly short period of time.

6. Be specific.

"Pay attention" has little meaning to a four year old. In fact, he may not even know what "attention" is. Instead use specific, concrete action phrases like *sit still, sit on your bottom, don't touch others, put your hands on your lap, don't touch the equipment, look at me when I'm talking,* and *raise your hand if you have a question.* By being specific and designating an action that the child comprehends, you teach him the actions that comprise paying attention.

7. Give reminders.

Don't be afraid to remind a child to follow the rules. A student who is having serious problems paying attention is going to need constant reminders at first and occasional reminders as his behavior improves. Rather than using verbal reminders, try to formulate "secret" signals or single word prompts. Instead of reminding a child not to talk out, simply make strong eye contact and make a zipping motion across your lips. Use a single word like "hands" to remind a student to keep his hands to himself.

When giving a reminder, keep your demeanor neutral. Do not scold or appear overly encouraging. Let the child see that you are on his side, but don't let him feel too much like you are his "buddy" or his poor behavior makes him special. Anything other than a quick, neutral reminder will deter his progress toward a longer attention span.

8. Provide immediate feedback.

Quick feedback, whether negative or positive, is very helpful in changing a student's attention span. By providing praise for paying attention or giving a reminder when a child is drifting, you make him more conscious of his behavior. As with reminders, praise can be given with a single word or a secret signal, like a "thumbs up" sign. This works especially well for older children who are sometimes embarrassed by being praised for good behavior in front of their peers.

9. Use natural consequences.

If a child is not paying attention, let her suffer the natural negative consequences like not knowing the rules to a game or what to do next in class or how to perform a movement. Once she realizes that everyone else is doing something and she does not know what to do, point out that her confusion is the result of not paying attention to what was just said or demonstrated.

Asking a child to repeat or explain what you just told the class is another way of calling attention to their distraction. Positive consequences can also be acknowledged when a child has paid attention and is performing a movement correctly, remembers a sequence of techniques or is able to explain what you have just told the class.

Giving Directions

Give directions one at a time for young children and no more than three at a time for older children and adults.

Poor direction giving:

I want everyone to go get their sparring gear, put it on, do five minutes of warm-ups then face a partner of the same rank and height for two five minute rounds of free sparring.

Young children directions:

Everyone put on your sparring gear. When you're ready, I'll tell you what we're going to do next.

Older children directions:

Everyone put on your sparring gear and do some stretching while you wait. When everyone is ready, I'll assign your partners.

Learning Disabilities

Adapting to student needs

See also . . .
Methods of Learning . . . . page 74
Factors Affecting Learning . . . . page 76

What is a learning problem?

A learning problem is a difficulty in acquiring skills. It can be very subtle to the point of being barely noticeable or it can be so severe that it prevents a child from learning skills like reading or memorization. Learning problems have many causes, including emotional, environmental and biological causes. The term "learning problem" refers to a wide array of problems and root causes.

What is a learning disability?

A learning disability is a learning problem that can be traced to the inefficient workings of the brain. It is not caused by limited intelligence, severe emotional disturbances or a physical handicap, such as blindness. The technical definition used by many school systems characterizes a child with a learning disability as someone who is functioning two or more years (grade levels) below the expected level for his age and IQ. A child with a learning disability may in fact have a very high IQ or be very intelligent for his age, but these characteristics are not manifested in his day-to-day work.

What are the signs of a learning disability?

Learning disabilities affect as much as twenty percent of the population, although boys are more likely than girls to be afflicted. Since children develop at different rates, a learning disability may not be noticed in school until a child has fallen well behind or begins to exhibit emotional or social problems such as avoiding certain activities (like reading aloud, class discussions, writing essays). Learning disabilities must be diagnosed by a trained professional in conjunction with input from a child's teachers and parents.

Some of the signs of a learning disability that a parent or instructor might note include general disorganization, seemingly intentional forgetfulness, underachievement, refusal to do certain types of school work, excessively slow completion of work, inattentiveness, anger toward school, poor self-esteem and regression to earlier social developmental stages. Taken individually, these symptoms can often be the result of other causes or part of the child's temperament so a professional evaluation is always necessary.

Are learning disabilities caused by trouble at home or emotional difficulties?

No. Learning disabilities are caused by the way the child's brain functions not by his environmental or emotional state. However, children with learning disabilities may have emotional problems such as low self-esteem, feelings of being stupid or a failure, anger, confusion and frustration.

Is there a cure for learning disabilities?

Unlike ADD, there is no medication for treating learning disabilities. Children with learning disabilities must develop work strategies to counteract the areas of weakness. The treatment strategies are highly individualized depending on the child, his teachers and his family. Great inventors and scientists such as Albert Einstein and Thomas Edison had learning disabilities that made them slow learners and poor students, yet they went on to succeed in their chosen professions.

How does a learning disability affect the ability to learn martial arts?

There are many types of learning disabilities, so each child's experience is different. Children who have difficulty with reading, writing or math, display no signs of the problem in martial arts class until they need to complete an essay, study terminology or take a written rank exam. In fact, you may be surprised when an otherwise stellar student turns in her black belt exam that reflects writing skills well below what you expected of her age level. Before you fail her, speak with her parents to see if there is a learning problem that you had not been informed of.

Other types of learning problems are more evident in class, including students (child or adult) who have difficulty remembering patterns, determining right from left, modeling an instructor's movements or remembering sets of skills, like step sparring, in order.

When a student has trouble in a particular area, speak with him privately to work out a system of teaching skills that works for him. Students who cannot remember the order of a form may be helped by diagramming the form on paper or using verbal or visual cues. A student who cannot follow the instructor's lead when he is facing the class may be helped by having the instructor demonstrate facing in the same direction as the student (with his back to the student).

Keep in mind that learning disorders can be modality-specific so that information taken by a particularly modality (a method, like sight or hearing) is not remembered while information taken in by another modality is processed and remembered without difficulty.

For example, a student is able to repeat a sequence of movements after seeing someone perform them, but he cannot repeat them when he is given spoken instructions. Or he can follow spoken instructions, but the order of the techniques is not carried out correctly. Similarly, once a sequence is learned, some children cannot rearrange the techniques into a different order.

When dealing with modality-related disorders, don't hesitate to try a variety of approaches— verbal directions, drawings, photos, key words, visual cues, physical demonstrations or video tapes—until you find the modality that works best for the child.

A final class of learning disability is the physical learning disability. Some children are afflicted by a lack of muscle strength, uncontrollable tics or limb tremors. More common, however, are coordination disorders. Children with gross motor coordination disorders have difficulty in running, walking or jumping, movements that require use of the large muscle groups.

Fine motor coordination disorders cause difficulty in manipulating things with the hands, for example writing or tying the shoes. Children with gross motor coordination problems initially have quite a bit of difficulty learning martial arts movements. However, the structured, progressive nature of the martial arts can benefit them greatly. Patience and a slow but steady approach is more rewarding for this child than participation in competitive sports.

In addition to the difficulties in learning caused by these disorders, afflicted children may have social or behavioral problems. A learning disability can prevent a child from learning the rules of the classroom, understanding how a line works, lining up with a partner and other simple tasks.

Again, it is necessary to change your approach. A child who always seems to be cutting into the middle of the line after his turn at target kicking may not grasp the concept of maintaining his place in line by returning to the end. Instead of telling him to "stay in line" try telling him to "stay right behind John" since John is a tangible object and a line is a vague concept that the child cannot grasp. When repeated corrections are not working with a particular child, look at how your approach might be affecting the child's ability to follow directions.

Dealing with Aggression

When children get physical

See also . . .
Reinforcement or Punishment . . . . page 92

All children have occasional verbal or physical clashes with siblings, friends and even teachers or parents. Outbursts that include crying, arguing, pushing, hitting and shouting are a normal part of growing up and learning social behavior. Some children, however, are angry or antagonistic almost all of the time. They overreact to even the smallest frustration or provocation with physical or verbal outbursts. They may cry, scream, use obscenities, lash out with punches and lose their temper on a daily basis.

Unchecked aggressiveness in children who are learning martial arts is particularly concerning. In fact, in cases where you feel learning martial arts might worsen the problem, you should ask the child's parents to withdraw him from class and seek professional therapy to control his anger and aggression.

If you are confident that the child is not an immediate danger to himself or his peers and teaching him martial arts does not increase the likelihood of his harming someone else, work with him and his parents to teach him how to manage his anger. Some strategies for controlling aggression include:

1. Never punish aggressiveness with physical punishment.

Many children who resort to hitting in anger are being hit at home by a parent, older sibling or other authority figure. On the other hand, a child's behavior may have nothing to do with the way he is treated at home. While it goes unsaid that you should never strike a student as punishment, be aware of other physical signals you may be giving off.

Try not to appear angry or aggressive when dealing with an aggressive child. Beyond the touching necessary to remove the child from an immediate physical interaction, do not touch him in any way. Be particularly conscious of seemingly innocuous gestures like leading him away by the arm or grasping him by both shoulders to get his attention. Any aggressive body language on your part will only cause his anger to escalate.

2. Use negative consequences to punish aggression.

Always give the child a time-out or another negative result of his behavior. Even the most stubborn child soon tires of being sent to sit and face the wall every time he puts a hand on someone. Consistently suffering negative consequences while the rest of the class goes on without him will eventually make him think twice about hitting or pushing in anger.

3. Do not allow the child to express aggression toward you.

If a child shows hostility toward you verbally or physically, immediately send him to a time-out in another room (such as the waiting room or office) with the assistance of another instructor. Remove yourself from his line of fire as quickly as possible. It is important for you to retain your position of authority in front of the class and to allow him to cool down before continuing any interaction.

4. Help the child label his feelings.

Talk about what it means to be angry, frustrated and sad. Ask the children to give examples of what makes them mad and what responses are appropriate. Suggest alternative calming behaviors a child can use when he feels like hitting someone. They can be conventional like counting to ten or silly like singing "Happy Birthday" in his head or martial arts related like "kihaping" (shouting) his anger away.

5. Praise.

Find opportunities to praise the child for controlling himself in a difficult situation. If someone cuts in front of him in line and he does not push the child away, praise him and reward him by letting him come to the front of the line. If you see a group of children pushing to get to a target or the water fountain, praise the children who are waiting politely behind them and let them get a drink or a target while the others wait until last.

6. Identify problem situations.

Some children have difficulty with certain situations such as forming a line, taking turns or moving from one place to another in an orderly manner. Try to spot patterns. If you identify what types of situations cause a particular child to become aggressive, you can develop specific strategies for staying in control or eliminate those types of situations.

7. Reduce partner contact activities.

A child who has an aggression problem should not be allowed any opportunity to have contact with a partner, such as in self-defense or sparring practice. Though everything may seem to be going well, some children are very adept at getting their shots in as soon as an adult turns their back or gets distracted.

The only circumstances in which this type of child should be allowed to practice with a partner are those times when you can assign one instructor to supervise only that child full-time. They should not be left unsupervised for even a few seconds.

8. Reduce target contact activities.

Aggressive children may "feed off" of heavy bag drills or target practice. Some children kick the heavy bag, then kick the wall, then punch one or two people in line on the way back to the end of the line. These children find hitting the bag so much fun that they look for as many other objects as possible to hit between turns.

Other children with aggression problems find it a relief to be able to hit something without getting in trouble. Evaluate each child individually and consider what impact contact activities have on his overall behavior.

9. Seek professional help.

If a child has a serious aggression problem, recommend to his parents that they seek professional counseling, as his aggression might be symptomatic of a larger behavioral or emotional problem. When in doubt, it is best to err on the side of caution to avoid being responsible for teaching an aggressive child how to be more potentially destructive. While martial arts can have the effect of reducing aggression in many children, some children need professional help that is beyond the scope of twice weekly lessons.

Separation Anxiety

Easing the transition

See also . . .
Shyness . . . . page 113
Managing Parents . . . . page 160

This is a problem that often occurs with new students, particularly very young children. A youngster suffering from separation anxiety does not want his parents to leave his sight during class. He may cling to his mother before joining the class, insist that she sit where he can see her, refuse to enter the class at all or break down in tears the minute he enters the school.

The most frustrating aspect of separation anxiety for an instructor is the crying that it brings every time you try to get the child to join the class. In addition to being generally disruptive, a crying child often upsets other students in class causing the problem to multiply.

By the age of four, a child should be able to leave his parents for a short period of time without anxiety or distress. In about four percent of children however, separation anxiety is so overwhelming that it prevents the child from participating in normal daily events like school or recreational activities. Many of these children's parents feel that their child is "shy" so they sign them up for martial arts lessons in hopes of making the children more assertive and raising their self-esteem. Consequently, an instructor may find that more than the average four percent of children in class have problems with separation anxiety.

Children with separation anxiety are preoccupied with thoughts that harm will come to them when they are away from their parents. They find it difficult to go to school, to sleep alone, to visit a friend's house or to participate in sports. They may exhibit physical symptoms including stomachache, diarrhea, rapid heartbeat, dizziness and recurring nightmares. In class, you will see these children

"It is important to remember that children with separation anxiety are not afraid of going to martial arts class."

108

frequently checking to see if their parents are still waiting for them in the waiting area, fidgeting, being easily distracted and bursting into tears without an identifiable cause.

It is important to remember that children with separation anxiety are not afraid of going to martial arts class. In fact, they may be very excited about learning and enjoy class when they are able to focus on it. What they are afraid of is leaving their parents. Reassuring them that class is fun, they won't get hurt, or that they'll make lots of friends is of little use in getting them to join in and enjoy class.

In fact, the easiest way to differentiate a child with separation anxiety from a child who is afraid of class is to notice if the symptoms (crying, fidgeting, refusing to join class) disappear when the child's parents are present and reappear suddenly and often violently if the parents say they are leaving. The symptoms of separation anxiety range from mild clinginess to an absolute refusal to join the class complete with crying and screaming. If untreated, severe cases of separation anxiety in children are often precursors to adult cases of panic disorder. And children of parents with panic disorder are three times more likely to have separation anxiety, suggesting a biological link between the two.

In most cases, separation anxiety can be dealt with and resolved if the student, parent and instructor work together. The easiest approach is to find a way that the child can comfortably participate in class, for example if his mother sits in a chair in the waiting room where he can see her. Some other tips to overcome separation anxiety:

1. Rituals

A ritual that helps the child get ready for class, like taking off his shoes, hanging up his coat, kissing his mother good-bye, checking his attendance card and meeting an assistant instructor on the mat for warm-ups is reassuring. A child with separation anxiety does not like change or unexpected events. By having a ritual that is always the same, the child begins to feel that he can predict the outcome of separating from his parent and it becomes less frightening.

2. Timing

Children who have separation anxiety should not be brought to class too early. Downtime before class gives them more time to conjure up frightening scenarios in their head and increases their anxiety. Arrange for them to be brought to class one or two minutes before it begins so they have just enough time to take off their coat and shoes and join in the action. The less time they have to think about class, the more smoothly the class will go.

3. Remove anxiety models.

Often, the crying, whining and distress exhibited by the child rubs off on their parents. Soon, parents are nervous and anxious about bringing the child to class and the child senses this. While the parents are anxious about the scene or struggle that they know is about to take place, the child misinterprets their parent's nervousness, thinking that if their parent is also nervous about going to martial arts lessons, there must be some credibility to his fears.

This increases their anxiety all the more and is the beginning of a downward spiral in which the parents' and child's increasing distress feed off one another, each causing the other to become more upset. Emphasize to the parents the importance of remaining calm and not getting emotionally upset by their child's behavior.

4. Make a behavior contract.

In the most difficult cases, a behavior contract between the instructor, student and parents can help change the child's behavior.

First, acknowledge to the child that you understand he is afraid of leaving his parents. Then reassure him that you and his parents are going to help him overcome his fear and that you are all on his side. Gently point out to him that the other boys and girls his age are able to come to class without crying or protesting and you think he can too.

Type up a contract for everyone to sign specifying how each person is expected to behave. It might read something like:

> "James will put on his karate uniform at home at 4:30 on Tuesday and Thursday without his mother's help. At 4:45 he will be ready to go to karate lessons, with his shoes and coat on. When he arrives at karate lessons, he will put his coat and shoes away by himself and give his mother a hug. His mother will wait in the waiting room in the chair closest to the office for the whole class. James will come into the class without crying and Mr. Smith will help James warm-up until class starts. James may leave the class once without permission to see his mother in the waiting room if he needs to. James will receive one star for each task he completes for a maximum of 4 stars for each class. When he earns 10 stars, his mother will take him for ice cream after class."

This contract spells out a number of very important issues for James. It tells him exactly what he must do, not only at class but at home before class. Children with separation anxiety often begin creating problems getting ready at home in hopes that their parents will become exasperated and give up on ever taking the child anywhere. By starting the contract behavior from home, you make the parent's job easier and take away one of the child's methods of short-circuiting the process.

The second important point is that the contract spells out the adults' expected behaviors, so James does not feel like the only person who is making an effort. By specifying your and his parents' behavior, you give James the right to expect certain confidence boosting behaviors from you in return for his effort.

Third, the contract gives James the opportunity to earn a reward that is doubly reinforcing because it is given after class. This means James has something to look forward to when class is over. If he doesn't make it through the class, he can't get the reward.

The contract is most effective if James has some say in creating it and if the behaviors you require from him are within his reach developmentally. You may have to go through several contracts that create a series of smaller goals. In the above example, you may eventually rewrite the contract, specifying that James' parents will come in with him and then leave once class is under way, specifying the time they will return and how James is expected to behave until they do.

5. Attitude

Your attitude towards the child's behavior can have a great impact on how quickly you are able to resolve separation anxiety. If you baby the child, appear nervous or give too much attention to his behavior, you run the risk of reinforcing it. On the other hand, belittling him, yelling at him or ignoring him may reinforce his conviction that it is not safe to be around anyone other than his parents.

Do your best to maintain a neutral attitude. Do not show any emotions other than a calm, welcoming demeanor. Do not beg the child to come to class or make bargains with him. Show him that you expect him to come to class, you are on his side and you want to help, but there is no special treatment for crying or whining. When he shows signs of positive behavior, praise him lavishly.

Dealing with separation anxiety can be made more difficult by the parents of the child. The parents may feel frustrated, guilty or confused. Sometimes one parent blames the other for babying the child or the child only exhibits symptoms with one parent because the other parent does not tolerate it.

Some parents resort to avoiding anything that upsets the child and would sooner pull him out after a few unsuccessful lessons than work on solving the problem. Unfortunately, this only reinforces the child's fears and delays the inevitable day when the problem must be faced. Children cannot be kept at home forever and overcoming separation anxiety as early as possible is the best approach.

When parents want to pull their children out of lessons, remind them that they have to face the problem sooner or later and you are willing to help them do it now.

Successfully dealing with separation anxiety generally happens quickly once the child realizes everyone involved is serious about it. Most children who cry before class in the beginning happily coming to class in a couple of weeks with the right approach. In fact, the majority of cases that can be solved by the instructor and the child's parents are resolved in four weeks or less.

If a child is still having problems after four weeks of consistent effort, he may need professional counseling to overcome his anxiety. However, don't be alarmed if a child has been doing well for a couple of months and suddenly shows up one day in tears. There will be setbacks along the way and you may need to go back to the basics for a few classes, including a new contract if necessary, to get the child back on track.

Shyness

Encouraging socialization

See also . . .
Separation Anxiety . . . . page 108
Managing Parents . . . . page 160

Some degree of shyness is normal. Everyone experiences feelings of social anxiety at one time or another: having to give a speech, meeting new people and putting on a demonstration can all be sources of stress.

Some children, however, suffer for an almost paralyzing shyness. They rarely talk, and even then only in grunts or monosyllables. They won't stand up and do anything in front of the class, they won't raise their hands to answer questions, and sometimes they won't even perform new skills in class for fear of making a mistake. Testing, tournaments or demonstrations are a particularly difficult time for shy children, with many refusing to participate and even quitting lessons they otherwise enjoy to avoid these events.

Overwhelming shyness is rooted in the child's feelings that she is being judged by others, watched all of the time or appears stupid to others. The child is afraid of being made fun or becoming the target of more socially adept children. Shy children often know they have problems interacting with others, but feel it is "silly" behavior or makes them weird so they are unable to seek help or guidance.

There are two types of shyness: some children are generally shy and avoid social contact as much as possible while others are shy only in certain situations like speaking to authority figures or performing in public. Shy children generally have trouble making friends, become the target of bullies, have difficulty in school, exhibit low self-esteem and lack assertiveness. Again, a disproportionate number of children in martial arts classes suffer from excessive shyness because their parents are bringing them to class to correct these traits.

There are a few ways you can help children overcome shyness and more fully enjoy their lessons and their life:

1. Relaxation

Shy children are very tense in social situations. Teaching them some simple breathing techniques as well as introducing them to mediation before they face anxiety-inducing situations may help them to relax in difficult situations.

2. Visualization

Shy children are afraid they will "mess up" when asked to do anything that draws attention to themselves. Mentally rehearsing a successful performance can lessen this fear. Ask the child to spend time thinking about (visualizing) how he might successfully react in a tough situation, like if you asked him stand up and demonstrate a kick in front of the class.

Have him practice in his mind, seeing himself doing the kick correctly and seeing the class applaud when he finishes. After he has practiced successfully in his head, give him the opportunity to stand up and demonstrate the kick.

3. Goals

Help the child set goals that encourage social behavior. An achievable goal might be to raise his hand once every class to answer a question, say "hi" to each new white belt at their first class, volunteer to demonstrate a self-defense technique he knows well in front of the class or help another child learn a new form. Small goals that can easily be accomplished build the child's confidence and lessen his fear of failing in public. Rewarding the child for reaching his goals may be necessary at first, but even more valuable is the outcome. When a child succeeds in front of others, and more importantly when he learns that he can fail and the world does not come to an end, he becomes more confident.

4. Limit surprises.

Many teachers treat shyness by forcing the child to participate, dragging her unwillingly out in front of the class to answer questions or show off her skills. For very shy children, this only increases their fears by taking away any power they might have over their social interaction. Instead, limit surprise social interactions and praise the child when she takes the initiative in interacting with the class or others. The more in control she feels, the more likely she is to try to overcome her fears.

5. Practice

Although shy children often know what is expected of them, they may forget everything under pressure. Every instructor has seen an otherwise competent student miserably fail a belt test in front of an audience of parents. The form he did perfectly in class last week suddenly flies from his head and he stands stone still.

Practicing the form in class is not always enough for very shy children. They need to practice under "game day" conditions. Occasionally invite a few parents in from the waiting room to simulate test or competition situations. Give all of the children the chance to practice under pressure so they feel like they have already "been there" when the real event comes around.

6. Avoid performance assessments.

When a child is overly focused on his performance, his instructor and parents should avoid performance-assessing questions like "How is your form coming along", "Who did you practice with today? Was he good?" or "Does your instructor think you're ready to test?" Instead, focus on questions like "Did you have fun today" and "What's new?" Give the child the opportunity to talk about something other than his performance.

Shyness is not something children grow out of as most parents think. It needs to be actively worked on by both the child and the adults in his life. By creating a safe, respectful atmosphere, martial arts class is an ideal place for shy children to overcome their fears and experiment with social behaviors they might find frightening in school or on their baseball team.

Children develop at different rates, but there are some general developmental guidelines that can help you select age-appropriate activities for your children's classes.

Ages 4-6

Children in this age group are discovering the world around them and learning new physical, emotional and social skills at a furious pace. They are eager to learn and ready to absorb whatever you throw at them. However, they have short attention spans and some limits to their cognitive and physical abilities.

Physical

Children in the 4-6 year old group:

- Are interested in perfecting gross motor skills including running, jumping, skipping, tumbling, throwing and catching. They enjoy games like *Mother May I, Red Light/ Green Light, Tag* and *Follow the Leader* which allow them to practice their emerging physical skills. Develop martial arts games that use gross motor skills and practice basic movements.

- Work to develop hand-eye coordination. Use gross motor skills for target contact activities.

- Use all five senses in activities. Activities that rely on watching and listening are good practice for their emerging senses.

- Tire easily, especially when working on new or challenging skills. Short learning periods interspersed with play periods work best.

- Enjoy practicing new skills. They frequently role-play skill practice, for example they may play "karate school" with neighborhood children, teaching and practicing what they have learned. Caution them only to practice their skills when an instructor or parent is supervising.

- Understand concepts like over/under and in/out but may not be ready for right and left. Use simple instructors and visual cues when explaining and leading activities. Children at this age are also just learning to count to higher numbers, so keep sets of exercises in groups of ten and encourage counting aloud.

- Enjoy playing games involving directions such as Simon Says and the Hokey Pokey.

Social

Children in the 4-6 year old group:

- Want the world to be structured like their home is structured. View all authority figures in parental roles and enjoy role-playing.

- Develop many short-term friendships based on common interests. They easily bond with other children in their martial arts class based solely on the fact that they both like learning martial arts.

- Enjoy playing with children of any age. They readily partner with older or younger children for classroom activities.

- Want to be "big boys and girls" and assert their desire to do things by themselves, but they still need the reassurance of an adult nearby.

- Express their feelings through behavior, making them vocal students. They are likely to hit others in frustration, throw a tantrum or jump up and down with excitement. Their strong emotions often pass quickly and are soon forgotten. You'll be most successful if you quickly deal with outbursts and move on.

- Seek out recognition and praise. Use reward systems, verbal praise and other means of recognition to encourage good behavior.

- Enjoy pretending and have vivid imaginations. Playing games that involve imitating animals or simple role-playing are excellent teaching techniques for this age group.

- Understand the concepts of taking turns and sharing.

- Are full of questions. Give simple specific answers that help the child expand his understanding of the world.

Ages 7-9

Children in this age group have a wide range of physical skills and enjoy using them. They intensely interested in rules, how things work and the world around them, but often have difficulty seeing through the eyes of others.

Physical

Children in the 7-9 year old group:

- Enjoy learning new sports. While they are still too young to engage in highly competitive sports, they work hard to master the basic skills and rules of a new sport.

- Have good hand-eye coordination and are able to use a wide variety of sporting equipment to supplement their learning. This is a good age to begin partner target drills because children now have the strength and understanding to hold a target correctly.

- Have longer attention spans and are more willing to see a task through to completion. Begin emphasizing perfection of techniques, in addition to accumulation of new skills.

Social

Children in the 7-9 year old group:

- Gravitate toward same sex peers. Beginning at this age, boys will prefer to work only with boys and girls only with girls, especially for contact activities like self-defense.

- Tend to form friendships based on peer group acceptance and common interests. May begin to form cliques or ostracize certain children.

- Feel they can do no wrong and often stubbornly cling to their opinions, even when proven wrong. They are quick to point out what others are doing wrong, but take corrections of their own actions as a personal attack. Take care in correcting behaviors or movements, but not criticizing the child personally.

- Learning to use words to express their feelings, which makes name-calling and teasing a primary weapon for use against peers. Children this age need to be taught the hurtful power of words and how to defend themselves verbally against taunts.

- Enjoy being helpful to younger children. Occasionally let older children help or "teach" younger children to build leadership skills.

- Very interested in rules. If you allow certain children to be exempt from classroom rules or you are not consistent in your behavior, children at this age will not hesitate to point out that you are being unfair. Knowing and following rules are important to them.

Ages 10-12

Children at this age begin to look to adults for role models and enjoy imitating adult behavior. They also enjoy testing their skills and are eager to compete.

Physical

Children in the 10-12 year old group:

- Can handle more complex skills and understand more detailed rules of competition.

- Demonstrate complex thinking patterns which allow for greater capacity for instruction in fine motor skills. They are able to use constructive feedback on their performance.

- Are ready for adult type skills and should not have difficulty memorizing patterns, such as forms or step sparring sets as they reach the upper range of this age group.

- Show increased interest in and ability for competitive sports. They actively seek out competition and are eager to test their physical skills. This is a good age to begin competing in martial arts tournaments.

- Start maturing rapidly, increasing in size, strength, coordination and reaction time.

Social

Children in the 10-12 year old group:

- Are curious about the world at large. This is a good age to introduce the cultural aspects and traditions of the martial arts.

- Begin to understand characteristics like respect, trustworthiness, loyalty and honesty but sometimes have difficulty showing these traits because of peer pressure. They need a strong emphasis on character development.

- Often develop intensely loyal friendships and small cliques that result in some children feeling left out or "uncool." Martial arts class is a good venue for addressing the hurtful nature of this behavior and the value of diversity.

- Tend to compare themselves to adults in terms of self-concept and skills. They are eager to imitate adults in many ways as they search for their own identity. Many children at this age are ready to join an adult class and respond well to being treated "grown-up." Be careful, however, to remember that they are still children and are not capable of all that they would like to believe they are.

- Enjoy researching, inventing and testing new ideas. At this age, children enjoy sparring as a chance to test out their skills and develop new ways of using them.

- Enjoy being members of clubs and having secret or made up rituals, languages and codes. Children of this age will work hard to be part of a black belt club, competition team or demonstration team, especially if they are allowed special privileges as part of the group.

Class Management

Development and Planning

In this section . . .

121 The Ideal Schedule
125 Setting Objectives
126 Class Intensity
128 Class Structure
129 Teaching New Skills
132 Teaching Complex Skills
134 Roll Tape
136 Educational Goals
140 Evaluation
142 Effective Promotion Testing

The Ideal Schedule

Adapting to changing needs

See also . . .
Class Intensity . . . . page 126

Finding the ideal schedule for your classes is an ongoing task. What worked well when you had fifty students does not work for two hundred. When you have hundreds of students, the challenge of scheduling can become an ongoing headache. By breaking your scheduling down according to a few simple factors, you can determine the best schedule for your school.

The most common factors to consider are age, rank, subject matter and intensity. The most necessary division to make is age division. A commonly heard complaint among adult students is the nuisance of training with children and children are bored with an adult curriculum leading to dropouts.

Age Divisions

If your school is small, you only need to make one division: children's class and adult class. However, if you have more than fifty students, begin breaking the children's classes down into age appropriate groups like 4-6, 7-9, and 10-13. Teens do best in the adult class, but for children over twelve, make placements on a case-by-case basis.

"What worked when you had fifty students does not work for two hundred."

By dividing classes into age appropriate groups, you achieve several desirable goals. First, adults who want to learn mature skills in a serious atmosphere are satisfied. Second, children are excited about learning in a fun, kid-friendly atmosphere. Third, parents are happy because you are providing an educational curriculum designed just for their child's developmental level. Finally, you are happier because you spend less time thinking of ways to satisfy everyone in one setting and more time teaching age appropriate lessons that students are eager to participate in.

121

Rank Structure

Structuring class by rank also has many benefits. When there are only one or two skill levels in a class, students learn faster because you are focused on teaching them exactly what they need to know without worrying about what other students need at the same time. Students also feel that they are progressing faster because they are learning progressive skills at each rank.

When you structure class by rank, you can shorten each class and teach more classes in one day. Because you are teaching each class in a very focused manner, less time per class is spent teaching skills that might take longer in a mixed class. Teaching only the necessary curriculum also prevents lower ranks from watching and practicing risky advanced skills before they are ready. Finally, when students "graduate" to the next level class, they have a sense of pride and achievement, leading to a renewed desire to learn.

If your school is small, create a beginner group and advanced group, roughly dividing the students in half. If you have more than seventy-five students, make more levels. The most commonly used designations are beginner, intermediate, advanced, pre-black belt, black belt, leadership team and instructor. Both junior and adult classes need rank designations, though not at all levels. For example, four to six year olds need only a beginner and intermediate class, while older children need advanced levels and adults need instructor training. A sample schedule:

- Tiny Tigers (4 – 6 year olds, all)

- Peewee Beginner (7 – 9 year olds, up to green belt)

- Peewee Advanced (7 – 9 year olds, blue belt and higher)

- Junior Beginner (10 – 12 year olds, up to green belt)

- Junior Advanced (10 – 12 year olds, up to blue and red belt)

- Junior Black Belt (10 – 12 year olds, black belt)

- Adult Beginner (teens and adults, up to yellow belt)

- Adult Intermediate (teens and adults, green and blue belt)

- Adult Advanced (teens and adults, red and brown belt)

- Adult Black Belt (teens and adults, black belt)

Depending on the balance of juniors and adults, you may have more adult levels and only two for juniors or vice versa. As the school grows, re-divide and adjust your schedule accordingly.

Intensity

Some schools offer classes for more serious students. These come under the heading of competition training, demonstration team practice, instructor training or black belt club classes. Unless you are running a professional fighting gym, the general student population is interested in recreational martial arts training. Things like full contact fighting, breaking a stack of cement blocks or attending class every day aren't that appealing to the majority of students. If you want to teach more intense areas of the arts, create separate classes for students to attend in addition to or in place of regular classes.

Subject Matter

Do you teach more than one martial art? Do you have separate weapon, yoga or cardio kickboxing classes? If so, this is an important factor to consider when scheduling classes. For large schools, classes can be scheduled in multiple classrooms during the same hour. Having additional classrooms is a huge benefit in scheduling. The only drawback to consider is the noise level. If yoga students are listening to relaxing music, they probably don't want the cardio class next door to crank up a hip-hop song. Schedule noisy classes concurrently and block out time for quieter pursuits, either during off peak hours or in a soundproof room.

For smaller schools with only one training area, alternative classes may end up getting scheduled at off peak hours or instead of conventional martial arts classes. How you work alternative classes into your schedule depends on what your priorities are and how profitable each class is. If cardio classes are more profitable than adult beginner classes, there is a temptation to give the cardio classes the most desirable time slot. But before you make that decision, look at the long-term ramifications. What is the retention rate for cardio versus martial arts? Will giving the better time slot to cardio classes kill off your martial arts classes forcing you to advertise more heavily to keep new cardio students coming in? Take both a long and short term view of scheduling to ensure that decisions you make today don't come back to haunt you in a year.

Open Classes

With structured classes, there is always the risk of boredom. Students tend to see the same people every day, learn a limited curriculum, and come to class at the same time of day. To introduce some variety and allow for scheduling conflicts, create a few open classes a week.

Open classes fill many student needs: the need to train with a variety of people, the need to see higher ranks for motivation, the need to learn to assist lower belts, the need for a flexible schedule, the need for learning varied subjects and the need for specialization in training.

There are two types of open classes: a general open class and open class by topic. A truly open class permits anyone to attend regardless of rank, but perhaps limited by age. The focus is on a workout type atmosphere with a lot of conditioning, repetitions of basics, heavy bag drills, controlled sparring, self-defense and drills that safely allow partners of different ranks to mingle. The curriculum should be suitable for even the lowest rank in the class to keep up, although not necessarily excel.

The best time to schedule general open classes is on a weekend morning, Friday evening, or after the last class on a weekday. Encourage students to use these classes as make-up classes, extra workouts, conditioning for competition or to burn off excess stress.

The other type of open class is open by topic. The class is open to students of any rank and focuses on teaching a specific subject like sparring, weapons, forms or stretching. Depending on the nature of the subject, you may need to limit students by age or rank. A topical class can be held one time, weekly or for a period of weeks. Or you can schedule a special weekly slot for topical classes, with the subject changing weekly or monthly.

To ensure regular attendance and prevent overcrowding, require students to sign up for topical classes, even if you don't charge an extra fee.

Flexibility

When planning your schedule, balance structure with flexibility. The majority of students should be coming to their regularly assigned class every week. However, there are always people who have varying schedules, including college students, medical personnel and law enforcement officers. Fluctuations in their weekly schedule make it impossible for them to stick to a regular class schedule. Be flexible with these students so they do not quit because of a scheduling conflict.

While you cannot accommodate every student, do your best to keep the majority happy and remember to evaluate your schedule every six months to see if it still meets your needs.

Setting Objectives

Student and instructor goals

See also . . .
15 Retention Strategies . . . . page 145
Building Leadership . . . . page 291

To teach, you must have two sets of objectives, student objectives and teacher objectives. If you have difficulty planning, begin **from your final goal or objective** and work backwards to the beginning of the plan. If one of your objectives is for all white belts to learn how to do low block correctly, identify the elements of a correctly executed low block and create a plan to develop those elements in the performance of your students.

Based on your teaching objectives, create objectives for your students individually and as a group. There are several established guidelines for setting student objectives.

1. Objectives work best when students are **aware of them**, treat them as directions to learn specific material and **feel they will aid in learning**.

2. Objectives work best when they are **clearly communicated** and the **task is suitable** to the skill of the students (i.e. not too easy or difficult).

3. **Average students** benefit more from objectives than above or below averages students.

4. Objectives lead to improvement in **intentional learning** (stressed as important) and decline in incidental learning (not emphasized as important).

According to these guidelines, objectives are most effective when students are aware of them. Communicate your student objectives clearly to the class. If you want them to learn front kick and middle punch in a class, tell them this at the beginning of class and remind them throughout the training session. They will have a goal oriented work atmosphere and improve quickly.

Class Intensity

Setting the pace

See also . . .
Setting Objectives . . . . page 125
Educational Goals . . . . page 136

The intensity of training varies at each school based on the background and personality of the instructor and students. Schools range from highly disciplined military style programs to informal drop-in gyms, with many degrees of structure in between. While no style is any better or worse than the others, each has its positive and negative aspects. To help you choose the most suitable style, look at the pros and cons of various style schools.

Highly Structured

A highly structured school is one in which the structure, customs, discipline and etiquette of the style take precedence over the skills taught. Characteristics of a highly structured school include rigid routines surrounding all aspects of training: a ban on non-essential talking, extensive use of the native language for the art to describe techniques, strong hierarchy among students, ban on approaching the instructor with questions and use of discipline for rules violations.

PROS:
1. Students are highly disciplined.
2. Learning is efficient.
3. Techniques are uniform.
4. Skills taught are readily accepted.
5. Students respect tradition.
6. Culture of the art is preserved.

CONS:
1. Little innovation is possible.
2. Many people are intimidated by rigidity and demanding structure.
3. Students who need help or clarification cannot receive it.
4. Atmosphere prevents social bonding among students.

Moderately Structured

A moderately structured school is one in which the need for structure is balanced with the need for individuality. It is characterized by a system of formal techniques, the use of some native customs/language of the art, students are allowed to ask questions of higher belts, students socialize at school events, and instructors are encouraged to upgrade/innovate skills used.

PROS:
1. The average person feels comfortable.
2. The system of skills is in continuous development.
3. The tradition of the art is preserved in modern context.

CONS:
1. Skills may not be consistent.
2. Students may be confused by the mix of traditional and eclectic.
3. May not be serious enough for some students.

Loosely Structured

A loosely structured school is one that is run on a drop-in basis, like a gym. It is characterized by students of many different styles, a high level of socializing, interaction and innovation between styles, and sporadic attendance.

PROS:
1. Many people enjoy coming and going as they please.
2. Not confined to any one style.
3. Many chances for personal and stylistic interaction.

CONS:
1. Little structure to maintain consistent attendance.
2. Lack of guidance from a single instructor or system.
3. Increased risk of injuries.
4. Potential for cliques to develop.

When creating your school culture, there is no right or wrong style, only what is best suited to your students end your style of teaching.

Class Structure

A varied lesson plan

The minute-by-minute structure that you use in class is heavily influenced by how your instructor taught. If you started learning martial arts a decade or more ago, your classes probably started with warming-up, followed by stretching and conditioning, then basic movements. Any time left over after the fundamentals were covered was spent on sparring, forms or self-defense practice. Your instructor might even have followed the exact same lesson plan every day. While this ensures good basics, it can get boring quickly.

A varied and well-planned class structure keeps things fresh and exciting. Rather than planning a one-hour class, look at the hour as a series of mini-classes, each about ten minutes long. The first mini-class is always a warm-up but that doesn't mean using the same warm-up every day. An adult class might use a music based cardio warm-up on Monday, a more traditional calisthenic warm-up on Wednesday and a skill based warm-up on Friday. Running races and games make fun warm-ups for children's classes. Vary the warm-up so that it is not repeated during the week.

Reserve the last five to ten minute mini-class for cool down and a message or wrap-up. Cool down activities include stretching, light movement and mediation or relaxation. While leading the cool down, review important class points or share a message for the students to think about.

The remaining four or five mini-classes form the core of the class. Each one should have a brief introduction, a core activity and a short wrap-up or review. For example, a kicking mini-class begins with you introducing the kick or kicks to be practiced then moving the students quickly into a core practice activity like target drills. When the core activity has been completed, summarize the key points in two or three sentences then wind down the activity by having students put away equipment and prepare for the next segment of class.

By segmenting the class, you create a familiar rhythm. The energy of the class purposely builds then falls, eliminating unintentional lagging in the pace. Working in segments also eliminates downtime, when students are not doing anything productive and makes the hour pass quickly.

Teaching New Skills

Observational learning and shaping

See also . . .
Methods of Learning . . . . page 74
Teaching Complex Skills . . . . page 132

The essence of teaching is passing skills and knowledge to others. Every instructor should develop a comfortable method of teaching new skills and employ it consistently throughout the curriculum. Consistency in teaching style makes it easier for students to follow instruction and adapt to new skills and ideas.

The standard method for teaching new skills is to first demonstrate the task to the class and give some key points necessary for successful task completion. Next, arrange the material in a series of steps to be practiced and provide ample practice time. Finally, supply feedback to reinforce correct behaviors and evaluate the completion of the task based on the predetermined evaluation criteria.

Introducing Skills

1. Demonstrate the skill

2. Explain key points

3. Break into simple steps

4. Give practice time

5. Provide feedback

Observational Learning

The methods for carrying out these various steps are provided in several widely accepted theories. The first theory is that of **Observational Learning**. Observational Learning is predicated on the idea that students will imitate a suitable model, thus the method of demonstrating a skill before requiring the student to perform it.

Observational Learning requires four components:

1. **Attention.** The student must pay attention to the model's behavior and have the conscious intention to imitate it.

2. **Retention.** The student must encode the behavior in the memory.

129

3. **Production.** The student must select and organize the movements and then refine them.

4. **Motivation.**

    a. **Direct reinforcement** occurs when the student watches the model, imitates the movement and is reinforced by the model.

    b. **Vicarious reinforcement** occurs when students anticipate a reward for a behavior because they observe a classmate being praised for the behavior.

    c. **Self-reinforcement** occurs when the individual strives to meet personal goals regardless of others.

The Observational Learning theory indicates the importance of both the instructor and the senior students in acting as role models for lower ranking students. The instructor naturally is seen by the students at the ideal model of a martial artist. New students admire his skills and endeavor to imitate them. But if the instructor or senior students project a negative image, the new student may assume that the martial arts make people negative and may turn to other pursuits for self-improvement.

Shaping

The next stage in teaching a new skill is guiding the student in practice and eventually perfection. For this area, we can draw on the work of the famed behavioral scientist B. F. Skinner. Skinner proposed the concept of shaping in which the teacher reinforces actions that are similar to those of the desired skill to be learned. The actions that are reinforced are strengthened and contribute to the perfection of the skill.

Shaping can be broken into several distinct steps:

1. Select the skill to be learned

2. Establish the standard of performance

3. Select reinforcers to be used

4. Reinforce approximations of the movement each time they occur

5. Reinforce the newly learned movement each time it occurs

6. Reinforce the movement on a variable (random) reinforcement schedule

Through this process you gradually guide students to the correct behavior. Once they begin to grasp the movement, reinforce it through positive feedback and encouragement. For martial arts training, reinforcement is most effective when given each time a student reaches a predetermined goal. This type of reinforcement encourages the student to work consistently toward the goal knowing that he will be rewarded for reaching it.

A good example of this is promotion to the next belt level. A student knows what is required for promotion and strives to learn it as efficiently as possible. However, immediately after a promotion is given, the student experiences a brief period of little or no progress. To counter this, reset his goals immediately and begin teaching new skills to rekindle his desire to improve. Make goals consistent with progress and provide rewards at appropriate times to keep students interested in long-term training.

.

"Reinforcement is most effective when given each time a student reaches a predetermined goal."

Motivation

Motivation is enhanced when success in training is the result of reasonable effort but is decreased when success is attained only through sustained effort.

If a task is difficult to master, design a series of short term, easy to master steps that lead up to the ultimate goal.

Rewards

Overuse of extrinsic rewards is a demotivator. Adults see excessive extrinsic rewards as controlling while children become desensitized and lose the motivation to perform without them.

Teaching Complex Skills

Advanced methods for advanced students

See also...
Teaching New Skills . . . . page 129

Teaching complex or advanced skills can be frustrating for both a student and instructor. There are several strategies that reduce frustration and enhance students' ability to learn complex skills without giving up.

Teach Conditioning Exercises

Before teaching a complex new skill, ensure that each student has the physical capacity to perform the skill. Skills that involve jumping, turning, falling, or contact with a partner are all activities that can result in a serious injury if a student is not physically ready.

In addition to warming up and calisthenics, make time in each class for conditioning exercises that are directly related to new or soon to be learned skills.

Relate New Skills to Basics

New skills are easier to learn when students relate them to skills they already know. For example, students who have a good understanding of front kick find it easier to learn jumping front kick because the front kick is the foundation for the mechanics of the new technique.

Teach in Steps

Break a complex skill into a series of increasingly difficult steps. *Example:* To teach jumping roundhouse kick, break the technique into logical steps: lift the left knee, hop with the right leg, rotate and kick with the right leg, land with the left foot followed by the right foot.

To teach the first segment, have the student practice jumping by bringing the left knee up followed by the right knee and landing with the left foot then the right foot. When he can do this well, add the hip turning motion by bringing the left knee followed by the right knee which turns into a chambered position in the air. When this step is mastered, move onto practicing the kick in the air then on light targets.

Since some complex skills cannot be taught in slow motion be creative in finding the logical steps in the learning process. The best approach is to work from gross motor skills (stepping, jumping, turning, leg lifting, body positioning) to fine motor control skills until you reach the final stage of the technique.

Students as Role Models

Students can be good teachers, both through example and by being supportive. If you are having difficulty in reaching someone, assign another student to work with him. Everyone has different learning styles and a fellow student may communicate the technique in a way you cannot. Also, students are less self-conscious among themselves than they are in front of their instructor so they are more likely to relax and perform better when you are not watching over them.

Call on higher-ranking students to demonstrate new skills. By doing so, the class feels that the skill is more attainable because they relate more closely to their classmates than to their instructor who they perceive to be at an entirely different skill level.

Use Video Tapes

Instructional video tapes or DVDs are excellent teaching aids because the performer on the program is usually highly skilled. Students can view a perfectly performed technique hundreds of times without tiring. Video has the advantage of slow and stop motion to analyze complex techniques in minute progression. DVD allows instant access to chapters (specific sets of skills) and a clearer image in stop motion than video.

If you have a camcorder, you can video tape each students' performance and let them compare it with the performance on the instructional tape. Seeing themselves on tape reveals errors that you might spend days or weeks trying to explain.

Roll Tape!

Using video in the classroom

See also . . .
Learning Disabilities. . . . page 102
Teaching Complex Skills. . . . page 132

The 80s brought the dawn of the video revolution in the martial arts. Video tapes now exist for every conceivable martial art and DVDs enable instant access to specific techniques without fast forwarding and rewinding. It would seem that anybody could learn dozens of styles without ever leaving the comfort of their home.

While this is an exaggeration, videos have changed the way many people learn martial arts. Students use videos and DVDs to practice and review at home. Instructors use tapes as a classroom or practice aid. Does this teaching technique have a positive or negative effect on the students?

In most cases, video tapes and DVDs are an invaluable aid to the instructor. First, instructors can broaden their knowledge without traveling hundreds of miles to train with the expert teachers found on the tapes.

Second, students see that what they are learning is a standard skill being practiced by thousands of other martial artists. Seeing it on television reinforces their confidence in your instruction. Finally, students can practice and refine their skills on their own, freeing you to spend more time with others.

However, video instruction has to be used correctly to be effective. If you turn on the video or DVD and leave the classroom, the students soon realize they can practice with the video at home in the same way. Use the tapes for specific purposes:

Review Skills

Use tapes to review skills you have already taught. This is especially helpful for people who have trouble keeping up or remembering things like forms and step sparring. Instead of spending endless hours working one-on-one with them, teach the skill and let them work with the video at their own pace until they feel comfortable. Then follow-up with a few pointers they cannot get from watching the video to reinforce the necessity of personal instruction.

Introduce New Skills

A new skill can be shown on video followed by in class instruction. By introducing the skill on video, students see different angles as well as slow motion. While you cannot perform complex skills in slow motion, the VCR can be used to break the movement down into manageable steps for students to practice. Since videos are generally made by experts, the movement is clear and correct.

Provide a New Angle

Once a skill has been practiced hundreds of times, students need new motivation to continue to work on it. By showing them new applications or viewpoints, you spark their interest again. For example, if you teach taekwondo and find your black belts are getting bored with basic kicking, show them a video of high level competitors using those basic kicks to score in international competition. Seeing the speed and skill of top level performers, will motivate them to new heights.

Motivate Children

Children like to watch television and it is a form of communication they are comfortable with. Show them the movement on video and ask them "Do you want to be like that?" They invariably respond positively and this is an excellent starting point for learning a new skill.

When used correctly, video can enhance your teaching and provide your students with a change from the class routine. Always keep in mind, though, that video tapes are a teaching aid and should not be overused. There is no substitute for personalized teaching from a qualified instructor.

Educational Goals

More than physical skills

See also . . .
Teaching Children . . . . page 73
Building Leadership . . . . page 291

In 1956, the White House Conference on Education convened in Washington, DC to assemble a list of goals for education of America's school children. The following are those goals which apply to martial arts education:

1. Respect and appreciation for human values and the beliefs of others.

2. Effective work habits and self-discipline.

3. Social competency as a contributing member of family and community.

4. Ethical behavior based on a sense of moral and spiritual values.

5. Intellectual curiosity and eagerness for lifelong learning.

6. Aesthetic appreciation and self-expression in the arts.

7. Mental and physical health.

8. Wise use of time, including constructive leisure pursuits.

9. Understanding for the physical world and man's relationship to it.

10. An awareness of our relationship to the world community.

(U.S. Committee for the White House Conference on Education, 1956)

If martial arts are to be valued as a legitimate form of education, we must implement these and other values into the teaching methodology. Consider them one by one to see they can be implemented in your teaching martial arts.

1. Respect and appreciation for human values.

Martial arts teaches respect for human values through a system of etiquette and seniority among students and instructors. Students are taught to respect their instructor and the senior students from the first day of class. They learn to bow to their seniors and to respect the spirit of the training hall by bowing when entering and leaving. In addition to respect in the class, they are taught to respect all life and never to use their skills to harm others without cause.

2. Effective work habits and self-discipline.

Discipline, like respect, is one of the building blocks of martial arts education. Without discipline, a student cannot master the difficult and demanding skills of the arts. To succeed in the class, he must work hard and discipline himself constantly. You instill discipline in the student by teaching him to set goals and work toward them until he achieves his plan.

3. Social competency.

Martial arts students are members of an organized society that teaches social responsibility and interaction. In many schools student have responsibilities such as keeping the school clean and caring for equipment. They learn to contribute to their school by making a pleasant and safe atmosphere in which to learn.

4. Ethical behavior based on moral and spiritual values.

Teaching combat arts to students who do not understand the importance of ethical behavior is very dangerous. Students must understand the correct uses for their knowledge, including what constitutes a self-defense situation in which harming another person is justifiable. Make it clear to every student when he is justified in using his knowledge and what amount of force is necessary to protect himself. Do not tolerate attitudes that take martial arts violently.

5. Eagerness for lifelong learning.

Martial arts is well-suited for students of every age and ability. Consider the needs of students of different ages when planning curriculum. When you teach each age group according to their needs, you encourage students to study the arts throughout their life because they continue to find new goals and achievements at every level.

6. Aesthetic appreciation and self-expression in the arts.

In teaching martial arts, do not forget that it is an art. Instill in students both the practical aspects of the art as well as the aesthetic aspects. Art is highly valued in every society from the most primitive tribesmen to the great Renaissance masters. Every person should cultivate his artistic perspective to develop a well-rounded personality.

7. Physical and mental health.

Physical and mental health is the most obvious and greatest benefit of martial arts practice. Students feel healthier from their first class. They learn how to exercise, how to tone their body, how to move naturally, how to improve coordination and much more. Provide supplementary material like nutritional information, exercise guidelines, and weight training programs to increase students' health even further. As their physical health improves, students begin to feel better about themselves. They gain more confidence in their physical being, have less stress and feel at ease with themselves.

8. Wise use of time including constructive leisure pursuits.

Marital arts is an excellent leisure pursuit and is becoming recognized throughout the world as such. It encourages a healthy life-style and a sound mind. It also teaches students how to manage their time by introducing the concept of setting and achieving goals regularly. Most martial arts can be practiced by all ages and are a good activity for families to participate in together.

9. Understanding the physical world and man's relationship to it.

Martial arts is based on natural movements. It has been derived from in depth study of the human body and the principles of nature. The student can be taught about his relationship to the world around him through explanations of natural phenomena and how they relate to training.

10. An awareness of our relationship to the world community.

Martial arts are practiced throughout the world. By encouraging students to meet and exchange ideas with each other on a global scale, such as international seminars and competition, we are encouraging the development of a truly global community.

Beyond these goals of mainstream education, the martial arts have goals that are unique. They include perfection of skills, self-fulfillment though self-improvement and betterment of the art. So, we can summarize the goals of the martial arts as follows:

Physical Goals:

1. Perfection of skills

2. Physical and mental health

3. Betterment of the art

4. Understanding the physical world and man's relationships to it

Intellectual Goals:

1. Effective work habits and self-discipline

2. Social competency

3. Eagerness for lifelong learning

4. Wise use of time

5. An awareness of our relationship to the world community

Value Oriented Goals:

1. Respect and appreciation for human values

2. Ethical behavior

3. Aesthetic appreciation and self-expression through the art

4. Self-fulfillment through self-improvement

With specific proven goals like these, you can feel confident in presenting your program to parents, schools, outreach programs and potential students.

See also . . .
Effective Promotion Testing . . . . page 142
Instructor Assessment . . . . page 287

To be a good teacher, you must consistently evaluate both the progress of your students and the progress of your teaching. Average teachers realize the importance of student evaluation, but often neglect evaluation of their teaching skills. **Self-evaluation** is essential for improvement in teaching. If you are deficient in your teaching skills, your students suffer and, if they have a choice, may leave for a better teacher.

To evaluate your teaching, first consider the quality of your students. If they are performing poorly relative to others at similar skill levels, your teaching is insufficient. Of course you have slow students, but your average student should easily meet the minimum standard of performance. Next, consider attendance. Consistent attendance of large numbers signals successful teaching in most cases. A large number of students is relative, but the number should grow steadily. The quality of your teaching can be evaluated by your ability to satisfy the needs of all students from beginners through senior students.

Once you have evaluated your teaching, you can set standards for promotion testing. If you find in your self-evaluation that you do not teach sparring well, you have to lower your expectations of your students' sparring skills. Similarly if you place heavy emphasis on self-defense skills, make the self-defense portion of the exam more rigorous than average.

After setting the standard for evaluation, decide what type of test you want to use. For martial arts, **performance assessment** (physical testing) is essential. In addition to physical testing, you may add a written test on philosophy, terminology, etiquette, and personal essays. In planning your test, consider why you are testing your students. Testing can be used to find deficiencies, check the level of accomplishment, set new goals for performance or assess the quality of instruction being given. In martial arts, testing is frequently a combination of these four objectives.

There are two categories of performance assessment tests: simulated performance and work sample. **Simulated performance** is a test intended to reproduce exactly, under controlled conditions, the response that should be made in real life situations. Simulated performance is well-suited to skills like sparring and self-defense where realistic performance may result in undue injury to the testing students. **Work sample testing** reflects the highest degree of realism in that it requires the student to perform samples of skills under real conditions.

This type of test is appropriate for forms, one-step sparring and skills that are inherently noninjurious.

After selecting the type and purpose of the test, design the testing syllabus according to your curriculum. Grading the test can be done in two ways. The most common method used in martial arts testing is **Criterion Referenced Grading**. The student is evaluated based on set standards for his level of achievement regardless of the skill level of others. Conversely, **Norm Referenced Grading** refers to evaluation based on the average ability level of the group. Superior performing students receive superior grades regardless of their ability to meet or exceed standards for that level. Under most circumstances, criterion referenced testing is preferred. Norm referenced testing is most suitable for selecting team members or candidates for advanced training.

Testing Objectives

1. Identify deficiencies in student performance

2. Identify performance levels

3. Establish new goals

4. Assess the quality of instruction

In the martial arts, rank advancement is one of the primary goals. It is a rare beginner who does not ask or at least wonder how long it will take to reach black belt level. Yet while many students want to advance in rank, they experience anxiety at testing time. In fact, fear of testing causes a significant number of dropouts.

Professionally administered testing boosts student morale and increases intrinsic motivation. The following are steps to ease your students' fear of testing and increase the value of your tests beyond rank advancement.

Plan a testing schedule in advance.

Plan your test dates six to nine months in advance. Give students at least four weeks notice of an upcoming test so they may prepare mentally and physically. Avoid holidays, vacations and competition seasons. When tests are scheduled during busy seasons, they cause undue added stress.

Schedule tests conveniently.

The best time to schedule a test is during the regular class period. Students have already freed that time on their calendars and parents do not have to rearrange their schedules to attend.

Make the testing syllabus clear

Students at every belt level should know exactly what is expected of them in terms of skills, terminology and essay questions. Provide students with both mandatory and optional requirements. *Example:* Everyone is required to perform their highest-level form and one lower level form to be selected by the examiner. This creates a manageable challenge.

Use a consistent test format.

Test the same types of skills at every test. *Example:* Each test consists of a basic outline of forms, basic skills, sparring, breaking, self-defense and an oral essay question. With a standard format, students feel much less anxiety than if you focus on self-defense and breaking one test then forms and sparring the next time.

Set a concrete standard of evaluation.

Martial arts testing is largely subjective because it is based on the instructor's evaluation of the student's performance rather than a strict true/false type of criteria. Set minimum standards of performance for each item on your syllabus and grade with letter or other quantitative grades.

Provide feedback.

Students need more than just a new color belt to continue improving. Give feedback during and after the test. When you award the belts, take time to point out at least one positive point and at least one area to improve for each student.

Never recommend a student for a test until he or she is fully ready.

Your students trust your judgment and assume that when you recommend them for testing, they are ready to move to a new level. If a student fails, he looses faith in his ability and your judgment. If he is not ready to test, suggest areas to improve and encourage him to keep working hard.

Reevaluate your teaching skills.

A promotion test is an excellent time to evaluate your teaching skills. There are always areas where your students are lacking in general. Take each test as an opportunity to upgrade your teaching skills in these areas.

Student Retention

Development and Planning

In this section . . .

145 15 Retention Strategies
151 Retaining Female Students
154 Black Belt Retention
156 Analyzing Student Retention
160 Managing Parents

Preventing Dropouts

Often, when a student comes to you to say that he wants to stop training, he is asking for help. If he really wanted to drop out, he would not be sitting in front of you.

When you encounter this situation, ask the student why he wants to quit. Once you find the true reason (this may not be the first reason he gives), propose a solution that will benefit him and allow him to continue training.

View a conference of this type as a chance to improve your communication skills and strengthen the student's commitment to training.

15 Retention Strategies

Coping with the common causes of dropouts

See also . . .
Analyzing Student Retention . . . . page 156

The single greatest threat to the stability of your school, club or program is a high dropout rate. Many instructors concentrate on bringing in large numbers of new students without regard for their retention rates. This strategy works in the early stages because everyone is new and classes full of white belts are a sign of successful marketing. As those students lose interest, they are replaced by new students and class sizes remain pretty much the same.

The trap here is that the school never matures past the white and yellow belt stage. There are many beginners, but few advanced students and almost no black belts. Without black belts, there can be no assistant instructors or branch schools. The school will be stuck in that beginner stage forever.

To develop a mature student community, you have to give as much attention to retention as you do to recruitment. The best place to start is by looking at what you may be doing to cause students to quit.

Instructor Related Reasons

There are five key instructor related reasons that students quit.

1. Poor treatment of students

Some instructors have preconceptions about certain types of students and carry them over into what they do or do not teach.

Prevention: Look at your curriculum. Do you reserve certain skills for only certain types of people? Do you favor a few talented students over others? Do you ignore or patronize slower students? Do you frequently punish one or two kids while letting others get away with similar offenses? Do you allow higher belts to bully others? Often, these trends develop quietly and don't catch your attention until someone speaks up. By then it is too late. Take time at least once a month to examine your treatment of each student in relation to the others.

2. Lack of technical knowledge or teaching experience

During the first years of teaching, you naturally lose students due to lack of teaching experience or technical knowledge. This is a necessary process and one you should take every opportunity to learn from.

Prevention: Continue to study and advance in the martial arts you teach. Never settle for being one step ahead of your highest student. Also, study other subjects like teaching, personnel management, and business. Strive to project a professional image and don't be afraid of increasing the depth and breadth of your knowledge. As you become more experienced in teaching, there is a temptation to "coast" through classes and drift away from the teacher your students met when they first came to your school. To prevent complacency, have at least one new challenge in front of you at all times.

3. Personality clash with a student

As in your personal life, there are people in your professional life whom you do not like and/or who do not like you. In your personal life, you may be able to avoid contact with people you do not get along with, but as an instructor, you bear the responsibility for overcoming a personality conflict with a student.

Prevention: The best way to deal with a personality conflict is to change your attitude. Since the student has come to you to learn, the ultimate goal is to change him for the positive. However, you cannot help him if you cannot get along with him. Ask yourself just what it is that causes you to dislike him. Is it something you can live with? If it is, acknowledge his right to express his personality and try to live with it or at least ignore it.

4. Major policy change

A change in the school schedule, location, size, class organization, curriculum, instructor, teaching style, or belt system is a major upset in the lives of the students. People favor stability and familiarity over change.

Prevention: Make changes gradually and prepare students and parents for their implementation. A major planned change like moving to a new building or rearranging the schedule should be well publicized at least one to two months in advance. When you announce a major change, also emphasize what will remain the same.

5. Improper balance of discipline

Discipline is the backbone of most martial arts. Parents bring their children to you to learn discipline. Adults come to improve their self-discipline. Striking a balance between discipline and individuality is important.

Prevention: Set rules for your school based on the character of your students. For young students, set more and stricter rules than for adults. Rules for children should emphasize safety, courtesy, respect and organization. Adults do not need as many specific rules, but they appreciate an atmosphere that allows them to practice without fear of injury or invasion of their privacy or practice time.

Student Related Reasons

The next set of retention issues are student related. These are reasons that are initiated by the student or of which the student is the primary source. There are five primary student based reasons for quitting:

6. Problem with other students

This results from a personality conflict, an argument, a situational confrontation, or personal bias. Whatever the source, interpersonal conflicts have a tendency to polarize others in the group as well. Once people begin taking sides, the potential for additional dropouts increases significantly.

Prevention: Before this happens, you must take one of two actions. The first is to attempt to mediate the conflict and help the students resolve their differences amicably. If mediation fails, the best alternative is to separate the students into two different classes, so they do not have to see each other regularly.

Staying in Touch

Contacting students who are absent encourages regular attendance.

During the first four to six weeks of lessons, contact any student who misses two consecutive classes. A firm commitment to learning takes time to form and the beginner period is the most vulnerable to dropouts. Once a regular schedule has been established, contact people after one week of unexcused absence.

Everyone needs occasional encouragement and people feel that you care about their welfare when you check to see why they are absent. However, be careful not to take responsibility for the student's training. Remind the irregular student that he made a commitment to training that only he can fulfill.

7. The student is injured in class

This is a problem faced by almost every martial arts practitioner at least once in the course of training.

Prevention: Some injuries are minor and can be dealt with in a few days or less. Others are significant time-loss injuries, requiring time off and even surgery or prolonged rehabilitation.

For minor injuries, modify the student's training plan temporarily to take into account any weaknesses created by the injury. For serious injuries, contact the student at regular intervals to provide support and encourage his rehabilitation efforts. Suggest he come by to observe class and stay involved in school events. If you have more than one or two time-loss injuries per month, reevaluate the intensity and safety of your curriculum. There may be flaws in the structure of the class that are causing students to be injured at a greater than normal rate.

8. The student is dissatisfied with training

Sometimes a student is just not happy with her training, due to your inability to meet her needs or her inability to adapt to class. The difference between the two is a fine line.

Prevention: First have the student restate her initial goals. Evaluate whether those goals have changed significantly. If they have, restructure her training plan to meet his new goals. This is a case of you failing to meet her needs.

If the student's goals remain the same, then she is failing to adapt to the process necessary to meet those goals. This generally means she has reached a plateau and is having trouble overcoming it. Try breaking down her goals into short-term objectives.

9. The student is bored

Boredom is the result of stagnation. If the student does not feel she is progressing toward her objectives, she feels bored.

Prevention: To overcome boredom, give the student a new personal challenge to meet. Once she is committed to a goal, she is less inclined to feel bored because she has a strong sense of motivation.

10. The student cannot keep up with the class

Some people learn more slowly than others, in certain areas or at certain times.

Prevention: If you find that an average student is suddenly getting behind, you have three options:

1. Give him a few private lessons to help him catch up.

2. Move him to an easier level class until he feels more comfortable.

3. If more than one student experiences similar difficulties, reconsider that area of your curriculum. You may be teaching skills before the students are fully prepared.

External Factors

The most difficult student retention challenges are those where the student's reasons for quitting are not directly related to your teaching. Often these are cases where you have to wish the student well and let him go. These reasons generally fall into five categories:

11. Financial reasons.

When a new student registers for class, you arrange a payment plan with him based on his current financial situation. However, this situation can change over the course of the contract, leaving the student unable to meet his financial commitment. Because martial arts lessons are not a necessity, they are one of the first things to be cut from the budget when a student's financial health worsens.

Prevention: In many cases, the student has paid off some or most of his contract allowing you to rearrange the remaining payments over a longer time span. Try to find some way to work out a suitable arrangement. If you cannot, consider setting up a scholarship fund or giving the student a few months at reduced tuition until he gets back on his feet. Often financial hardship is temporary and when the student is able to recover, he appreciates those people who helped him when he was in need.

12. Non-martial arts related injury

Sometimes students are injured on the job or while playing other sports.

Prevention: If the injury is minor, the student may obtain her doctor's permission to continue training with limitations. Discuss these limitations and clarify how training should proceed. For example, if the student is recovering from an ankle injury, you can give her permission to sit out of activities that require bouncing, jumping or quick direction changes.

If the injury is serious and the student requires total rest, it means missing weeks or months of class time. In this case reassure the student that she will receive credit for the classes missed and you or an assistant instructor will spend time with her when she returns to help her catch up. This is especially important in maintaining the motivation of injured students. When the student returns, she will find that not only have others moved ahead but that she has lost ground as well.

13. Long distance move.

Occasionally students move to another city or state for school or work related reasons.

Prevention: In this case, the only thing you can do is wish the student well and if possible help him find a school in his new area. He may also need documentation of his previous rank to continue in a new school. Be supportive and create a positive climate for his departure.

14. Major life change

Everyone experiences changes that have major consequences on their lifestyle. These changes include marriage, the birth of a child, a career change or a critically ill family member.

Prevention: A major life change means less or even no time for martial arts classes. In this case, reduce or restructure the student's schedule to accommodate her new lifestyle. In time and with your understanding and support, she will adjust to the changes and return to a more regular schedule.

15. Change in priorities

All students experience a change in priorities where something else takes precedence over martial arts.

Prevention: At this time, it is your job to refocus the student on his original goals and reiterate the value of martial arts in his life up to this point. If you cannot persuade the student to continue, accept that some students lose interest in learning and try to pinpoint the cause for future reference.

Although you cannot change every student's mind, you can discover the major causes of dropouts in your school and take steps to prevent them in the future.

Retaining Female Students

Addressing common concerns

See also . . .
15 Retention Strategies . . . . page 145

Women's sports are on the rise and perhaps nowhere more so than in martial arts. In addition to looking for self-defense, women are now joining martial arts schools for the fitness and competition.

Offering cardio kickboxing and women's self-defense programs is a big step toward making a school female-friendly, but there is a lot more to retaining women in the long run. Women have very different concerns than children or men, who are traditionally the mainstays of most schools.

In fact, some instructors who think they are helping women may be alienating them. Do you let women teach, but only children's class? Do you include women in demonstrations, but only as the "victim" in self-defense skits? Do you have separate test requirements for women because the men's requirements are too difficult? All of these seemingly helpful practices may be damaging your retention of female students.

While women as a group should not be stereotyped, there are certain concerns that women are more likely to have than men. Review the questions below to see if your school is answering the most common concerns of female students. The more questions you answer yes to, the better your school ranks in the area of female student retention.

Important Concerns of Female Students

1. Is the parking lot well lit?

2. Is there secure parking?

3. Is there a safe and well-lit bus stop nearby?

4. Is the school clean?

5. Are the locker rooms secure and private?

6. Are there adequate changing facilities for women?

7. Is the equipment in good shape? (women are turned off by the blood spattered heavy bags still found in some schools)

8. Are the bathrooms clean and well stocked?

9. Are there many other female students?

10. Are there female instructors?

11. Are there women of all ages or just young women?

12. Do the instructors treat men and women equally?

13. Is there parity in the curriculum (testing, for example) for men and women?

14. Do women have the option to attempt the male breaking or sparring requirements if they are different from the female testing requirements?

15. Do you expect students to treat each other fairly regardless of gender?

16. Do you have a written sexual harassment policy for staff members?

17. Do male students treat female students in an unbiased way?

18. Are women free from offensive comments or unwanted come-ons?

19. Do women have the opportunity to practice with partners of all sizes and genders?

20. Are self-defense skills practiced realistically?

21. Are there safety rules in place to prevent the use of excessive force?

22. Is the amount of contact in sparring reasonable and consistent?

23. Is adequate safety gear required?

24. Can women purchase female-specific gear at the school?

25. Are safety rules followed in sparring?

26. Can people observe class before signing up?

27. Can people try out a lesson before signing up?

28. Is an instructor available to talk about concerns or problems?

29. Is there a female instructor or senior student available for women to speak with about problems that may be sensitive or embarrassing?

30. Are there teaching opportunities open equally to men and women?

31. Do women have the opportunity to teach adult classes in addition to children's or self-defense classes?

32. Do the techniques taught in class work well for women of small stature?

33. Are women paired with partners of all sizes for realism?

34. Are variations for smaller students taught and practiced?

35. Are women offered the option to practice grappling skills with another woman if they are uncomfortable grappling with a man?

36. Is excessive contact during practice pointed out and discouraged?

37. Are there opportunities for women to attend competitions?

38. If you have a competition team, is there at least one female coach?

39. Are women encouraged to participate in and lead demonstrations?

40. Are women given leadership roles in class?

Adult Motivation

Adult motivation is based on 5 factors:

1. Are the outcomes of the action valued?

Example: Does the student want to learn what you are teaching?

2. Does the student believe that their actions will result in the desired outcome?

Example: Does the student think you are competent and that the classes are progressively taught?

3. Do the outcomes meet expectations?

Example: Does the student feel able to defend herself with the skills she is learning?

4. Do the benefits outweigh the costs?

Example: Is the result of learning valuable enough for the time invested or is getting to class more hassle than it's worth?

5. Has the passing of time changed the cost-benefit balance?

Example: Are lessons still valuable six months after initial enrollment?

Black Belt Retention

The future of your school

See also . . .
Building Leadership. . . . page 291
Outreach Programs . . . . page 302

Some of the most difficult questions instructors face are the ones about their black belt students. Because black belt is often set up as a major goal in the martial arts, it offers special challenges for instructors. Once students reach black belt, they may feel they've finished their training or know everything there is to know about an art. Black belt retention is essential to a strong school. Let's look at common questions instructors pose about their black belts.

Q. "I taught that kid for three years and then he gets his black belt and quits a week later. I don't understand what went wrong."

A. There are two possibilities, the first is that you made earning a black belt seem like the only goal of training during those three years and when he got his belt, he thought there was nothing else to learn. Sometimes, parents contribute to this problem by telling a child that he must continue taking lessons until he reaches black belt then he can quit and try something else. It is important to communicate to both students and parents that black belt is a goal, but not the only goal, of martial arts training.

The second possibility is that he found there were fewer things to learn as he reached black belt and was beginning to lose interest anyhow. Once he got his black belt, he felt that he had achieved most of what he wanted and was no longer being challenged enough to stay interested—a mixture of apathy and burnout.

In either case, the groundwork for continued training after black belt is laid long before the student reaches that level. Adopt a challenging curriculum and a philosophy that black belt is a long-term goal, but it is only one step on the road of self-improvement.

Q. "One of my black belts just quit and opened a school down the street. I don't know what to do."

A. A common occurrence, this is generally motivated by the feeling that your school does not offer growth opportunities for black belts and instructors. If your student had a teaching opportunity in the safe environment of your school, why would he risk going it alone?

Providing teaching opportunities, instructor training and career options for black belts is essential to protecting your investment in your future. Teaching opportunities include part time positions in your school, a recreation or after school class in town or a full time branch school.

Q. "I have a lot of beginner students but almost all of them quit before they get to black belt. What can I do to make some black belts without lowering my standards?"

A. Instructors with few or no black belts often insist they have such high standards that no one can meet them. Perhaps it is not their standards that are a problem, but their teaching methods. The average student loves a challenge and will rise to meet it when equipped with the proper tools and skills. Some instructors cannot create students who are black belt material because their teaching methods are faulty or incomplete. To create quality black belts, you must have a wealth of background knowledge in your art as well as a continuously growing ability to teach and motivate your students.

Q. "I have a lot of students who become black belts, but most of them quit."

A. The instructor, who produces dozens of black belts, only to see them all quit, is not meeting the needs of the average black belt student. Black belts expect to learn complex skills, to be better than lower ranking students, to command respect with their proficiency and to continue to advance as they did before they reached black belt.

Analyzing Student Retention

Identifying causes

See also . . .
15 Retention Strategies . . . . page 145
Defusing Anger . . . . page 277

Think about the last time one of your students quit coming to class. What was the reason? Too much homework? New job schedule? Soccer practice every day after school? Unreliable transportation?

At the time, you probably considered the student's excuse briefly and forgot about it. But did you stop to think about whether the excuse the student gave was the real reason for quitting or just an easy way to avoid talking about his true feelings about your teaching, your school, his classmates or whatever made him want to quit?

As an instructor, you owe it to your students—the ones who quit and the ones who stay—to research and act on the elements of your school that are turning students away. Of course, many students really do quit because of time pressures or family obligations. But others might have rearranged their commitments if their martial arts classes were important enough.

For example, a student who has new job hours might go to the trouble of giving up another activity if he really wants to keep learning martial arts. Perhaps he would quit his bowling league to make time for martial arts. If martial arts class is getting boring, he might quit to make time for bowling. Either way, he blames his work schedule.

Look beyond his excuse. After some thought you realize that he has been at the same belt level for about six months due to an injury and he has not been progressing as rapidly as he used to. On top of that, your new assistant instructor yelled at him last week for not knowing his form and he has not come to class since.

"When analyzing dropouts, remember that most people respect you as a teacher and do not want to hurt your feelings."

156

When you consider the whole picture, not just the face value of the excuse he gave, you see areas where you might have taken action to prevent his dropping out. While it might be too late for him, you can still prevent the same thing from happening in the future.

In this case, consider several key changes: better communication with your assistant about students who are not progressing on course, special attention to injured students when they rejoin class, a more flexible schedule to allow for make-up classes and personal instruction for students who are falling behind. You can do all of the above and still lose students, but at least you are improving your school and your teaching skills along the way.

Identifying Causes

Whenever a student quits or drifts away from class, contact her and politely ask if there is a reason she has been missing classes or does not want to continue attending. If you have good communication skills, most people give a specific reason. A few avoid giving a reason, but promise to return and never show up.

If you get a reason, write it down on an index card along with the student's name, date of last class and belt rank. Under these facts, list the other possible reasons the student may have quit. Some areas to consider:

1. Your teaching manner and personal treatment of the student:
   • too personal
   • not personal enough
   • forgot her name
   • yelled at her
   • disciplined her
   • ignored her
   • offended her parents

2. The curriculum:
   • too hard
   • too easy
   • too boring
   • too irregular
   • too physical
   • not physical enough

3. The physical environment of the school:
   - dirty
   - sweaty
   - dusty
   - unkempt
   - broken equipment
   - lack of equipment
   - unsafe area
   - poor parking
   - too many observers
   - noisy
   - crowded

4. Business management:
   - payment problems
   - lateness
   - unprofessional
   - too professional/impersonal
   - too system oriented
   - no system at all
   - too merchandise oriented
   - not enough classes
   - poor scheduling

5. School social environment:
   - too lax
   - too disciplined
   - gender bias
   - too crowded
   - not enough students
   - irregular class sizes
   - children in adult class
   - too many ranks in one class
   - bullies in class
   - higher belts mistreat lower belts
   - cliques among students
   - high pressure atmosphere
   - too competitive
   - too traditional

When you do each student's analysis it is for that student only. What is too physical for one person is just right or too easy for another. Without judging any of the areas objectively (i.e. for everyone), list how you think this particular person felt about the above areas.

Analyzing Trends

When you have a number of cards that represent about twenty-five percent of your current student numbers you are ready to look for trends. If you have fifty students, you need at least twelve cards to do a good analysis. Spread the completed cards out on your desk.

Look at the cards and group them according to obvious trends. Did you make a note that ten out of twelve students might have quit because there was too much contact in class? Did six students quit because they had personality conflicts with a certain instructor?

If you did an honest analysis of each student at the time of quitting, you will recognize a few definite trends that need correcting in your school. If you cannot pick out trends, refine your analysis procedure—perhaps by having an assistant instructor or senior student help out.

Taking Action

When a trend emerges, ask yourself what can be done to correct it or prevent it from reoccurring. While you cannot satisfy everyone and prevent every drop out, you can make sensible changes that prevent some students from quitting.

When you analyze dropouts, remember that most people respect you as a teacher and do not want to hurt your feelings. Therefore, they may tell you that you are always late, or you insulted them, or their mother doesn't like you, or they are getting bullied by an assistant instructor. As you gain experience in analyzing dropouts, you will find that more often than not, students have a valid and preventable reason for quitting. Discovering each one can mean the difference between the success and failure of your school.

When you accept a child as a student at your school you are accepting his parents as well. Parents can be a valuable partner in your instruction of their child. They can also be a serious impediment.

Parents who enroll their children at your school are interested in improving their child's life in some way. Some want their child to learn to protect themselves, some want them to make more friends/have fun, some want them to be more confident, some want them to be more disciplined, and some just want their children to have something to do after school. Whatever the reason, they are spending their hard earned money for their child to learn martial arts and that means they care about their child's welfare.

Unfortunately, the way some parents express their concern is a hindrance to their child's learning experience. Let's look at some of the conflicts that occur between parents and instructors.

1. The parent thinks his child is ready to test/compete before you feel they are.

In every sport, there are parents who believe they should be the coach/teacher and who make their opinions known. This problem is especially common among parents who have past martial arts experience. Once a parent feels the child should test, he may tell the child so, creating confusion in the child's mind. Two important role models are giving him opposing opinions and he must choose a side.

Solution: Before the child begins to doubt your authority, speak to both the child and parent together in private. Acknowledge that you understand the parent's concerns regarding the upcoming test/competition and that you have considered the child's eligibility with regard to the minimum requirements. Point out the specific areas where you feel the child is not prepared, then lay out a plan of action as well as a target date for the next testing/competition opportunity. Ideally the parent will acknowledge his agreement in front of the child, so the child is no longer confused about his status.

2. The parent insists on teaching the child to do it his way.

Some parents enroll their children for lessons because the parent has some martial arts experience. Like the little league father who played college baseball, these parents often think they know what is best for their child and proceed to contradict and "improve" on your teaching.

Solution: The first step is to acknowledge the parent's previous experience and express your appreciation for his desire to help his child learn more quickly. Then emphasize that not all martial arts are the same and the skills you are teaching his child might be quite different from what the parent learned. Suggest that he focus on helping his child *practice* skills at home, which is different from teaching the child at home. There are many ways a parent can help a child practice without teaching, including holding a target or following along with a form on videotape. Another way to channel a parent's interest is to suggest he sign up for lessons and learn alongside his child. Then they can practice together.

3. Parents are noisy during class.

If your training area opens to the waiting room or you allow parents to observe, there is the danger of the noise level becoming too high. Even a small group of parents can make a good amount of noise if they get an enthusiastic conversation going. Add to that cell phones, younger siblings with noisy toys and crying babies and the waiting room noise can easily drown out the instructor.

Solution: The most direct approach is to walk out to the waiting room and politely ask the parents to keep the noise down. If you find yourself doing this frequently, hang up a little "Quiet Please" sign in the waiting room as a reminder.

4. The parent repeatedly communicates with the child during class.

Some parents like to catch their child's attention with hand signals, encouraging smiles and stage whispers. This is not only distracting to the child, but it can pull the attention of the class away from the instructor.

Solution: Speak with the parent in private before or after class. Explain that while well-meaning, her interruptions are distracting to the child and are doing more harm than good. Suggest that she bring something to do while waiting, like a book to read, so that she won't feel tempted to communicate so frequently during class. An occasional thumbs up from the waiting room is helpful, but not so often that the child becomes dependent on constant parental feedback.

5. The parent wants you to fix their child.

Most schools advertise the benefits of martial arts for children, including discipline and confidence. Some parents take this a bit too literally, expecting an instructor to fix their child in twice weekly lessons, while they allow him to run wild the rest of the week.

Solution: When a parent comes to you to complain that it's been two months and their child isn't disciplined, explain that martial arts lessons can do only so much. Teaching a child discipline is a team effort that includes the child, parents, martial arts instructors and academic teachers. Point out the positive elements that your curriculum includes and give the parent a specific list of behaviors that she can work on at home with the child. Some parents are unaware of what steps they can take at home to reinforce what the child is learning in class. Additionally, consider developing a parent-child contract or list of tips for parents.

6. The child who can do no wrong.

Every once in a while, you run across a child whose parent thinks he is a little angel. No matter what he does wrong, the parent finds a way to blame it on someone else. If little Johnny hits a classmate, the other child started it. If he forgets his test form, you didn't remind him. If he's lazy in class, he must be coming down with the flu. Never once does this parent consider that their child might be at fault.

Solution: Hold this child to the same standards as the rest of the class and let the parent know that the rules apply to everyone. Don't adopt an attitude of general disbelief toward his excuses, but don't allow him to get away with everything either. Don't make a special effort to punish or avoid punishing his misdeeds. In these situations, having a written set of rules, rank expectations and behavior policies is a big help. Another strategy is to rotate instructors, so the child and/or parent don't believe you are "out to get" the child. Be positive but firm.

7. The child is too attached to the parent.

This problem is most prevalent at the preschool age. The child is so attached to the parent that he cannot join the class without crying, constantly checking on his parent's presence, sitting near the parent during breaks, or misbehaving to draw the parents' attention. If not handled quickly, this child will either quit after a few lessons or cause other children to behave similarly.

Solution: Tell the child that this class is for children only and that mommies and daddies wait in the waiting room or go home. Ask him to be your assistant for the day. Give him a target to carry around then begin the class with a fun, low-key activity. Introduce him to other children and assign him a buddy to keep his mind off his parents. With encouragement, the average child will adjust in two or three classes and his parents will be delighted to see his improvement.

8. The parent watches every class, causing their child to be distracted/self-conscious.

A few parents insist on watching every class from beginning to end, much to the dismay of their children. A parent's constant attention makes a child feel self-conscious, distracted and pressured to perform.

Solution: An ideal solution is a one-way viewing window so parents can watch from the waiting room. One-way windows are see-through on one side and mirrored on the other side, so parents can watch their children without the children being distracted by an audience.

If this is impossible, try to find a balance between allowing parents to observe occasionally and giving children the parent-free practice time they need to create a low-pressure learning environment. If the classroom is not in full view of the reception area, set specific days for observation (test days or the first Monday of the month) or request that parents observe for a few minutes then return to the waiting room. If the classroom opens into the waiting area, suggest that parents go out shopping or bring something quiet to do while they wait, like knitting or a book. That way, though parents are present, their children do not feel pressured to "perform" for them.

9. The parent pushes the child to be better than everyone else/perfect.

While most parents are supportive, some are overly enthusiastic, pushing their child beyond her limits. When this happens, classes become a chore and the child decides to move on to another activity to avoid the pressure.

Solution: If the child is giving one hundred percent in class, point this out to the parent. Emphasize that martial arts are noncompetitive, encouraging each individual to do her personal best. Remind the parent that you, as an instructor, know what areas the child needs to improve and you have a specific plan for improvement. Give an example of one of a short-term goal and suggest she encourage, but not nag, the child toward improvement in this specific area only.

10. The parent uses classes as a reward/punishment.

Some parents use martial arts classes as a weapon. This problem usually takes the form of "If you don't (finish your homework, clean up your room, share with your brother), you can't go to karate this week."

Solution: Remind the parent that martial arts classes are more than just a fun pastime. Martial arts teach the discipline and responsibility the child needs to perform his chores at school and home. Suggest a more positive system like "If I don't have to remind you to clean your room for three weeks, you can get a new patch for your uniform."

By taking a positive approach to working with your young students' parents, you increase their enjoyment of classes and help them understand their relationship with their parents better. Every parent appreciates this in the long run.

11. The parent enrolls the child then "disappears."

Every instructor has at least a few of these parents. They enroll their child and that's the last time you see them. The child is dropped off and picked up in the parking lot, brings in notes from their parent and asks to take home anything that has to be signed. These parents may not even show up for promotion testing or other special events.

Solution: There are a couple of reasons why parents disappear. A common one is that they are simply too busy to do more than drop off and pick-up their child. If they work, have other children in after school activities or a toddler to care for, they find it difficult to make time to drop in and watch class. Another reason may be that the parent is shy or intimidated by the school atmosphere.

For busy or reluctant parents, a soft touch works best. Personally call to invite the reluctant parent to the next promotion testing or tell her about something exciting her child did in class. If you have a lot of absent parents, consider holding a parent open house or a parent-child event like a target kicking class, a parent appreciation party, an annual parent-teacher conference or a bring your parent to class day. With a little encouragement and a personal invitation, most parents make an effort to be more involved in their child's classes.

Unfortunately there is another type of parent that falls into this category: the neglectful parent. These parents are absent because they have "better things to do." Not only do they never set foot in the school after enrollment, but they are often late to pick up or drop off their child, forget to send in paperwork and payments, send the child to class in a dirty uniform, arrange for their child to get rides from an ever-changing list of people and are generally neglectful.

This parent is very difficult to deal with because their child is fairly low on their list of priorities. If you have more than a few of these parents, set up some school policies to deal with them and ensure their children's safety. Create a pick-up policy stating that children will only be released to a parent or guardian inside the school building. Children should not be allowed to wait in the parking lot or to run out into a dark parking lot looking for a parent. Require parents to renew their child's lessons in person every six or twelve months. Use this opportunity reinforce your expectations of the parent's role. Contact the parent by phone and diplomatically express your concerns. Don't give up on neglectful parents because it is their children who need your guidance the most.

Fortunately the parents listed above are in the minority. Most parents are helpful, well-meaning and eager to support their children's martial arts lessons in a way that does not make your job more difficult. Don't forget to show your appreciation to them!

Public Relations

Your Reputation Depends On It

In this section . . .

167 The Value of Publicity
170 Types of Publicity
173 The Press Release
180 Targeting the Right Media
194 Professional Phone Tips
197 Power of the Internet
200 Creating a Professional Image

The Value of Publicity

Branding your school

An active, targeted and ongoing publicity campaign is essential to the survival of a professional martial arts school. In fact, a strong publicity program has the dual effect of reducing your need for advertising while bringing in dozens of excited and motivated new students. In the long run, that means more new students at less cost to you.

Publicity can be used to achieve many important goals for the school including:

Improved Name Recognition

Ongoing publicity makes your school name a household word. Think about the businesses in your community. Do a few immediately come to mind? Were some of those that came to mind businesses that you have never even set foot in? These are the businesses that are using publicity to build name recognition. You may have never bought carpet at XYZ Carpet, but if they have done their publicity homework, XYZ Carpet is the first place you think of when you *do* need carpet.

"Make your school name so familiar that people in your community automatically think of you when they think martial arts."

This is your goal as well. Make your school name so familiar that people in your community automatically think of you when they think "martial arts." Name recognition has two benefits. First, it brings in new students on a regular basis. Remember, when people think martial arts, you want them to think of your school first. Second, it creates a positive reputation for your school in the community. Your school is seen as an active contributor to the good of the community and this makes people feel good about patronizing your business.

1. Credibility

Publicity builds credibility for your school in the eyes of your students and their family members. Everyone likes to be a part of something good and your publicity efforts remind your students that they are members of a reputable and admired group. Every time they see you, your school or maybe even themselves in the newspaper, they will say to their friends "That's where I learn Karate" with a proud smile. The credibility you create through publicity helps retain students in the long run.

2. Authority

If you use publicity to make people aware of your knowledge of the martial arts, you will become a local expert—an authority in your field. People feel comfortable joining your school knowing that they are learning from a true expert, not just some run of the mill black belt. This gives you an edge over the local competition.

3. History

Each article run in the newspaper or public recognition becomes part of your school's history. Proudly display your publicity efforts on the walls of the school waiting rooms. News articles create the impression that your school has a long and reputable history. Being a well-established business is important in the eyes of potential students. Nobody wants to trust their time and money to a fly-by-night operation. New students often assume that the more history you have, the more likely you are to be around for a long time. And they're probably right!

4. Expansion

When it comes time to expand your school to a second location, you will have the background to negotiate a favorable lease, meet the requirements of the zoning board and clear the hurdles of breaking into a new community. Your past publicity efforts are an asset in convincing your landlord, town officials and your new neighbors that you are an asset to their town.

5. Diversification

Every instructor is eager to diversify his or her programs. Many instructors set up contracts with schools, corporations and recreation departments to teach classes on salary. These outreach programs are an excellent supplement to school income and a great way to get more people interested in the martial arts. Unfortunately, they can also be very difficult to set-up. Most organizations have strict guidelines to follow in creating programs and hiring instructors, especially programs that work with children. The credibility and authority you develop through publicity gives potential employers confidence in hiring you, especially if they are comparing your resume with that of other instructors.

6. Growth

At certain times in your school's life cycle, you may feel like the school is going nowhere; It is not growing in size or perhaps it is shrinking. These periods can lead you to feel frustrated or disappointed with your teaching and business skills. Publicity is a great way to stimulate the growth necessary to break out of a slump. Good publicity creates interest in your school and, if nothing else, makes you feel good about what you do. And if you feel good about what you are doing, your school will most likely get back on the right track.

There is one additional way that publicity can benefit your school. It can generate interest in an event you are hosting by giving the event credibility, authority, name recognition and, most of all, excitement. So, when planning your publicity, remember to make both general plans for your school and specific plans for each event—seminar, demonstration, tournament, kick-a-thon—that you organize.

Ultimately, all of your publicity efforts should be geared toward a positive contribution to your community. When you are making a contribution to the world around you, you become part of something bigger than yourself and discover many new opportunities to grow.

Publicity should not be confused with advertising or marketing, both of which are paid means of communicating with the public. Publicity is editorial, meaning you are not paying for it. If you are paying, no matter what form the media takes, you are advertising.

However, beyond that, publicity can be hard to quantify because it takes many forms. Every type of media—newspaper, magazine, radio, television, online—can be used to gain publicity if you know the tricks of the trade. In fact, much of what you read in your daily newspaper is the result of publicity. Next time you read an article that cites an expert opinion, consider whether this person might have gotten into the article, or even inspired the article, through good publicity. Although the expert probably initiated the contact with the newspaper, and possibly even provided the idea for story, most readers assume that the reporter contacted the expert because the subject matter is important. This is why publicity is infinitely more valuable than advertising. It carries an implied endorsement of the media that reports it.

There are four major classes of media in which you may get publicity:

1. Newspapers

This is the first choice for most martial arts schools because the local newspaper is accessible and always in need of information. It has dozens of pages to fill in every edition, making it the perfect place to start for those new to public relations. The types of newspapers to consider include shoppers/freebies, local weekly papers, daily metro papers and national newspapers.

2. Magazines

Magazines are more selective in choosing their content and often less plentiful than newspapers, making them harder to break into. On the other hand, magazines have a larger circulation and stay on the newsstands longer than newspapers. Types of magazines include local/regional news magazines, local or national special interest magazines and national news magazines.

3. Radio

Radio is very difficult to break into for a martial art school. The best bet is to get a radio station to cover one of your events live, particularly a charity event. The next best route is to get on an interview or call-in program as an expert.

4. Television

Television is by far the most difficult medium. Not only do you have to have a dynamic and timely story, you have to create a visual story that is appealing to a broad audience. The best approach is to start with a local cable access program and try to work up to the local news or feature shows.

5. Books

The public perceives a book, and by association its author, as an authority on a subject. Being associated with a book on martial arts gives you an aura of authority. You can write a book if you have a great deal of time and the required knowledge. You can become part of someone else's book, by contributing editorial material or artwork or posing for photos. You can get someone to write about you in their book, as an expert or authority. Or you can endorse a book, by writing a preface or giving an endorsement to put on the cover.

6. Video Tapes

The same methods can be used on videotape. You can produce your own video for sale or you can become involved in another instructor's video. Again, you will gain the benefit of being seen as an expert in your field.

7. Internet

The internet is a fast growing medium that provides easy access public relations. By participating in a newsgroup, mailing list or online forum or hosting a special interest web site, you can establish your reputation as an expert and create name recognition.

The above methods, however, carry one prerequisite: an outstanding knowledge of your art. Before you can establish yourself as an expert, you have to have the knowledge, experience and credentials to back up your reputation. This may not be possible or even desirable for every instructor. The best plan of attack is to concentrate on the conventional media first and use the non-conventional media as a reinforcement.

Types of Stories

There are a few common formats that you should understand when pitching a story to the media. Before you write your press release, consider what type of story you are looking for.

1. Interview
A reporter or editor interviews a subject and prints the interview line for line. Another option is to use outtakes from an interview to develop a feature story or to edit the interview for length and content.

2. Feature story
A feature story focuses on a person or event with the emphasis on the human interest side of the story rather than hard news. A feature is likely to appear in the people, lifestyle, business or sports section of the newspaper. Feature stories are often used for filler on slow news days or to tie-in with a national trend, event or holiday.

3. Event announcement
A one to five paragraph article detailing the who, what, when, where and why of an upcoming event.

4. Post event report
This type of article gives the details about what happened at a recent event, including who attended, what took place and what benefits the community reaped from the event.

5. Hard news
Hard news is a pressing regional or national event of interest to the general public. It is often related to politics, crime or international relations.

6. Business news
Business news, mostly found in the business section of the newspaper, is any story about the economic side of doing business. Most business news revolves around large corporations and the government, however many newspapers do human interest stories on unusual careers, industries or business people.

7. Sports news
Sports news records the previous days sporting events and sometimes upcoming local contests. It focuses primarily on major sports. Few newspapers consider martial arts to be a major sport, but you may be able to convince the editor otherwise, especially for a human interest story.

The Press Release

Over 100 ways to get fit and beat boredom

See also . . .
Types of Publicity . . . . page 170
Targeting the Right Media . . . page 180

A press release is the fundamental tool used to get publicity. It is usually one or two pages long and serves as your introduction to the press. A good release communicates your message while generating interest in your story. It should be informative and concise. Reporters and editors are busy people who don't have time to waste reading long, boring press releases.

Format

Press releases have a very specific format that is accepted throughout the media industry. The following points should be observed when creating your press release:

• The release should be typed or laser printed on an 8 ½" by 11" sheet of white paper.

• The lines should be double spaced.

• If you are using a computer, select a standard font like Times or Arial. Use at least 10-point type. If you will be faxing your release, consider 12-point type because it's larger size makes it more legible when reproduced.

• When possible, limit your release to a single page. Never print on the back of the page.

• Date your release in the upper left corner. If your release is time sensitive, indicate it by typing "For release no later than _____." The date indicated should be at least one day before your event. If the release is not time sensitive, type "For immediate release" in place of the date.

• Place the name and telephone number of a contact person in the upper right hand corner of the page. On the first line type "For further information contact:" On the next line type your name and a telephone number where you can be reached. Make it very easy for the media person to reach you. Do not give a phone number that will be answered by an answering machine or your children or no one at all. Remember, reporters are busy people and they will not waste time trying to reach you repeatedly.

- Make your release easy to read. Do not use fancy formatting techniques or unusual type styles.

- Use italics or bold letters for emphasis. Avoid using all capitals, except in the headline. Long strings of capital letters are hard to read.

For an example of the above format, see below and right.

Sample Press Release for an Event

For immediate release   For more information contact:
                                         Gail Green at 555-5555

Martial Arts School Raises Over $1000.00
to Benefit South Middle School

"During March and April, Green's Martial Arts hosted a self-defense seminar to benefit the South Middle School PTO. The seminar, led by Gail Green, head instructor at Green's Martial Arts, taught self-defense skills and assault prevention techniques to over 100 mothers and daughters from Middleborough. Mrs. Green and eight assistant instructors volunteered their time and expertise to raise over $1000.00 for the PTO. According to Helen James, president of the South Middle School PTO, "The seminar proceeds will be used to benefit the children and families of Middleborough through the activities of the PTO."

For more information, contact Gail Green, Green's Martial Arts, 57 Broad St., Middleborough, 555-5555.

Also enclosed is a letter from Helen James to Mrs. Green detailing the use of the donated funds and a photo taken after the seminar. See the back of the photo for caption.

# # #

Sample Press Release for a Feature Story

For Immediate Release

For information contact:
Joe Smith 555-5555

Local Martial Artist Achieves International Notoriety

Local Karate instructor Joe Smith just returned from Spain where he won the European Open Karate Cup tournament, defeating 40 other fighters from 17 countries. The tournament, sponsored by the Spanish National Karate Federation, is hosted annually to crown the International Open Karate Cup Champion in three weight classes. Mr. Smith defeated all comers in the middle weight division, earning the title of 2001 International Open Karate Middleweight Champion. As champion, he will receive a feature profile in the European martial arts magazine *Kickers* and be invited to return to Spain next year to defend his title.

Mr. Smith is the only martial artist from Iowa ever to win the European Open Karate Cup tournament and only the fourth American to hold the title. The lightweight title was won by Frederico Perez of Portugal and the heavyweight title was won by Jean-Claude Dion of France. Mr. Smith, owner of Smith's Karate of Anytown, is an avid competitor and a lifelong martial artist. Since beginning his competitive career at the age of 8, he has won over 200 tournaments including 16 national and international titles. Says Mr. Smith of his victory, "I love to compete and I won this one for my students back home. They have been a great help in my training and I want to thank them for all of their support and encouragement. I couldn't have done it without them."

For more information contact:
Joe Smith, Smith's Karate of Anytown, 12 Main St., Anytown, 555-5555.

#

The Headline

The first thing a reporter reads is the headline. This is not the headline that the actual article will use, but it should draw attention to the key points of your story. Good headlines tell the whole story in one sentence or phrase. If you cannot summarize the point of your story in the headline, you need to focus your story more tightly.

A good headline is catchy. "Karate Instructor Wins National Championship" is a boring headline. Besides the instructor involved, nobody really cares about this story. It doesn't call attention to any particular points and could describe almost anyone. On the other hand, "Local Resident is Top Martial Artist in the Country" has more punch. It indicates that the story has a local angle and that someone in the community has made a significant national achievement. Successful headlines convey the subject of the release in a unique and exciting way.

The Body of the Release

When you have a great headline that sums up your story, write the story. That's right, the headline comes first. Remember, if you cannot tell your story in a sentence or phrase, your story needs more work. So once you write a successful headline, you can be sure that you have given your story sufficient thought and planning. Now you are ready to create the body of the release.

Every news release has to have an angle. The angle is what makes the story interesting. The angle is sometimes referred to as "the hook."

A story is not inherently interesting just because it exists. It must have a human interest point. For example, a promotion test at your school is not news. The fact that one of the students promoted is the first woman in town to reach black belt is news. The fact that one of your students just won a tournament is not news. The fact that he is only eight years old is. The fact that you are holding a women's self-defense seminar is minor news. The fact that all of the proceeds are going to a local charity is major news for your community.

The angle can mean the difference between a one-paragraph announcement of your event and a half page feature story with photos. Most reporters know nothing about martial arts, so they do not necessarily see the potential interest in a martial arts story. Your job is to tie together your story with the readers or viewers of the media you are approaching.

How can you make your story noteworthy? A common technique is to read your headline out loud then ask yourself "So what?" For example, "Mother of three achieves black belt" is a nice, catchy headline. Now, who cares? Well, not only is she a mother of three, but all three of children are involved in the martial arts. And she has been coming to class for four years despite a serious injury suffered in a car accident that almost ended her hopes of reaching black belt. And she works at the local bank. And so on, until you have enough material to create a dynamic story and support the story.

Of course, not every story is dramatic or exciting. Some stories are more routine, like an upcoming demonstration or tournament. In these cases, look for a story within the story. Does the tournament have a "challenger" division for handicapped students? Is the demonstration going to feature a group of kids who are all honors students and black belts? Look for an element that sets your story apart from the rest. This element is invariably a human one.

With that in mind, there is an exception to the rule for using an angle. There are times when you just want a simple mention of an event that has happened or a listing of an upcoming event in your local paper. In this case, there is no need for an angle. Just type up a straight "who, what, when, where" paragraph and send it to the local paper. In most cases they will reprint it exactly as you submit it. In general this is most common at small newspapers with just a few staff members. But, all publicity is good publicity so don't overlook these opportunities.

Supporting Materials

In most cases, supporting materials are not necessary for your press release. In a few instances, the media will want photos to reproduce or video to preview. Send supporting materials in the following cases only:

- When you are sending in an announcement of an event to a small, local paper as discussed above, include one or two appropriate photos. Small newspapers do not have the staff to send on photo shoots and often use whatever material is provided. Remember to caption the photos accurately, including the names of each person featured.

- If you have written a release or news article for a martial arts magazine, send appropriate photos. Again, include captions. Most magazines require a release form stating that the persons in the photo as well as the photographer give their permission for publication. You can obtain the necessary form from the magazine. Until you receive it, indicate on your press release that permission has been granted by all involved parties.

- When you are pitching a story to television, it can be helpful to provide a short, representative video clip. Do not send the video with your press release, but indicate on the release that video is available for review. The video should directly relate to the story or event. If you are pitching your tournament, provide video of last year's event. If you have a story about a student, provide video of that student doing what he will do on camera for the reporter, whether it is talking or performing or both.

Identify your supporting materials clearly and provide a postage paid envelope if you expect them to be returned. Never send photos to major daily newspapers, they are barred from using them. If a reporter for a major newspaper is interested in the story, the newspaper will arrange for a photo shoot.

Presentation

There are two accepted ways of getting your press release into the hands of the media. If you are not on a tight deadline, you can **mail the press release**. For a one page release, fold it and place it in a regular business envelope. Address the envelope to the correct person at the media outlet and drop it in the mail. If you are sending photos or other supporting materials, include a brief (not more than three paragraphs) cover letter stating who you are, why the enclosed materials are important to the reporter and what you are sending, for example photos of the event or press clippings from another article.

For news events on a tight deadline, **fax the release** to the media. Prepare a simple cover sheet that indicates who the fax is intended for. If the news outlet is very large, specify the person's title and department. That way, if they are not in the office, someone else in the sports department or feature department will take a look at the release and not just drop it on the intended recipient's desk. Some news outlets also accept press releases by email, but use this method only if the news outlet has specifically requested it and you have a direct email address for an appropriate contact.

Follow-up

Every press release you send out should be followed by a phone call to the appropriate reporter, editor or producer. If you fax your release, follow-up later the same day. If you mail your release, call a few days after the release goes out. When you call, keep your inquiry simple. The best approach is "Hello, this is _____ from _____ and I am calling to confirm that you received the press release that I mailed/faxed to you today/recently." This will prompt one of several responses:

- **Yes, we received it but we're not interested.** This is not good news, but politely inquire about why the reporter is not interested. This feedback will help you to prepare your release more accurately in the future. It is not a good idea to argue with or try to persuade the reporter because you want to make a good first impression and create an ongoing relationship with each media contact. There are many reasons why you might be turned down and you are unlikely to change the reporter's mind. In fact, it may not be his decision to make so you only aggravate him by pursuing the issue. On the other hand, most reporters do not mind sharing their reasons for turning down a story. Remember to thank the reporter for his time at the conclusion of the call.

- **I don't know if we got that or I don't remember seeing it.** This is a mixed blessing. It means that your release was not exciting enough to catch the reporter's attention, but it also means that you have a chance to pitch your story to the reporter over the phone. Before you call, be prepared for this answer by having a two or three sentence summary of your story idea. Keep it simple and be enthusiastic. Once you have presented your idea, ask the reporter if he is interested in covering the story.

- **I have it right here on my desk or I was going to call you.** This is the ideal answer. Your press release was so impressive that the reporter knows exactly who you are and what your story is about.

Writing a Professional Press Release

DO:

- Keep it short, a single sheet of paper if possible
- Have a catchy headline
- Include your name and telephone number
- Indicate the release date
- Type your release in double spaced format
- Use a laser printer
- Make it easy for the media to get in touch with you
- Follow up with a phone call
- Address your release to the correct person
- Include supporting materials when appropriate
- Include little known facts that might interest the reader
- Have a unique angle for your story
- End your release with # # #

DON'T:

- Hand write your release
- Type on both sides of the paper
- Use fluorescent or unusual paper
- Use italics or small type
- Use a hard-to-read font style
- Type in all capital letters
- Be pushy or aggressive when contacting the media

Using this Section

When you are ready to send out your press release, consult the following pages to determine what category of media is best suited for your story and how to approach that media type. Each industry has customs and practices to follow if you want to be taken seriously.

Review the "Best Approach" steps, then consult the drawbacks to assess what the impact of your release might be and what the pitfalls for that industry are. Knowing the drawbacks ahead of time helps you form reasonable expectations for the impact of your publicity efforts.

Targeting the Right Media

Getting results

See also . . .
Types of Publicity . . . . page 170
The Press Release . . . . page 173

Finding the right media for your story is the most challenging aspect of securing publicity. This section will review each type of media in detail, analyzing the strengths and drawbacks as well as the best approach.

Weekly Free Newspaper   (i.e. shopper)

Most likely to run:

1. Event announcements such as a grand opening, seminar or tournament

2. Post event reports, especially with a photo

3. Community related events

4. Frequent short releases and mentions

Drawbacks:

1. Free weekly papers are usually made up of primarily classified and display ads. They provide little, if any, news and are not regarded as news sources by the community.

2. Because they are free, they may give the impression that they are "cheap" and your event may be seen as low budget by association.

3. Free papers appeal to bargain hunters who have only bargain hunting in mind.

4. Many free newspapers are briefly glanced through then thrown away by the majority of recipients.

Best Approach:

1. Send your press release far in advance (at least 2 to 3 weeks) because these types of newspapers work on a very long deadline and tend to be understaffed. Make it easy for the staff to use your information.

2. Include good quality black and white photos with captions identifying each person in the photo.

3. Send photos and stories that mention local residents. Prominently include hometown affiliations for residents.

4. Appeal to the newspaper's community interest. Stress the benefits that the community will gain by reading your story or learning about your event.

5. Whenever possible, send photos with children (always get parental permission) in them. Photos of children are much more likely to be run than photos of adults.

6. Many small papers don't have a fax or don't accept releases by fax. Allow enough time to mail your release.

7. You may not be able to reach a reporter or editor by phone. If there is a voice mail machine, leave your follow-up message and a telephone number where you can be reached. Don't expect to be contacted unless there is a problem or question.

8. In most cases, small papers will run your release in the format you submit it in, so write the release with this in mind.

Local Weekly Newspaper (single or several town circulation)

Most likely to run:

1. Event announcements

2. Features on local residents

3. Events with community impact or benefits

Drawbacks:

1. Circulation is often small, limited to a single town.

2. Most weekly papers have a small staff with limited resources.

3. Community papers are often conservative and hesitant to run unusual stories.

Contact Information

If you plan to do regular publicity for your school or events, develop a contact database, either on your computer or in an index card file.

The first place to start your data collection is the local media. Pick up a copy of each one of the print media you plan to target at your local news stand or library. From each publication, copy the address (make sure it is the editorial office address, not the subscription address), telephone, fax, e-mail and editor's name.

For publications that are not available in your library or newsstand, consult one of many directories available at large libraries. In addition to *Writer's Market*, there are directories that list contact information for television stations, radio stations and associations. Ask a reference librarian to help you locate the appropriate directories.

Best Approach:

1. Send a one-page release focusing on a local angle.

2. Put your local connection in your headline.

3. Direct your release to the editor because many reporters at small papers are free-lance or part time.

4. Follow-up with a call to the editor.

5. Make a note on your release if photos are available. Do not send photos with your release. If the editor wants to use them, she will request them.

6. Provide both day and evening phone numbers. Some reporters may work part time and prefer to call you in the evening.

Your county may have a local daily paper or a metro daily paper or both. A local daily paper focuses on community news, reports local sports, local features, etc. A metro daily has more of a national or regional focus, reporting on national sports, stock markets and international news.

Local Daily Newspaper

Most likely to run:

1. Late breaking news

2. Regional events

3. Feature stories

4. Human interest stories

5. Interviews

Drawbacks:

1. You have to move fast to meet the short deadlines of a daily paper.

2. You must be available to the reporter on his schedule.

3. Daily papers have wide coverage areas and much of the impact of your story falls outside of the intended audience.

4. There are dozens of other articles competing for attention with yours.

5. The paper is read and saved only one or two days. This gives you a very compressed time period in which to make an impression.

Best approach:

1. Fax a one-page release to the appropriate editor or reporter. To find the right person, consult the articles in the section where you think your story fits best. Choose the section editor or a reporter who writes similar articles. Many daily newspapers run contact information in each section or on their website to make it easy for readers to get in touch with reporters and editors.

2. Do not send photos. Daily newspapers have their own staff and will send a photographer if they want photographs taken.

3. If your event or story is photogenic, mention this in the release. Newspapers are always looking for great photos to run in every section.

4. If your story takes place within the newspaper's primary coverage area, mention this prominently in the release.

5. If your story ties in with regional or national events making it a timely topic, point this out in the release.

6. Follow-up with a call to the person you sent the release to. If that person has passed it along to someone else, get his or her name and telephone number for follow-up.

7. Bear in mind that dailies work on short and ever-changing schedules. Your article could be added or dropped at a moment's notice.

Metro Daily Newspaper

Most likely to run:

1. Hard news

2. Stories with statewide, regional or national impact or interest

3. Broad human interest stories

4. Departmental stories (sports, business, feature)

Drawbacks:

1. Metro dailies are difficult to place a story in because they place a great deal of emphasis on national news and receive hundreds of press releases a week.

2. Metro dailies have a life span of only a day or two, after which they are discarded.

3. Because of the size of a metro paper, your story may be lost amidst the clutter.

4. The area of coverage is broad and much of the impact of your story falls outside of the target audience.

5. The frequency with which you can place items in a metro daily is very limited. If you get one story every couple of years, you are doing very well. Large newspapers are very sensitive to providing coverage to a wide range of businesses and topics.

Best approach:

1. Fax a one-page release to the department or section editor where your story fits best.

2. Do not send photos. Daily newspapers have their own staff and will send a photographer if they want photographs taken.

3. If your event or story is photogenic, mention this in the release.

4. If your story takes place within the newspaper's coverage area, feature this prominently in the release.

5. If your story ties in with regional or national events, making it a timely topic, point this out in the release. For a feature story, try to tie in with a current trend, fad or news item.

6. Follow-up with a call to the person you sent the release to. If that person has passed it along to someone else, get his or her name and telephone number for follow-up. If that person is not in, ask to speak to his or her assistant.

7. Emphasize the seriousness of your story and the number of people it impacts.

8. Bear in mind that dailies work on short and ever-changing schedules. Your article could be added or dropped at a moment's notice.

National Newspaper (USA Today or The Wall Street Journal)

Most likely to run:

1. Hard news

2. National events

3. Significant human interest story

4. Stories on national trends or fads

Drawbacks:

1. National newspapers are extremely difficult to place a story in because they emphasize national news and receive thousands of press releases a week. Many of their human

interest stories are pitched by professional public relations people and feature national experts.

2. National newspapers have a life span of only a day or two, after which they are discarded.

3. Because of the size of a national newspaper, your story may be lost amidst the clutter.

4. The area of coverage is very broad and almost all of the impact of your story falls outside of your target audience.

5. The frequency with which you can place items in a national newspaper is very limited. If you get one story in your entire career, you are doing very well.

6. Most national newspapers will not do an article with only a single source of information. The reporter will take your release and contact many other people in the same field, so be prepared to share the spotlight.

7. There is a chance for your story to be twisted into a controversial angle to build readership (i.e. a tabloid type story).

Best approach:

1. Fax a one-page release to the department or story editor where your story fits best.

2. Focus on a unique point of interest or a trend with broad national appeal.

3. If you have had a local article done already on the same topic, fax it with your release to support the story's newsworthiness.

4. Emphasize your credentials, especially if you have been featured in regional or national media. Portray yourself as an expert in your field.

5. If your story is picked up and does not appear right away, keep following up. Some large news organizations keep feature type stories on file for later release.

6. If you do not have any luck with news reporters, approach one of the newspaper's columnists who write on topics similar to yours (sports, family life, business). Columnists face daily deadlines and are always looking for new ideas to fill their space.

7. Be persistent. You may not catch a reporter's attention on the first try, but perhaps your fourth or fifth story idea will be just what the reporter is looking for.

Maximizing Publicity

Once you get great publicity, your job is not done. The first thing you should do is arrange to get a copy of the publicity. This may mean buying copies of the newspaper, ordering reprints, taping a television show or getting a tape from the radio station you appear on.

Good publicity can be used many times over. If the publicity is print, make copies or purchase reprints to display them in your school. You can also use quotes from them as part of promotional handouts to new students and parents. Consult with the media about restrictions on the reuse of their stories.

Another way to reuse your publicity is to develop a media kit, which is simply a collection of past publicity to send out with new press releases. Media people like to be part of a trend and a thick media kit will persuade them that you are a great story waiting to be told.

Regional Martial Arts Magazines

Most likely to run:

1. Event announcements

2. Event reports

3. Local martial artist profiles

4. Stories on up and coming young martial artists

5. Rank promotions

6. Tournament results

Drawbacks:

1. Coverage is only within the martial arts world, not to the general public from which you might draw new students.

2. Coverage may fall far outside your intended target area, with little to no coverage in your immediate geographic area.

Best Approach:

1. Regional martial arts magazines are a growing trend and a good way to break into the martial arts media scene.

2. Regional magazines are often understaffed and will print a solid article as is, including the pictures you submit.

3. Focus your story on a regional angle, highlighting the connection in the headline.

4. Fax or mail the release to the editor. If you have photos, send both the release and the photos by mail.

5. Follow-up with a call to the editor.

6. Offer to become a regular contributor to the magazine, reporting on events in your area or writing a column.

7. Regional magazines are often given away free at tournaments within the region, so coverage is tightly targeted.

8. Because regional magazines are hungry for content, especially photos, they provide a good opportunity for repeat exposure.

National Martial Arts Magazines

Most likely to run:

1. Event listings

2. Post event reports

3. Feature articles

4. Mentions about charity donations, fund-raising seminars, etc.

Drawbacks:

1. Some magazines require payment to run event listings.

2. National magazines are often difficult to get into for feature articles. Try submitting an event report or a two to three paragraph news item about an event before trying a feature article.

3. Repeat coverage in the same magazine is unlikely to occur more than once a year. Approach different magazines for different occasions.

Best Approach for a listing or event mention:

1. Send a short press release (not more than three paragraphs) with photos if you have them. Include the "who, what, where, and when" of the event in the first sentence.

2. Direct event mentions to the editor or reporter who writes the "events" column or "news" column.

3. Follow up with a phone call to confirm that the material arrived safely. If the editor indicates that your story will appear, ask for the date of the issue it will run in. Professionally run magazines will send you a copy, however, you may have to buy your own at the newsstand.

Best Approach for a feature article:

1. Send a query letter (see the end of this section for an example) to the editor or assistant editor. Check the contents page of a recent issue to find the correct person.

2. The best article to send for a first submission is a how-to article, focusing on a tightly defined topic that you know well.

3. If you are sending the query letter to a number of magazines at once, which is a good idea to save time, it is courteous to mention in your letter that you are making multiple submissions. If your article is accepted by one magazine, be sure to notify the others immediately.

4. If you have photos available, mention this in your letter.

5. Many martial arts magazines are open to receiving finished articles, particularly from new writers, to get a feel for the writer's skill level and the quality of the photographs. If you choose to send a finished article instead of a query letter, enclose a postage paid envelope for the return of your materials. If you don't send a return envelope, do not expect to get your materials back.

6. When sending photographs, be prepared to have each person in the photograph sign a release (provided by the magazine) giving their permission for the magazine to use the photo. Minors need a parent's signature.

7. If your article is accepted, you may be paid. To get details on payment and other guidelines, write to the magazines and ask for their "writer's guidelines." You should never pay a legitimate magazine to run an article.

Other Magazines

Most likely to run:

1. National or regional magazines may be interested in running an article by you or about you. Many types of magazines occasionally run martial arts, fitness, safety or self-defense related articles.

2. You may have more luck starting with a regional or statewide magazine.

Drawbacks:

1. A mainstream magazine is more difficult to get an article in than a martial arts magazine and the writing standards are higher.

2. Many magazines accept only assigned articles or articles from published writers.

Best Approach:

1. Always send a query letter first.

2. Focus your query letter on why the article appeals to the magazine's readership. Read a copy of the magazine before you write your query.

3. If the magazine runs short articles or "fillers" try getting in this section first. Many magazines use these short articles to scout new writers.

4. Pick up a copy of the most recent year's *Writer's Market* from your library or bookstore. The contact names and addresses for major magazines are listed, along with valuable inside information on what each magazine is looking for and brief submission guidelines.

Sample Query Letter for a Magazine

Jane W. Writer
123 Main St.
Anytown, CA 90023
555-5555

John Q. Editor
Martial Arts Illustrated
789 Broadway
Anytown, NY 10098

Jan. 15, 2001

Dear Mr. Editor,

"Successful Business Tactics for Instructors" is a 2000 word article I have written on the timely and informative subject of running a martial arts school. The article is aimed at the professional martial arts instructor planning to open a new school or struggling to make an existing school profitable.

The article offers both specific tips and general advice on how an instructor can master the business aspects of running a school without taking an MBA course. I have spoken with a number of successful instructors and interviewed the owner of XYZ Funding Company to gain insight into the typical problems faced by instructors in today's martial arts business climate.

I have been a free-lance writer since 1985 and my credits include articles in martial arts magazines including *Karate Fighter* and *Masters Journal*. I am also a regular columnist for my city newspaper, the *Anytown Register*.

Enclosed is a brief summary of the article as well as a copy of an article that I wrote for *Karate Fighter* last year. I would be happy to send you the full text of "Successful Business Tactics for Instructors" as well as the high quality black and white photographs (model releases on file) I have taken to supplement the article. I have enclosed an SASE for your reply.

Sincerely,

Jane W. Writer

Radio

Most likely to run:

1. Interviews on timely or informative topics

2. Event promotion or tie-in

Drawbacks:

1. Radio exposure is very short lived. It is difficult to motivate listeners to write down important information, like your school phone number, because many listen in the car or while relaxing.

Best Approach:

1. To arrange an interview with a local radio station, first select the show you think best fits your topic. Call the station and get the producer's name.

2. Fax a three page press release to the producer: a cover letter, a release detailing what information you can provide to the show's listeners and a list of questions for the host to ask you. Select attractive questions such as:

   • When are women most likely to be attacked?

   • What are three things women can do to reduce their chances of becoming victim?

   • Is it a good idea to carry pepper spray?

3. Of course, you have to answer the questions on the show, so prepare answers for each of the questions.

4. A call-in show is a good way to encourage interaction with listeners in your community. The host will promote your school or an upcoming event that the public can attend.

5. Consider offering a free giveaway such as a safety tips handout that callers can get by calling or visiting your school. Distribute the handout with a brochure and coupon for lessons.

6. After you have some experience as an interview guest, you may be able to arrange your own weekly show on a topic like public safety, self-defense or martial arts.

Public Access Television

Most likely to run:

1. Informational shows like a self-defense show, safety show, kids martial arts instruction, basic martial arts instruction

2. Community interest programs like video of demonstrations or seminars put on within the community

Drawbacks:

1. Public access shows prohibit advertising.

2. Most public access channels have limited audiences and the schedules can change at the last minute.

3. Homes without cable service subscriptions do not receive public access channels.

4. Most public access channel broadcasts are limited to one or two towns.

5. Some public access channels are run by small groups of volunteers who are not very open to newcomers. Consider becoming a regular volunteer at the station.

6. The quality of public access broadcasts is lower than that of regular television stations, which may make your program (and your school) look cheap.

Best Approach:

1. Public access channels are required to provide airtime to residents in the viewing community as long as the show to be broadcast is not commercial or offensive in nature.

2. Contact the president or director of the public access group that covers your town. Ask him or her to provide you with guidelines and paperwork necessary to get a show on the air.

3. Inquire about using the equipment that the station has and about the availability of volunteers for taping and editing.

4. Plan your program and set up a schedule for taping and editing.

5. Speak with the person in charge of scheduling to get your tape broadcast.

6. If you have time, schedule a weekly show or a series of shows that are progressive, such as a ten-week course of lessons or a weekly call-in program.

Local Cable and Broadcast Channels

Most likely to run:

1. Event related stories if there is a very strong visual element

2. Human interest stories

3. Educational pieces about safety, especially child safety

Drawbacks:

1. Television has a short-term impact.

2. The greatest impact may fall outside of your geographic area or your demographic target, depending on the show's viewers.

3. Your story may be preempted or canceled if a big news story breaks on the same day as your event.

Best Approach:

1. For event coverage, notify the appropriate producer by fax at least one week in advance. Follow-up with a call to see if they are interested in the story.

2. For a feature or human interest story, fax a press release to the appropriate producer and follow-up. Mention that the story is timely, but can be run any time during the next couple of weeks. The larger your time frame, the more likely the station is to pick-up the story as filler material for a slow night.

3. In the press release, highlight the visual element of your story.

4. Give detailed information about why this story is important to the community served by the station and what benefit it has for viewers.

5. If your event is expected to draw a large crowd or a local celebrity, mention this early in the release.

National Network or Cable Television

Most likely to run:

1. Hard news

2. National events

3. Significant human interest story

4. Stories on national trends or fads

Drawbacks:

1. National television is extremely difficult to place a story on because it emphasizes national news and receives thousands of press releases a week.

2. The impact of your story is brief.

3. The area of coverage is very broad and almost all of the impact falls outside of your target audience.

4. The frequency with which you can place items on the national news is very limited.

5. Most national programs will not do a story with only a single source of information. The reporter will contact many other people in the same field and you will have to share the spotlight.

6. There is a chance for your story to be twisted into a controversial angle to build ratings (i.e. a tabloid type story).

Best approach:

1. Create a story that fits a specific angle, trend or niche.

2. The press release to the appropriate producer. It is acceptable to fax producers at different shows and stations simultaneously.

3. Follow-up with a call. Have a one-sentence summary of your story prepared in case the producer does not recall your release.

4. If the producer is even remotely interested, try to work with him or her to shape a story that is acceptable.

5. Stress the visuals of your story.

6. Keep following up until you get a definite (yes or no) answer.

Enrollment

People are more likely to enroll for lessons if the initial prospect interview is done in private. Many people sign up for martial arts lessons to solve a personal problem, such as being overweight or feeling fearful of their surroundings, which they are uncomfortable discussing in a public reception area.

Arranging the initial meeting in a more private office setting encourages each person to talk about the motivating factors behind their interest and gives you the chance to explain how your program can address those concerns.

Professional Phone Tips

Putting your best foot forward

See also . . .
Creating a Professional Image . . . . page 200

As a service provider, the telephone is your lifeline to potential customers. Every inquiry should be treated professionally and seriously. The impression you project over the telephone can make or break your school.

You do not need to stick to a preset script or use a hard sell over the phone. Be sincere, enthusiastic and honest. Create a sense of urgency in the potential student's mind and always encourage the caller to stop by to pick up literature or try a class.

Callers have many questions, some serious and some not. You do not have to answer every question in detail. Decide what information to provide over the phone and stick to it. When a caller asks a question you do not want to answer, politely explain that you do not have time to talk, but would be happy to make an appointment at your school to talk more in person. Most callers who are not serious politely excuse themselves at this offer.

In addition to these general guidelines, here are some specific tips to help you create a professional telephone image at your school:

1. Answer the telephone **politely and professionally**. A good greeting consists of three parts: salutation (Hello, Good Morning), identification (Mr. Smith speaking, Smith Karate) and solicitation (How may I help you?). *Example*: "Good afternoon. Smith Karate, how may I help you."

2. **Answer the phone within ten seconds** or between the second and fourth ring.

3. **Avoid putting a caller on hold** for more than sixty seconds and always ask first. *Example*: "May I put you on hold while I look up that information for you?"

4. **If you must put a caller on hold** for longer than sixty seconds, ask to call back instead.

5. When you return from a break in the call, **always thank the customer for waiting**. *Example*: "Thank you for waiting, Mrs. Smith. How can I help you today?"

6. Consider investing in an **on-hold system** that plays informative messages about your school.

7. **Avoid using a speakerphone**. Most people do not feel comfortable being put on speaker and the quality of the call reception is poor.

8. Speak at a moderate pace, slightly slower than you would in person, or **moderate the speed of your speech** to that of the caller. If the caller speaks slowly, respond slowly to avoid intimidating them. If they speak fast, quicken your pace a bit to match their energy.

9. A **lower voice** conveys authority and confidence.

10. **Sit up straight or stand** when you speak on the phone. Reclining or slouching in your chair makes you sound tense or distracted.

11. Be **sincere and friendly**. Smile when you talk.

12. Have a **brief but professional message** on your answering machine. Avoid long messages (i.e. press 1 for information, press 2 for a schedule) because many callers become frustrated and hang up instead of leaving a message.

13. Return all messages the **same day** if possible.

14. If you cannot reach the caller, **leave a brief message** to let them know that you tried to reach them. Offer to call back at a convenient time and give your office hours.

15. Learn the caller's **needs first**. *Examples:* Who are the lessons for? Are you a beginner? When is the best time to come to class? What type of classes are you interested in?

16. Based on this information, give the caller the best **class schedule and the price** of your introductory program.

17. **Make an appointment** to register for classes or participate in a trial lesson.

18. Give the caller **directions**, a contact name and what to bring.

19. **Do not hard sell** or be evasive. If the caller does not trust you, you will never hear from them again.

20. Honestly **address any fears or misconceptions** the caller expresses or implies. *Examples:* Isn't Karate violent? Won't my son hit kids at school? Aren't I too old for this? Can women do this too?

21. **Admit when you cannot offer** what the caller is looking for. *Example:* They want tai chi but you teach kickboxing or vice versa. Perhaps they are not interested in kickboxing, but their teenage son is.

22. If you are having difficulty understanding what a caller wants, **paraphrase** what you think he wants as a question. *Example:* "So you'd like to find out if your five year old daughter and eight year old son can attend the same lessons?"

23. **Set limits** on what information you are willing to provide over the telephone. This includes an appropriate schedule, a basic course price, directions and addressing any fears or misconceptions of the caller.

24. **Avoid using the word "no."** Instead use "I can't _____ but I can _____ ." *Example:* "I can't explain the full schedule on the phone, but I can give you an idea of what time your class would be at if you give me a little more information about yourself."

25. Do not dismiss **calls from youngsters**. If the child sounds old enough to write down the information, give him a simple price and time schedule. Ask him to stop by with his parents for a trial lesson.

26. Respond to hostility with **polite detachment**. Never get drawn into a fight with a caller. If you cannot defuse the caller's hostility or aggression, politely excuse yourself by feigning an unexpected visitor or a pressing appointment.

27. If a call is **dragging on** without focus, for example the caller is giving you her son's entire school history including everything bad his teacher has ever said about him, use a break in the conversation to redirect it. Rather than asking another question, use some affirmative statements to get the conversation back on track. *Example:* "Many of the boys I teach have the same difficulties in school that your Timmy is facing. I'd like you to bring him down to the school so I can meet him and we can talk some more in person. Is Wednesday after school good for you?"

28. **Train your staff** to answer as many common questions as possible. This is more effective than having to refer callbacks to you or another instructor. When they cannot help a caller, be sure they take complete and accurate messages.

29. **Avoid making outgoing calls** during busy times so callers don't get a busy signal. If you have two lines, making calls at off-peak hours frees you from having to juggle lines and put people on hold.

The Power of the Internet

Promote your school in the digital age

See also . . .
Creating a Professional Image . . . . page 200
Marketing Strategy . . . . page 217

There are two primary ways to use the internet to benefit your school: Promotion and Communication. A well designed website is the cornerstone in any internet strategy. Additionally, tools like email, discussion groups and mailing lists can be effective promotion tools when used correctly.

Promotion

When the internet first gained popularity, many businesses saw it as a selling tool. Martial arts schools quickly put up websites and registered with search engines only to be disappointed when no one signed up for lessons online. While you may not gain many new students as the result of a search engine listing or a random hit on your web site, you can effectively use your web site as a reference tool.

1. Put your **website address** on every piece of print communication that leaves your office including newspaper ads, yellow page ads, business cards, fliers, contracts, brochures, new student packets, free lesson coupons and handouts.

2. Use a **catchy tagline** like "More self-defense tips at www.smithkarate.com" or "Take advantage of our new student special at www.smithkarate.com. Give the reader a reason to visit the web site, something that immediately benefits them.

3. **Keep it simple**. Put the minimum amount of sales information necessary on your site and encourage people to call or visit for more details. Helpful information

"There are two primary ways to use the internet : Promotion and Communication."

includes a class schedule, introductory program cost, directions to the school and some general program information. You might want to include a FAQ for web savvy visitors. Avoid high bandwidth or annoying items like music and animations.

4. Offer something of **benefit** such as a coupon, tip sheet or kid's coloring page. Make people glad they took the time to visit.

5. Offer an **email newsletter** that contains special offers and informative tips. Some people sign up for the newsletter even if they do not call or visit your school. With regular contact, they may decide to take lessons at some point in the future as they "get to know" your school through the newsletter.

The goal of the promotion portion of your website is to give visitors a reason to pick up the phone or visit your school. Every aspect of the promotion portion of the website should be focused on this goal.

Communication

The second function of your website is communication with students and parents. There are many ways your website can make your job easier. While it cannot substitute for personal contact, it can lessen many of the day-to-day jobs that eat away at your time. Consider putting the following in a password protected area that is accessible to member students only.

1. Event promotion and scheduling

How many times have you had a student or parent call because they lost their tournament application or needed directions to a demonstration at the last minute? Spending a few minutes to put important event information on your website can save a lot of time in answering questions, taking phone calls and redistributing paperwork. If you have the technical know-how or can afford to hire a web guru, you can even do event registration online.

2. Class information

Post information about regular classes, team practices, promotion testing and special events in a monthly calendar so students have an "at-a-glance" way of seeing what's coming up for the month.

3. E-newsletter

Ask students to register their email addresses for a student e-newsletter. Topics for an email newsletter include training tips, an event schedule, announcements, special pro shop offers and student successes/news.

4. Referrals

Set up a "tell a friend" feature so students can send a short email note about your school to a friend.

5. Merchandise

A section that allows students to shop at home for merchandise can be a bonus to your bottom line. While the ability to accept payment online is a nice extra, it is not necessary. It's acceptable to create a nice display area that allows students to view and request items then pay for them when they come in for class.

6. Discussion Groups

The interactive nature of the internet is one of its most powerful features. Take advantage of it by creating student discussion groups or instructor brainstorming mailing lists. Discussion groups are a great way to build community and take the pulse of your school.

Maintenance

Whether your website is a simple three page set-up or a full-scale online e-commerce site, building the site is only the first step. Schedule regular maintenance at least weekly.

Daily or Weekly:

- Update the calendar or schedule
- Take down outdated event information
- Post new event information
- Update merchandise selection

Monthly:

- Change training tips
- Change special offers
- Send out email newsletter
- Check for broken links

The best part of having a web site is the ability to change or expand it on a moment's notice. Your web site will grow with your school and is only limited by your imagination.

Atmosphere

Create an exercise oriented atmosphere to keep students excited about their lessons.

Some suggestions:

- Display action oriented pictures and posters in the locker rooms, training areas and waiting room

- Post motivational sayings around the training area

- Provide mirrors in the training area for instant feedback

- Supply supplementary exercise equipment for use before and after class

Creating a Professional Image

First impressions count

See also . . .
Marketing Strategy . . . . page 217

First impressions count. When a student walks into your school, what is the first thing they see? Is it a motivational poster, a martial arts photo, the dirty carpet, the men's locker room door half open? Making a good impression through external public relations creates an image in the customer's mind. You have to follow up and fulfill that image to turn a curious visitor into a new student. The last thing you want is for the prospective student to walk in the door and think "Oh, is that all?"

There are a few simple ways to improve your image:

1. Know what your image is.

Is your style modern, traditional, fighters' gym, kid-friendly, something else? Creating a consistent image is important. Parents who read about your great children's program in the newspaper will be disappointed if they show up and find you teaching a full contact kickboxing class to a bunch of shirtless guys.

2. Be consistent.

Your image is made up of everything from the signs on the wall to your business cards to the color of your carpet. If your brochures, business cards, mats, staff uniforms and signs are all done in the same shades of red and blue, they project a consistent image. If you have blue business cards, green brochures and a purple and orange mat, the school feels disorganized.

3. Use a logo and slogan.

Put your school logo and slogan on everything: uniforms, t-shirts, gear, mats, business cards, brochures, ads, signs, handouts and paperwork. A logo and upbeat slogan project a positive, professional image.

4. Notices are more than information.

Everything that goes up on your bulletin board or gets handed out to students is part of your image. Spelling, grammar and design count. Keep things neat and simple. Avoid multiple fonts, small type, odd colored paper and slang. If notices need to be kept on the bulletin board for more than a week, replace them frequently so they do not get torn, yellowed, curled or dirty.

5. Get a second and third opinion.

Ask parents or staff members to recommend changes in the school design. Keep a suggestion box in the waiting room or have a brainstorming session. Form an improvement committee. Don't forget to spruce up outside as well as in.

6. Meet and greet.

As the head instructor, a large part of your image is you. Greet visitors, parents and students with enthusiasm. Don't hide out in your office between classes. Visit the waiting area and the warm-up room. And don't leave visitors stranded. You or a staff member should be on hand at all times to greet visitors in less than thirty seconds after they enter the school.

7. See with fresh eyes.

Try to see the school as a stranger. Stand out on the sidewalk and look at the front of the building. Drive by from all angles. Park across the street. Go outside at night. Walk in the back door. Do a sweep of the restrooms and locker rooms. Look for things you might not notice on a daily basis. Things that you take for granted may be a nuisance or eyesore to visitors. Do the huge special offer papers in the windows block the view of the training area from the street? Has a tree grown down over the spotlight that lights your sign? Are there lots of "lost and found" clothes left in the locker room? Seeing the school through "fresh" eyes can turn up many ideas for improvement.

Marketing

Attracting New Students

In this section . . .

203 Low Cost Marketing
217 Marketing Strategy
223 Myths of Advertising
228 Setting Tuition Rates
231 Summer Survival Tips
234 Economic Cycles

Marketing Types

The ideas in this section cover every area of school marketing including:

1. Advertising
2. Promotion
3. Publicity
4. Image Building
5. Niche Building
6. Customer Service
7. Product Promotion
8. Service Development
9. Merchandising
10. Competitor Intelligence
11. Student Recruitment

Low Cost Marketing

100 low or no cost options

See also . . .
Professional Telephone Tips . . . . page 194
Myths of Advertising . . . . page 223

As a martial arts school owner and instructor, you are aware that one of the biggest challenges of running a martial arts school, club or program is attracting new students. The second biggest challenge is keeping the students you have. Both of these challenges can be met through effective marketing. Marketing, not to be confused with publicity or advertising, encompasses all of your ongoing efforts to "sell" your school and your services, both to new students and current students.

The marketing ideas in this section are designed specifically with the martial arts instructor in mind. They are proven ideas that have been tried and tested by martial arts instructors. And they will not break your budget, a bonus for new or part time instructors. In fact, more than half of the ideas that follow are absolutely free. They require only your time and effort, not your hard earned money.

As you read through the ideas, you will certainly find many that you are already using as well as many that you never thought of or thought you could successfully use. However, do not be discouraged because a technique seems beyond your marketing ability. All of these ideas have been used successfully by instructors just like you. You never know until you try!

1. **Spruce up your school**. Every school has areas that could use a little work, even if it's just spring-cleaning. The appearance of your school can be the difference between gaining and losing a potential student. Nobody wants to work out in a place that is lacking in hygiene. Take a look around your office, the training area, the waiting room, the locker rooms, and especially the bathrooms. Start with a good cleaning, then consider what

types of furnishings or decorations could improve the school atmosphere. Next, take a look at your equipment. What needs to be replaced? What do you need more of? What new equipment would enhance classes? Invest a small amount each month to continuously improve your school image.

2. **Create a Product Display.** A product display can be as simple as pinning up patches, headbands and pins on a bulletin board or as complex as furnishing a glass display case. The important part is how it looks. Use your imagination to create a low cost display of the supplies and equipment students can buy at the school. If you have time, create monthly themes in your display. Be sure to include item names, descriptions, sizes and prices. And don't forget to secure the items (or permanently mark them in some way) so they don't "walk away."

3. Have a **free giveaway**. For example, everyone who drops by to tour your school and pick up information receives a free headband, key chain, sticker, trading card, poster or patch. The gift does not have to be expensive, especially if the recipients are children.

4. **Reward referrals.** Make a policy to reward student and parent referrals. When a student brings in a friend or relative to sign up, give the student a gift of appreciation, such as a   t-shirt, sparring equipment or a hand held target. As an added incentive, give a small gift to the new student as well.

5. **Create a tie-in with another business.** Contact a local business and offer to exchange coupons. For example, your students receive coupons for a discount on martial arts video rentals at the local video store and the video store gives their customers free trial lesson coupons. Tie-ins work well with video stores, restaurants, arcades, bowling alleys, movie theaters and other recreation businesses. A great place to start is with students or parents from your school who own businesses.

6. **Make your waiting room "parent friendly"** with a place for younger brothers and sisters to play and a comfortable reading area for parents. A play area can be as simple as a few child size chairs with a table. Ask junior students to donate suitable toys that they no longer use. Remember to inspect the toys for small parts that might be swallowed or sharp edges that toddlers might injure themselves on. For parents, purchase some comfortable folding chairs and perhaps a writing table for those who bring work to do.

7. **Make copies of news articles** about yourself and the school. Hang them on the walls or pass them out. Past publicity is better than any advertising or promotional literature you can create. Give copies of positive articles to everyone who comes in for information. Post articles on the bulletin board or frame them in the waiting room. Make students feel good about your school.

8. **Raise money for charity.** Not only do you help a good cause, you get plenty of free, positive publicity and exposure. Hold a kick-a-thon, do a demonstration, have a break-a-thon or think up your own exciting charity event.

9. Submit **press releases** to the local newspapers about a noteworthy event at your school or a human interest story. Did you get promoted to a higher rank? Do you have twenty junior black belts? Did your students compete in a tournament? These are all news. Tell someone in the media about it.

10. Give a **free self-defense or fitness seminar** at your school. Invite members of the public and students' family members to participate. A seminar gives them the chance to see your school and have a very positive introduction to what you teach. Don't forget to invite the local newspaper.

11. Offer a **class at lunch time, mid-afternoon, pre-dawn or late evening**. People who cannot arrange their schedule to attend evening classes at other schools in the area will be excited to find a convenient class and you will establish a unique market share.

12. **Give a demonstration** at least once a month. Inquire with the organizers of fairs, carnivals, public school events, town picnics, scouts, boys/girls clubs, YMCA, YWCA, expos, etc. Generally they will not come to you, you have to contact them and make a suggestion. Before you know it, you will have a reliable group of annually scheduled demonstrations.

13. **Sell products** that students need or want. Don't make your students go to a local supply store or mail order company to buy uniforms, gear, workout clothes, books, and videos. Call the manufacturers and catalog retailers listed in martial arts magazines to request a wholesale account. Stock the items your students need and enjoy extra income every month.

14. Put student and parent **testimonials** in your ads and brochures. They are convincing and add credibility to your marketing. Don't forget to get permission to use the student's or parent's name. Change your testimonials frequently so the public can see how many satisfied "customers" you have.

15. Never let a student quit without **finding out why**. Every student who leaves your school has a reason. Some reasons you cannot do anything about (moving away, going to college, lost job, having a baby) but many are things you might be able to fix or improve. By asking each student why he or she quit, you find ways to improve and expand your teaching, managing and marketing abilities.

16. Position yourself for a specific market—a **niche** in which you specialize. Niche markets in the martial arts business include: self-defense, full contact fighting, sport competition, health and fitness, children's classes, reality training, mixed martial arts, kickboxing, adult fitness, weapons training, law enforcement training, family classes, traditional instruction, drop-in workouts, gym style training, high tech facilities and community service classes. Your niche (or niches if they are compatible) depends on your background, abilities, preferences and goals. Whatever your niche, stick to it. If you believe in your school philosophy, don't get discouraged if a student decides your school is not for him. When you develop a niche, you cannot satisfy everyone, but you can satisfy students who believe

in what you are doing. A typical niche school has a strong, unified bond among the students.

17. Offer a **free trial lesson** to anyone who is interested in trying classes. The free trial lesson is the most powerful and economical method of enrolling an interested student. People are impressed that you are willing to let them try class without obligation, especially if the school down the street is charging for introductory lessons. And when the student has the opportunity to participate in the class he will be in, with the people he will learn with, he begins to feel comfortable about coming back for classes on a regular basis. He knows exactly what to expect.

18. Allow students to **observe a class** before starting. Although trying a class is the best way to interest new students, not everyone is adventurous enough to jump into something new without first seeing what it is like. If someone is hesitant about trying a class, offer to let him watch a beginner class to see what it is like first. After watching, he may want to try class or he may be ready to sign up right away. After he observes the class, suggest signing up for lessons and if he is hesitant, recommend a trial lesson.

19. **Write a column** for your local newspaper. Most town newspapers are happy to have local experts or business people write topical columns on a weekly or monthly basis. Instead of payment, which many small newspapers cannot afford, ask the paper to mention your school name and your credentials at the end of the column. Possible column topics include: health and fitness, children's safety, women's self-defense, martial arts philosophy, parenting tips, and self-improvement.

20. **Hold a drawing** for free memberships that people have to come in to your school to enter. For example, advertise a free one-year membership drawing. Anyone can enter the drawing by filling out an entry blank available in your school lobby. An on-site drawing gets people to stop by to see your facilities.

21. Follow up after the drawing with **free one-week memberships**. When the drawing is over and you have awarded the grand prizes, call the rest of the entrants, or a good portion of them, and offer a week of free classes as a consolation prize. If they took the time to come in and fill out the drawing entry form, they must be interested in signing up for classes for themselves or a family member.

22. Hold a **recruitment contest** among your students. The student who gets the most students to sign-up for classes during the specified period of time wins a prize. The prize can be free lessons, gear, equipment or another suitable item. If you have a large school, award second and third prizes as well.

23. **Pass out flyers** about your school at demonstrations. Make a special, time limited offer available only to people who saw the demonstration.

24. Write an **article for a national magazine** to establish yourself as an expert in the martial arts field.

25. **When your article is published** in a national magazine, pass it out to everyone at your school. Hang a copy in the waiting room in a nice frame where students, parents and visitors can read it.

26. **Follow-up** with every new student who joins. As your school grows, you may begin to neglect this simple task. For the first two or three weeks, make sure each new student is attending class regularly, fitting in with other students and progressing positively. The first few weeks are the most important in establishing a long-term relationship.

27. **Assign a buddy** to each new student. Select a student in the same class who is similar in age and personality to guide each student through the first few classes. Everyone likes to have someone they can turn to in an unfamiliar environment.

28. **Hold special classes** for advanced students. Often, instructors experience a high turnover rate among advanced students due to complacency. The best strategy is to have separate classes for advanced students and black belts. If you do not have the time or resources for separate classes, have a class on advanced skills weekly or monthly. A class open only to students who have trained at least two years is something advanced students look forward to as special time with you.

29. Invite **influential people** to train in your school. The meaning of influential may differ depending on your community. Consider the benefit of having the mayor's children or the police chief in your class. The participation of influential community leaders in your class lends credibility to your teaching and establishes your name in the community. Think about how many people in town the mayor talks to every day. Perhaps he mentions to associates that his children learn karate at your school. This is a tacit endorsement of your school and a great benefit to your reputation.

30. Include **excerpts from news articles** in your brochures. If you don't yet have any news articles about your school, include quotes from articles about the martial arts in general. There are plenty of articles and studies that tout the benefits of martial arts for children and adults. Go to the library and find some to quote in your brochure.

31. Place a **classified ad** in the town newspaper or local shopper newspaper. Most small newspapers have a classified heading like *instruction* or *education* in which you can place a short ad. For just a few dollars a week, you can run an ad that says something like "Self-defense classes forming now, all ages, affordable rates, 555-0000." If you get at least one new student a week, the ad is worthwhile.

32. Start a **school newsletter** to promote school events, announce student successes and introduce new products. A newsletter can be as simple as a single, photocopied 8 1/2" x 11" color flyer. Include upcoming school events, tournament results, test results, new products, and merchandise sales. If you have space, include short articles that are related to class topics and training.

33. Print **gift certificates** with your school name and promote them year round, especially during the holidays. If you can't afford custom printed gift certificates, buy generic ones and print your school name and address on them.

34. Make a **special holiday offer** for all gift certificate purchases. When a customer buys a gift certificate for a month or more of lessons, include a free uniform. Gift wrap the uniform and certificate in holiday paper. Or offer a bonus like buy a gift certificate for one month of lessons and get an additional week free.

35. Call your **local radio station** and inquire about being interviewed on one of their talk shows as a local expert. If there has been a rash of assaults or other crimes, offer to talk about safety and crime prevention. If it is near Halloween, talk about trick-or-treat safety for kids. If summer is coming, talk about getting in shape for the beach season. Radio stations are always looking for informative, timely guests and will mention your school and credentials during the show.

36. When you have some experience with the radio, approach the **local nightly news** the same way. Don't forget to mention your successful appearances on the radio as proof of your expertise and experience.

37. Be flexible with **payment schedules**. You should never lose a student because she or her parents are having a bad month financially. If the student has paid on time in the past and is facing a temporary financial crisis, offer to reduce or delay payments until she can get back on her feet. Both of you will feel good about your generosity.

38. Hold **clinics and seminars** on topics of interest to students. Inviting a skilled seminar presenter to your school can excite and invigorate your students' interest in the martial arts. A good seminar presenter shows students the potential for achievement in their art that inspires them to set long-term training goals.

39. Hold **in-school clinics** in which students, family members and community members can participate together. Not only does this bring non-martial artists into your school, it gives them a chance to see that your students are regular people, softening the sometimes mysterious aura surrounding martial arts. Good topics are: fitness, sports conditioning, self-defense, martial arts philosophy, and crime prevention. Try to achieve a 50-50 mix of students and non-students.

40. Give **discounts to civic groups** and organizations. Some groups to approach are police department, fire department, military, boy/girl scouts and boys'/girls' clubs.

41. **Start a club** or team. Some ideas: demonstration team, competition team, black belt club, junior assistants club, outstanding students club, leadership team, assistant instructor's team and outstanding attendance club.

42. **Send a note to new students asking for referrals**. The most exciting period for a student is the first few weeks of classes. Whenever we start something new, we like to

share it with our friends and family. This is also the time that a student is most likely to talk to other people about their martial arts lessons and when friends or family members consider trying out a class. Send a brief note to each new student mentioning your referral program (a free gift to all students who bring in a new student) to take advantage of the excitement she is feeling and sharing.

43. **Offer a money back guarantee**. If you have a strong school (and can take the occasional emotional and financial burden of having a student take you up on this policy) a money back guarantee is a good confidence builder for new students. Include conditions to protect yourself such as: the guarantee is good only during a beginner course or for the unused portion of the tuition.

44. **Accept credit cards and electronic fund transfers**. Many people like the convenience of paying by credit card or automatic bank debit. You are more likely to get a full payment if you offer a credit card option. The bank gets a small percentage of the amount charged, but your revenues increase overall.

45. Offer an **information package** for people to stop in and pick up. Everyone likes to get something for free and giving away a packet of information about your school is a good way to get prospective students to come in to meet you and see the school. The packet can contain a brochure, schedule, price list, business card, special offer flyer, newspaper/magazine reprints, safety/self-defense information and any other information that puts your school in a positive light. Pack everything in a 9" by 12" envelope or folder with the school name, address and phone number printed on it. When someone comes in for an information package, explain each item and ask the student about her interest in the martial arts. At some point during the conversation, ask her to try out or observe a class.

46. **Offer financing options and payment plans**. Always offer more than one method of payment. The majority of people cannot afford to pay for a year of lessons in one payment. Depending on what is customary in your area, offer a payment plan or financing plan. A payment plan is simply a division of the yearly payments over the course of a few months. A financing plan is handled by a bank or finance company for a percentage of the tuition. Pass this cost along to the student as interest or pay it yourself as the cost of collection. Both options offer a way to pay tuition over an extended period of time.

47. **Invite family members** sitting in the waiting room, to try out a class. Every school has at least a few family members who spend night after night waiting for a child, spouse, or sibling to take class. Once in a while, walk out into the waiting room during class and say something like, "Gee, it seems like you're here as often as some of our black belts. Why don't you come in try out a class next Tuesday? Getting involved in class with your _____ (son, daughter, husband) would be a lot more fun than sitting and watching." A casual low pressure statement like that gets people thinking about how much time they are wasting by sitting around instead of getting involved. Don't despair if your first suggestion doesn't get a positive response. Try again a few weeks later. Eventually, most people agree to at least give it a try.

48. **Be honest and ethical**. The martial arts have become notorious for unethical behavior by instructors. Although this is the result of a relatively small number of bad apples, it means everyone else has to be scrupulously ethical to counter public perception. Ethical guidelines for instructors include:

　　a. Establish consistent tuition rates and policies for all students.
　　b. Maintain a professional distance in teacher-student relationships.
　　c. Be honest about your background, training and qualifications.
　　d. Deliver what you promise in your advertising and promotional materials.
　　e. Avoid favoritism in and out of class.
　　f. Compensate students fairly for their professional contributions to the school.
　　g. Announce and consistently follow policies on refunds, dropouts and cancellations.
　　h. Keep your personal life out of the school.
　　i. Try not to mix business (who owes tuition, who always pays late) with teaching (who is eligible for promotion, who gets complimented/criticized in class).

These rules not only make you a better school owner and instructor, they create respect for you among students and parents.

49. **Advertise only when you are ready** to handle an influx of new students. Many businesses make the mistake of putting a lot of money into advertising only to lose customers when they respond to the ads. Have you ever been to the grand opening of restaurant where the service was terrible and the food arrived an hour after you placed your order? This is a common example of not being ready to handle the crowds that advertising creates. Before you place a big ad, be prepared to handle the increased walk-in traffic, the increased phone inquiries, the larger class size and the increase in trial lessons. If you are overwhelmed with inquiries, you may lose business to a more prepared competitor.

50. Start an **exercise class for senior citizens**. If you are experienced in the fitness field, start a senior fitness class at the local senior center or community center. Charge a small fee for a couple of classes a week and incorporate some easy martial arts exercises or self-defense information into the class. The seniors may not join your school, but many of their grandchildren will.

51. **Investigate your competitors** and find out what you are up against. If you want to compete with other schools in your area, know what your competition is up to. Find out what they charge, how many classes a week they offer, who teaches the classes, what they teach, what their strengths are and what weaknesses you can exploit. You may feel like this is unethical or akin to cheating, but it is common business practice in every industry. Through a thorough investigation of your competition, you strengthen your school. After all, the average person looking for a martial arts school calls and sometimes visits every school in town before making a decision.

52. **Make a student questionnaire**. Ask students about their classes, their opinion of the school and their future goals. Sample questions:

        a. Is your class schedule convenient? How would you change it?

        b. What is the biggest benefit of your martial arts training?

        c. What else would you like to see taught?

        d. Are the locker room facilities adequate for your needs?

        e. What part of class do you like best: sparring, forms, self-defense,...?

        f. What would you change or improve in our school?

        g. Do you want to achieve a black belt?

        h. Would you like to attend seminars? On what topics?

        i. What martial arts products would you like to see sold at our school?

        j. Why are you learning martial arts?

        k. Are you interested in competition? In sparring, form, weapons, breaking...?

There are two ways to use the student questionnaire. The first is to assess each individual student's progress and goals. In this case, each student should put their name on the questionnaire when they complete it. The second way is to use it as an anonymous survey to assess the state of your school. In this case, don't ask students for their name. Instead evaluate the questionnaires by demographics such as age, rank, gender, class schedule, and length of training. These demographics identify children's preferences versus adults' preferences, men's preferences versus women's preferences, or advanced students' preferences versus beginners' preferences. Use the questionnaires to make changes and improvements that the majority of students request.

53. **Be dependable**. Students want a teacher who is a role model, someone they can count on.

54. **Hold a competition** among your students. The competition can be in any event: forms, sparring, breaking, self-defense or demonstrations. Create added interest by having a team challenge like firemen vs. policemen, teachers (school, not martial arts) vs. students, town vs. town or another pairing. Emphasize friendship and fun over competitiveness. Get everyone involved by asking for volunteers to help run the competition (for those who don't want to compete).

55. Have a **suggestion box**. Put out a suggestion box (with a pen and pad of paper) for anonymous suggestions to improve the school. You don't have to use every suggestion, but knowing what people are thinking gives you insight into your students' needs.

56. **Show you care**.

57. **Give a speech** on discipline, confidence, or safety for a local school, civic group, or club. A speech, combined with a short demonstration, promotes your school and provides a public service at the same time.

58. **Propose a show** on child safety (or another timely topic) to your local public access cable television station. Don't forget to work in a few practical martial arts techniques everyone can use.

59. Send a **welcome letter** to each new student. Include an invitation to participate in an upcoming school event or other inviting message. Everyone likes to feel welcome in a new environment.

60. Hold a **parent-child class** once a month. Invite every student to bring their parent or child (depending on who is currently enrolled) to participate. Teach simple skills that everyone can follow without becoming frustrated or embarrassed. Relate the skills you teach to what the students are learning in their regular classes to give the non-students an idea of what a class is like.

61. Sponsor a **bring-a-friend** day. Invite everyone to bring a friend to class on a specially designated day of the month. If you are inviting children to bring a friend, make sure each friend has gotten a parent's permission to participate. Teach some easy, fun skills and give everyone a chance to be partners with the friend they invited. At the end of class, hand out flyers, information packets or free lesson coupons to the visitors.

62. Start a **pre-martial art class** for the three and four year olds who are too young for regular junior classes. Teach simple developmental skills like running, jumping, rolling, and coordination games. Introduce easy strikes and kicks then give everyone a chance try them out on the soft shield targets. When each child is ready, graduate him to the regular junior class.

63. Send a **thank-you letter** when a student re-enrolls. A short note thanking the student for continuing her training as well as a brief word of encouragement can be a great boost for long time students.

64. **Offer a bonus** for students who pay their membership in full. The bonus should be appropriate for the amount the student has to pay up front. For example, give a t-shirt for paying for three months, a uniform for paying for six months and an extra month of lessons for paying for a year. The value of the item should be about five percent of the amount of tuition paid.

65. **Publish a monthly school newsletter for parents**. Include upcoming school events, exciting student milestones, child safety tips, parenting tips and news of new merchandise or special sales. Children rarely tell their parents what is going on at the school and a parent newsletter keeps parents informed. An 8 1/2" by 11" colored flyer makes an inexpensive newsletter.

66. Make a **safety handout** with your school name, address and phone number printed on it. Include simple self-defense tips everyone can use in their daily life. Pass them out at demonstrations and speeches. Give them to parents, family members and new students.

67. **Teach your assistant instructors** and higher-ranking students about your school and style of martial art. Include the school history, your background, a brief history of the art, a summary of what is taught at your school and the benefits of learning the art. Higher belts and assistants are frequently asked questions by new students and parents. Imagine the difference these two scenarios might create: A parent asks one of your brown belts what type of martial art is taught at the school. The brown belt may shrug and say "some kind of karate" or he may be able to give a brief and exciting synopsis of the style, depending on what you have taught in class. Which will give a better impression to the parent?

68. **Be punctual**. Everyone's time is valuable. Start and end class on time. Open and close the school at the announced times. Show your students that you respect their time by placing a high value on it.

69. **Announce holidays and special events** two to three weeks in advance so everyone can plan accordingly. Most families juggle busy schedules and you need to give them plenty of notice if you want them to attend a special event. Students appreciate advance notice of closings on holidays so they can schedule accordingly. Set aside a special place on the school bulletin board for these announcements.

70. Learn and practice **professional telephone skills**. It is not necessary to invest a fortune in a school management course to learn good telephone skills. Go to the library and take out books on telephone skills, professional selling skills and people management skills. Especially helpful are short workbooks that cover specific topics like telephone selling, telephone attitude, handling disgruntled customers and customer service. Never answer the phone without being ready to use your best telephone skills.

71. **Treat parents and family members with respect and kindness**. Every student has a family that is supporting his or her training. Some family members, such as parents, are directly involved in driving the student to class and paying for lessons. Others are simply understanding enough to let the student pursue his or her classes without distraction. Whenever you come in contact with a student's relative, whether at the school, on the telephone or in the local shopping center, treat them with the same respect you have for your students. And don't forget to mention how nice it is of them to support their relative's efforts.

72. **Keep popular merchandise and supplies on hand**. Don't lose a sale because you run out of a common item like a uniform, head gear, patch, or target. Many people want to be able to purchase their gear right away and might go to the local supply store or sporting goods store if you are out of what they need.

73. **Have a liberal return or exchange policy** on gear, uniforms and supplies. Exchange unused items for a different size, color or style. Replace defective merchandise, even if the merchandise has been used a few times. (Occasionally you may get a piece of gear that is defective and breaks after a few uses. Call the supplier and ask for a replacement. If the merchandise does not work as promised, both you and your student are entitled to a

replacement.) Having a good return/exchange policy gives you an edge over the sports and department stores that sell martial arts equipment and uniforms.

74. Make a list of **Halloween safety tips** with your school name and address printed on it. Give the list out to local stores, schools and children's groups to distribute the week before Halloween. Tips might include: don't eat any candy before it is checked by an adult, always carry a flashlight, only trick-or-treat in neighborhoods you are familiar with, trick-or-treat in large groups, wear brightly colored clothing, go out with a parent or older sibling and never go into a stranger's house.

75. Print **doorknob hangers** and distribute them to local houses. A popular form of advertising in recent years, the ad is printed with a circle and slit at the top that fits around a doorknob or other fixture. They can be printed on one or both sides and economically distributed by hand to neighborhood houses.

76. Provide every student and parent with a copy of the **school rules**. Having and distributing clear rules is essential to preventing student misunderstandings and miscommunication. When the rules are publicly announced and displayed, they can be equally and fairly applied to everyone.

77. **Decorate your windows**. If you have large windows in the front of your school, decorate them with martial arts themed drawings and special offer signs. If you have a series of small windows, such as a second floor space, put a few letters or words in each window to form a message. Use window space creatively and change it often. Take advantage of the free exposure to drive-by and pedestrian traffic.

78. **Clean up the outside of the school**. Don't neglect your storefront and parking lot. Keep the windows washed, the parking lot free of garbage and shrubbery/flowers/grass neatly trimmed. The outer appearance is as important as the inside of your school when it comes to encouraging people to drop in.

79. **Make your school inviting at night**. Most classes take place in the evening, often after dark. Make sure your parking lot and any alleys next to the building are well lit. Light up all of the rooms inside the school as soon as it starts to get dark. Shine a spotlight on your sign if it is not illuminated. If you are in a bad neighborhood or students have to enter a parking garage or alley to reach their cars, offer student escorts for those who are hesitant to walk to their car alone.

80. Make it a policy to **freeze student memberships** when a student becomes ill or injured for a prolonged period. A personal emergency, like a long-term illness or injury, is very stressful. Your students will appreciate your concern when you offer to credit them for any time missed during their crisis. This policy can be the difference between keeping and losing several students a year. If you feel the policy might be abused, set limits. Require notification of how long the student expects to miss class or limit the amount of time that may be credited in a year.

81. Offer **different types of classes** to meet different needs. One size does not fit all when it comes to learning new skills. Classes should be broken down by age, ability (rank) and style (if you teach more than one). You can also offer specialized classes: women's self-defense, weapons, tournament training, sparring, street defense, full contact training or senior citizen's self-defense.

82. **Recognize student successes**. Acknowledge student achievements outside of class. Examples of important achievements include: graduations, sports awards/championships, honor roll candidates and job promotions. Everyone likes to receive recognition for their achievements and many people attribute these successes to their martial arts training.

83. Offer a **limited time sale** on products or classes. Setting a time limit on a uniform sale or seminar registration creates urgency and increases sales. The time limit should be at least ten days and not more than thirty days. Ten days to two weeks is ideal.

84. Implement a **dress code** for instructors and staff. A dress code creates a professional, unified look for your staff. The in-class dress code might be a black belt uniform with school and instructor patches. The out-of-class uniform might be a jogging suit or slacks and a polo shirt with the school emblem. Depending on your community standards, you may also choose to limit areas of personal grooming such as beards, earrings, jewelry, piercings and hair length. Create a neat, sporty, professional look that makes staff members easy to identify.

85. **After each promotion test** remind students of the equipment they need for their new level. If you teach sparring or weapons at a certain belt level, announce what equipment is needed to participate. If you allow students to wear different uniforms at different levels, tell them when they become eligible for a new style. If you have training aids that are appropriate for a certain level (books, videos, equipment) announce this after testing. A newsletter or bulletin board is a good forum for this type of announcement. Students are eager to do well and want to have every advantage in their training.

86. Offer a **family discount plan** for two or more family members. A discount of twenty to fifty percent enables entire families to join together. Use a flat discount with the first family member paying full price and all others paying forty percent off or create a sliding scale with each additional person getting a larger discount. Put the family discount policy in school advertising and promotional material and mention it to inquiring callers.

87. **Send letters** to all of the students who have stopped coming to class in the last year. Tell them that they are always welcome to restart classes at the same level and make a special discount offer if they return.

88. Hang **framed photos** of you and your students around the school. The pictures should give a positive impression of your school. Suitable pictures include you and your students having fun and succeeding at tournaments, demonstrations, seminars, classes, camps and other events.

89. Display your school, instructor and **rank certificates** prominently to give people confidence in your qualifications.

90. Offer to **mail your information package** to callers so they can read about the school before they come in for their trial lesson.

91. Track your success with **telephone callers** and look for areas that need improvements. What groups are you most successful with? Parents? Women? Men? What types of people are most likely to come in for a trial lesson? Those who want to learn self-defense? Fitness? Confidence? Fighting? Keep a careful log of each phone call and review your log monthly to look for weak areas.

92. **Donate short memberships to charity auctions**. An increasingly popular event with charities, auctions increase the visibility of your school name, bring in new students and contribute to a good cause.

93. Make a **school bulletin board** for important announcements. Put it in the most high traffic area of the school (like near the front door) in an easily accessible spot.

94. **Start a class at the local recreation center**, YMCA, YWCA, community center or elementary school. The sponsoring organization takes care of all expenses and pays you on a per student or per class basis. You risk nothing but your time and have a great source of new students at the end of each session.

95. **Make your school inviting** to passers-by. Encourage drop-in visitors to tour the school and pick up an information package. Prop open your front door to create a welcome feeling.

96. Offer private, **individually tailored courses** or seminars (self-defense, health & fitness, safety, stress reduction) for corporations or organizations.

97. **Offer private or semi-private lessons** at a higher rate than the regular tuition. Private lessons are a good way to get maximum benefit from your free hours during the day and the income from teaching a few private students is similar to that of a dozen or more group class students.

98. **Track where new students hear about your school** and adjust your advertising plans accordingly. Regularly evaluate your ads and drop non-producing advertisements from your budget.

99. Whenever someone calls to schedule a trial lesson, ask if he or she has **a friend who would like to come along**. Everyone likes to start something new with a friend or relative along for comfort and you have the chance to enroll two new students instead of one.

100. **Spend 15 minutes every day** on the marketing of your school. Never let a single day go by without finding or working on at least one way of improving your school!

Limit Options

Too many options cause people to avoid making a choice.

When offering a choice to students or prospects limit the options to two or three.

Marketing Strategy

A scientific approach

See also . . .
Economic Cycles . . . . page 234

A successful marketing strategy takes into account the "four P's" of Product, Price, Place and Promotion. A martial arts school's products are the classes it offers and the items (uniforms, gear, clothing, books, videos) it sells. Although a class is not a tangible item that a student can buy and take home, like a uniform, it is still very much a product that has to be advertised and sold.

There are four primary methods of marketing a product:

1. Market Penetration:

Market penetration means increasing the market share of your current classes. Market share is a ratio of a school's revenue to the total market revenue. If there are five thousand people in your market area (usually within ten miles of your school) and you have five hundred students, your market share is ten percent. To increase your market share, you need to convince a larger percentage of those five thousand people to sign up for your classes instead of taking lessons at another school in the area.

Market penetration is usually done through local advertising, demonstrations and publicity. It is the most common type of marketing done by martial arts schools.

2. Market Development:

Market development means interesting new markets (groups of people) in your current classes. For example, a

217

cardio class that attracts primarily women is advertised to 20-something men, a segment of the population that is under represented in the class.

Market development can be challenging because not all classes are suitable for all markets. A children's class has very limited potential for market development because it is limited to a certain age group. One way to approach market development is to change the tone or theme of your advertising. If you have always advertised the educational benefits of martial arts for children, try advertising the fun or competitive aspects. By changing your positioning, you attract people who might not have considered martial arts in the past.

3. Product Development:

Product development means creating new classes for an existing market (group of people). Some examples are enrolling parents in parent/child classes, beginning a yoga class for people bored with cardio kickboxing or bringing in a defensive tactics instructor to teach a supplementary workshop.

Product development is a very cost effective means of marketing because much of the advertising is done internally.

4. Product Diversification:

Product diversification means creating new classes for new markets. This is the most challenging type of marketing because you not only have to develop a new class, you have to find a new way to market what you are offering. If you have been offering primarily children's classes, a morning tai chi class for senior citizens fills unused class time, but it also requires market research to find out what senior citizens are looking for in a class and where to advertise to reach them.

Product diversification is recommended for mature schools that have reached a plateau in their marketing efforts.

In developing and marketing classes there are two aspects to consider: **tangible aspects** and **benefits**. Because classes are intangible, student satisfaction can be difficult to measure. A martial arts class is different from a product like a television. With a television, a person can readily see the quality of the picture, the size and style of the box and the technological features offered. With a service like martial arts instruction, it is important to create tangible things for a potential student to evaluate. Things like the quality of instruction, the flexibility of the class schedule, the qualifications of the instructors, the cost of lessons, the cleanliness of the facility, the variety of equipment available and the impression that the school makes are all tangible qualities. When creating your marketing materials, emphasize tangible areas that you excel in.

The benefits of lessons are more difficult for potential students to evaluate because they have not yet experienced them. Paradoxically, the perceived benefits are what motivate most people to look into lessons and to enroll. This is the reason that the trial lesson or introductory program is so successful in martial arts marketing. By inviting a potential student to try a class, you give them a chance to experience the short-term benefits of learning and can then better explain the potential long-term benefits.

In marketing martial arts lessons, product is the most important factor to consider. Without a quality product, no matter how great your prices, promotion and location are, your school will not survive.

Price and Place

Price and place have a symbiotic relationship. When you have a great location you can charge more for lessons. Conversely, when your location is poor, you have to lower prices to draw students. Unfortunately, moving to a better location is not the perfect answer to the price/place dilemma. While you can charge more in a better location, you also have to pay more rent, thereby limiting the advantage of a prime location.

First consider your current situation. If your location is poor there are several things you can do to overcome its limitations:

1. Charge less than your strip mall competitors. You can afford a price reduction, they cannot.

2. Build an excellent reputation based on your teaching skill, personalized service, family atmosphere, renowned competitors or whatever makes you special.

3. Do the best you can with what you have. If you currently rent a factory building because it's cheap, consider renting more space. Advertise your size as a plus. Concentrate on the possibilities, not the limitations.

4. Get involved in the community. Organize community events, teach at a local recreation center, make your name known to your neighbors.

If you are in the process of selecting a new location, look for improvements over your current place. If it is too small, get a bigger place. If it is on the outskirts of town, move closer to a high traffic area. If it is in a declining area, look for a more stable neighborhood.

You will not be able to leap to the top in one step. Look at the areas you are weakest in and try to improve them first. When you do, tell current and potential students about it. The biggest failure in marketing is to make improvements and not tell anyone. Emphasize the benefits to the students. Let them know you are improving the school for their convenience.

Once you settle down in a satisfactory location, you have to confront the issue of price. There are several factors to consider:

1. What do other schools charge? If you are on the high end, offer something special. If you are on the low end, you may have to counteract the impression of being a bargain basement outlet. Many consumers feel that a mid-range price indicates the most value for their dollar.

2. What are other similar activities charging? Your school is not only competing with other martial art schools, it is competing with little league, dancing, soccer and boy scouts. Parents are often forced to choose between martial arts and another activity. Stay competitive.

3. What can you offer? People are willing to pay more for quality or special services.

4. What is your bottom line? Come up with several estimates of how many enrolled students you need at each price level to run your school professionally and live comfortably.

The issues of price and place are complex and ongoing. Set a standard and maintain it. If you move to a new location every year or raise prices frequently, people will see you as unstable and unappealing. In making price and place decisions, think three to five years into the future.

Promotion

The function of promotion is to communicate the availability and usefulness of your classes to the public. There are five fundamental types promotion: advertising, publicity, direct contact, atmospherics, and incentives.

Advertising

Advertising is the first thing that comes to mind when most people think of promotion. It is also the most costly and often least effective means of promotion. Advertising includes many means of paid communication including brochures, TV commercials, newspaper ads, flyers, radio spots, and billboards. For a single school, the most effective means of advertising are the yellow pages, flyers, brochures and local newspaper ads. For a group of schools, radio and television ads can be cost effective.

Advertising has the advantage of being a market segmented, controlled message—you can say positive things about your school and be sure that they reach your intended audience. Unfortunately, your positive message may not carry a lot of weight with readers because they know that you paid for the ad and can say whatever you want. When using advertising as promotion, you have to increase the reader's will to believe you by encouraging some type of personal contact, like a trial lesson program.

Publicity

Publicity is a nonpaid message about your school that appears in the media. Most frequently it has to be initiated by you in the form of a press release. Occasionally the media will come to you, but don't expect it. Use events like promotions, camps, seminars, demonstrations, charity drives and tournaments to create publicity. Publicity is an extremely believable means of promotion, since people perceive it as news. However, it is also difficult to control and hard to keep up consistently.

Direct Contact

Direct contact is the best means of promotion. When you talk to a person face to face you can tailor your message for them and respond to their questions and concerns. You can also spend much more time interacting with them than the average few seconds of attention an advertisement draws.

The best of type of direct contact promotion includes two-way communication in which you and the prospective student have a dialogue. The second best type is when you speak to a large group of potential students, as in a speech or demonstration. When speaking before a large group, try to offer a question and answer period to facilitate at least some two-way communication.

Direct contact encompasses many aspects of promotion including drop-in customers, initial interviews, word of mouth, trial lessons, demonstrations, seminars, speeches, and casually striking up a conversation with a potential student. The more people you reach directly, the more chances you have to show people the benefits of martial arts.

Atmospherics

Atmospherics describes the location and ambience of your school. The best atmosphere for a martial arts school to project is one that is professional, clean, safe and family oriented. When a potential student walks into your school, they make a decision almost immediately about whether it is a place they want to spend a few hours a week. Make your school inviting and familiar. Hang up exciting posters, fill up your billboard with announcements, and clean, clean, clean. Never give potential students an obvious reason not to join your school.

Incentives

Incentives are things that add value and appeal to a product or service. They can be tangible, like T-shirts, uniforms, video tapes and trophies or intangible like free guest passes, trial lessons, and early payment discounts. Incentives are most effective for helping potential students make a final decision and in gaining repeat or word-of-mouth business.

The best incentives are tangible ones. If a potential student is having a hard time deciding whether or not to sign-up, offer a free uniform or T-shirt. Some people need to perceive added value before they can make a decision.

An Effective Mix

An effective promotion mix can be hard to strike. Too much promotion quickly breaks your bank while too little leaves you teaching in an empty room. The easiest place to start is with atmospherics. Spruce up your school and ask yourself what kind of image you want to portray. Your image attracts people who "fit" it. Next, look at your incentives program. Set up a give-away program for new and renewal students who make a commitment.

Then consider what you can do to gain some publicity. Look at your upcoming events for the next six months and target at least one that to get the attention of the local media. Finally, try to increase your direct contacts with potential students by increasing the number of interviews and trial lessons you schedule with prospective students. Give away a free lesson and use that time to make contact with your soon-to-be new student.

Up to this point, your entire promotion plan has cost you almost nothing but your time. If you try all of these methods and still find that you are lacking students, try a limited advertising campaign, offering good incentives and encouraging people to come down and see your school. When they come in, you already have an excellent promotion system in place and are ready for them.

When you have taken the time to prepare, the money you spend on advertising is much more effective. Bring new students into your school only when you are ready to excite them with your professional teaching, orderly school and terrific program.

Advertising is an area of running a school that is plagued by misinformation and myths. Understanding the secrets of advertising is an important factor in keeping a school running year after year. Yet many instructors and school owners approach advertising with concepts that are outdated. There are a number of common advertising myths that are hazardous to your bottom line.

Myth 1: Advertising brings immediate results.

Every beginning school owner assumes that you simply run an ad in the local newspaper and wait for the phone to start ringing off the hook. This expectation is inevitably met with disappointment when not only does the phone not ring off the hook, it barely rings at all.

It's not that your ad was poorly done or that no one saw it. **Advertising takes time to get results.** The average person must be exposed to an ad at least seven times before they decide to take action.

It does not necessarily have to be the same ad. They might see your ad in the paper a few times, drive by your school twice, see a demonstration you put on and get a flyer in the mail.

"The average person must be exposed to an ad at least seven times before they decide to take action."

After all of these exposures, they might take action on the offer you made in your flyer. This doesn't mean the flyer was any better than any other promotion you did, it means that they have finally seen your advertising enough times to confidently decide to act on it. Advertising takes weeks or months to work and consistency is the key.

Myth 2: Ads must change frequently to catch attention.

This is similar to Myth 1. You may be tired of reading the same ad, but the average person hardly notices it the first few times they see it. Newspapers are packed with ads and readers quickly scan most. After seeing the same ad a few times, they might finally decide to read it more thoroughly. **Using the same ad makes you look not boring, but reliable,** a trait that consumers like in a service business.

Run an ad for a minimum of four months, until the response starts dropping off (usually after about a year). Of course, this does not mean running the exact same ad. Vary your offer for the season to include summer programs, Christmas specials and back to school classes, but keep the overall look and message consistent.

Myth 3: Ads that don't show immediate results are a waste of money.

Advertising is an investment in your future. As in Myth 1, ads don't always get immediate results. Every ad you place has long-term value. As you establish your reputation, you will be able to identify and drop poor performing ads. But until that time, assume that each ad is taking you closer to your goal of getting **maximum exposure** in people's minds. Track the performance of ads by asking callers how they heard about your school.

Myth 4: Seasonal advertising gets then best results.

Many schools advertise according to season. Popular advertising times include back-to-school, summer vacation and the holiday season. Although interest is high during these times, schools that are not advertising at other times of the year are missing out on potential students.

If most schools in your area focus on seasonal advertising, pick up a big **share of the market** by advertising when they are not. Not only are you visible year round, you become the first choice of people who are looking for a school during off peak times, a necessity for operating a full time school

Myth 5: Ads should be catchy and humorous.

Many small advertisers try hard to get noticed by making their ads humorous or catchy. The reasoning is that the more outstanding or outrageous the ad is, the more likely potential customers are to remember it. However, the opposite is often true. Many times, the ad or commercial is so outrageous or humorous that viewers or readers get caught up in the joke and miss the message.

The point of every ad is to get potential customers to buy your product or service. If you can do this using humor, as many professional marketers can, then the use of humor or gimmicks is acceptable. However, if your message is buried in the ad, potential customers love the ad but do not know what action to take.

Myth 6: The more expensive the ad, the better it is.

Although the advertising sales reps that visit your school would like you to believe that their newspaper is better because they charge more for their ads, this is not necessarily true.

A big newspaper charges more for advertising because it has a large circulation area. But do you really need to reach people who live thirty miles away? If you have a typical school, most of your students come from less than five miles away. If you are spending money to advertise in areas outside of this 5-mile radius, you are throwing money away. Make sure you **only pay for what you need** when it comes to advertising.

Myth 7: The best advertising is in the local newspaper.

A martial arts school is not a mass-market business like a department store. Your advertising must be **tightly targeted** to your potential customers.

Often the cheapest forms of advertising like flyers, coupon books, doorknob hangers and window displays are more effective than expensive display ads in the local newspaper. In fact, for the cost of one good size display ad, you could print several hundred flyers and distribute them at a local shopping mall. This is a far more effective way of getting the attention of people in your community than a one time ad buried among hundreds in the local paper.

Myth 8: Television and radio advertising is worth the added expense.

While it may be exciting to see yourself and your students in television ads, you will not recover your costs if you have one location. If you have three or more locations within one market area (television or radio broadcast area), television and radio commercials can be a big boost for your image and generate interest in your schools.

Myth 9: People love new things.

Contrary to popular belief, most people do not want to be the first ones on their block to try something new. Everyone, however, wants to be a part of something successful.

To generate interest in your school, create the image that martial arts are not unusual or foreign. Give the impression in your advertising that everyone is doing it and everyone will want to join in. This is especially true of children. When kids find out that other kids at school are taking karate, they want to sign-up too.

Myth 10: Advertising is for new schools.

Many school owners invest thousands of advertising dollars for their grand opening then stop advertising once students begin to join. This is a fatal mistake. The students that sign up from your grand opening are just the start. Advertising is a **year-round process** that must be planned with long-term objectives.

At the beginning of each season, set aside one day to plan the next season's advertising. For example, at the beginning of summer, plan your fall advertising campaign. Choose what types of specials to run, which ads to use and where to run them. Once you have decided this, get the ads made up and contact the advertising representatives. When fall rolls around, your advertising will be ready to go while you begin planning your winter ads. By using this method, you avoid a post-grand opening slump and keep a steady stream of new people walking in the door year after year.

Myth 11: You must spend a minimum percentage of your monthly gross on advertising.

Many conventional businesses set aside a percentage of their income each month for advertising. Spending more does not mean more response. **Spend advertising dollars wisely.** If you can enroll twenty new students a month by spending fifty dollars a month on flyers, that's great. Work within your means and squeeze every cent out of your advertising budget, no matter how big or small.

Myth 12: Advertise more during slow seasons and less during busy seasons.

This is often the logic of novice business owners. The reasoning is twofold: when business is good, I don't need to waste money on ads and when business is bad, I must not be advertising enough. But for a seasonal business like martial arts, when you advertise is a major component of your plan.

When you anticipate a busy season like back to school or just after the new year, budget heavily for advertising. A busy time of year means interest is high and people are looking at ads to make a buying decision. When you anticipate a slow season like Christmas or late summer, do a minimum of advertising. If people are distracted by vacations or holidays, they are not looking for a new hobby or pastime. In this season, no matter how much advertising you do, you will not get them to make a serious buying decision.

Myth 13: If you get plenty of publicity, you don't need to advertise.

Some schools are masters at generating publicity in the local papers, so they don't bother to advertise. However, many people do not know how to contact you after reading an article or seeing a photo in the local paper. Running a regular ad ensures that your contact information is on hand for them to easily find you and your school.

Myth 14: You have to be a professional to create a successful advertising plan.

To create a successful advertising plan, you have to know your market and know what benefits your school offers. By following a few simple rules and knowing what your potential students want from your school, you can create an advertising plan to fit your budget and your expectations

Setting Tuition Rates

A smart guide

See also ...
Economic Cycles . . . . page 234

Setting tuition rates can be one of the most confusing aspects of starting and running a professional martial arts school. Charge too much and enrollment suffers. Charge too little and you find yourself working forty hours a week to barely break even. But how can you set tuition rates that are fair to both your students and yourself?

Planning a tuition structure begins with assessing monthly expenses. Plan to do this once when you start out and every six months thereafter. As expenses and student numbers increase, you need to raise your tuition to cover your costs and keep class sizes acceptable. Once you have established your monthly expenses, you have a basis for setting monthly tuition rates. There are two basic methods for setting rates:

1. Market Dependent

Market dependent rates are set based on what others in your area are charging. You can choose to meet or beat local prices, depending on your income needs. If you are in a less expensive location than your competition, you definitely need to beat their rates. Less expensive usually indicates less desirable, meaning you have to give people a reason to put aside the inconvenience of coming to your location instead of going to the school in the mall or shopping center. If you have a better location than the competition, meet their prices and emphasize more value for the money.

2. Break Even

The break even point is the point at which you can cover your monthly expenses and salary with tuition income. There are two ways to find your break even point:

Formula A

Add your estimated expenses plus your salary and divide by the number of students you expect to average each month in your first year in business. The figure you get is the minimum monthly tuition fee necessary to break even.

For example, if your monthly expenses including salary are $5000.00 and you expect to have 70 students average, you need to charge $72.00 per month per student average. This method is based on knowing how many students you expect to average in your first year of business.

Formula A:
expenses + salary = Break even rate
   # students

Example A:
$$\frac{\$5000}{70 \text{ students}} = \$72.00/\text{month}$$

Formula B

If you have an idea of what you want to charge, but do not know how many students you need to cover expenses at that rate, add your expenses and salary and divide by the average monthly rate to get the number of students you need to break even. For example, if you want to charge $75.00 a month and have $5000.00 in expenses and salary, you need to average 67 students a month to break even.

Formula B:
expenses + salary = Break even
monthly rate

Example B:
$$\frac{\$5000.00}{\$75.00} = 67 \text{ students}$$

Setting tuition rates case study:

1. Determine which formula to use
    a. Market Dependent
    b. Break Even Formula A
    c. Break Even Formula B

2. Calculate your base monthly rate

3. Develop a sliding scale

4. Plan special discounts or offers

Example:

Using Break even Formula A:

$$\frac{\$2500\ salary + \$7950\ expenses}{150\ students} = \frac{\$10,450}{150} = \$70.00$$

Sliding Tuition Scale:	Monthly	$75.00 per month
	6 mouths	$70.00 per month
	1 year	$65.00 per month

4. Discounts	1 year paid in full earns a free uniform
	6 months paid in full earns a free T-shirt
	Family rate: 1st person full price, others 40% off

When you set your rates, plan on allowing a few months to reach your break even goal, no matter how modest it is. To account for this, base your estimates on the average number of students you expect to have at the end of one year.

The long hot days of summer present special challenges for martial arts schools. Vacations, swimming, outdoor sports, summer camp, other fun in the sun activities are only available for a few months in many areas. Martial arts classes, on the other hand, are available year round. And, honestly, where would you rather be, sipping a cool drink on the beach or sweating out a hundred push-ups on the mat?

Overcoming summer training apathy is difficult but not impossible. Develop your strategy early, before the warm weather breaks.

1. Plan ahead.

Prepare for a decline in attendance caused by vacations and seasonal activities. Arrange lesson plans to suit smaller classes. Have a few special class plans to use in the event of a very small class. When class is especially depleted, those in attendance need to feel rewarded for their perseverance.

2. Allow for irregular attendance.

Create lesson plans that are less technically intensive, include lots of review and focus on personal improvement over technique accumulation. When students miss two weeks because of vacation or come back from four weeks of soccer camp, you don't want them to feel totally lost. If the rest of the class learned a new set of twenty self-defense skills while they were away, they will feel discouraged and behind when they return. Summer is a good time to work on individual improvement of existing skills so that the students who attend see a big improvement the quality of their skills while those who miss classes don't feel they are lacking in quantity of skills.

3. Emphasize consistency.

Promote the importance of regular attendance before the summer season and remind students of the long-term benefits they have amassed through their consistent training (i.e. improved flexibility, strength, coordination, technique). Many of these qualities decline rapidly when practice is stopped for even a few weeks. Incorporate new or unique activities into your summer lesson plans. Students who trained through previous summers will not only remember them, but will tell others.

4. Adapt to changing needs.

Adapt to the temperature. In hot weather, people feel lethargic, tire more easily and lose essential body fluids more quickly. Slow down the pace of class, emphasize technique over heavy conditioning, provide plenty of water breaks and keep the training area at a reasonably cool, but not cold, temperature. In some regions, there are days on which exercise is not safe. If the temperature is too high, substitute a non-exercise activity like viewing martial arts videos, educational readings, discussion groups, question and answer periods or theory classes.

5. Provide short-term goals.

Most importantly, provide all of your students with a short-term goal for the end of the summer. Give them something to work toward like a promotion test, competition or other results oriented activity. Or create a special reward for those with good attendance (for example, 80% or higher) like an invitation-only seminar or camp.

6. Cut costs.

If you find that tuition income drops in the summer months and your retention strategies are not working, try some of these cost cutting tips to get you through to the strong fall enrollment period:

1) **Involve employees.** Particularly if you have a large staff or multiple locations, your employees might be more in touch with the day-to-day operations of the school than you are. Make a deal with your employees to split any cost savings they initiate. *Example:* Staff members at three schools negotiate a discount with a supply company by promising to exclusively carry that company's products in all of the schools. Over the course of six months, the agreement nets $8000 in savings on merchandise purchases and you agree to give one third of the savings to the staff as a bonus. You are still ahead more than $5000 in savings and your staff takes home a nice bonus for their efforts.

2) **Examine your budget.** Sit down with your office manager and go over every expense. Are there places you could be saving more by using a competitor? Are there non-producing advertisements or marketing programs? Would purchasing items in bulk and storing them for future use save money? Are there jobs being done by outside vendors that staff members could be doing?

3) **Implement an audit system.** Every invoice and bill that comes into your office should be carefully examined by your office manager for accuracy. It is not unusual for service companies to over bill or bill in error.

4) **Look for discounts.** Many professional organizations offer discounts for members on a wide variety of things including insurance, office supplies, auto related expenses and business services. A small annual membership can lead to hundreds of dollars in savings.

Economic Cycles

Understanding how to capitalize

See also . . .
Low Cost Marketing . . . . page 203
Outreach Programs. . . . page 302

The martial arts business, like any other business, is cyclical. Some years are boom years and others are busts. The typical business cycle is composed of three stages: growth, saturation and decline. Each part of the cycle has ramifications for martial arts school owners, particularly the decline stage.

Anatomy of a Decline

A downturn in the martial arts industry is actually the end of a cycle and a predecessor to growth. This is the good news. The bad news is, many schools do not survive the decline to reap the benefits of the new growth cycle. During a downturn, many schools are put out of business by a lack of knowledge about surviving when times are tough.

A decline is characterized by a loss of interest in the martial arts in general and a drop in positive media exposure for martial arts, particularly in the movies and on television.

Signs of a decline in the martial arts industry include:

- Martial arts schools and programs close or reduce their offerings

- Box office receipts for martial arts movies suffer

- Martial arts magazines go out of business

- Suppliers reduce their advertising and range of products

- Organizations, such as instructor training groups, cease operations

All of these indicators mean that not only is the martial arts business suffering at the industry level, but the schools that support the industry are also suffering. As fewer students sign up, schools purchase fewer supplies and cut out expenses for extras like marketing support and magazine subscriptions.

But once you are done cutting expenses, how else can you adjust your business plan to stay alive during the decline?

Strengthen the Foundation

If your school has been open a few years, you have a good chance of surviving a short to moderate downturn because you already have a student base. During a period of low enrollments, it makes sense to focus on keeping every student you already have.

At the first signs that a downturn has set in, turn your attention to strengthening your base of students:

- renew or upgrade students to longer memberships

- emphasize the long-term benefits of training

- help students set long-term goals

- spend time before and after class to give marginal students extra attention and secure their interest.

Do everything in your power to make each student feel like an integral part of the school. It is much easier to keep an enrolled student than to sign up a new one during tough times.

Increase Internal Marketing

During a downturn, advertising is less effective. Contrary to conventional wisdom, this is not the time to increase your advertising; it is time to decrease it. Advertising during a downturn is like throwing money out the window. You cannot enroll nonexistent students.

Instead of advertising, focus on internal marketing and public relations. Encourage students to recruit new members. Hold a contest to see who can recruit the most new members or offer a special deal for anyone who enrolls on the recommendation of a current student. This type of marketing is very cost effective, because it only costs you advertising dollars when someone enrolls. If you are a good instructor, your students will be happy to spread the word.

Other methods of internal marketing and public relations include:

- seminars for students or the public

- in-school tournaments

- demonstrations or speeches in the community

- merchandising

- special interest classes

- charity event, like a kick-a-thon

All of these activities serve the dual purpose of increasing student interest (and commitment) and generating extra income to make up for a lack of enrollment.

Pick up the Pieces

As the decline in your area progresses, schools will close. Be prepared to pick up the pieces by taking these students into your school. Perhaps the only time to advertise heavily during a downturn is in the weeks after a local school closes. Many of its students will be anxious to find a new instructor quickly so their training is not interrupted. And many schools in your area may not be too eager to welcome them, especially if they practice a different style.

Accommodating these students benefits both of you. They gain a welcoming new home to continue their training and you gain a new group of enthusiastic and committed students. Accommodation can mean anything from allowing them to keep their rank to offering private lessons to help them catch up and feel comfortable in your school. If there are a large number of students who want to move to your school as a group, consider offering a few weeks of group lessons for them, perhaps after regular classes end or on weekends. A temporary class is a good way to get the new students up to speed with your teaching style and curriculum and to let them adjust at their own pace. Changing schools unexpectedly is a difficult and discouraging experience. Your sincere efforts to ease the transition will create a base of loyal students.

Improve Yourself

Typically, during a slow period, you have a lot of time on your hands. Instead of using it to worry about how difficult it is to make ends meet, use it to improve yourself and your staff and prepare for the coming growth period:

- take a business course

- buy some training tapes

- learn a new curriculum element

- improve your teaching style

- train your staff

- read management books

Another great thing to do during a down time is to spruce up your school:

- put up a fresh coat of paint
- hang new pictures or posters
- create a new merchandise display
- build an equipment rack
- make some low cost stretching/training devices
- do a thorough spring cleaning
- straighten up the parking lot
- repaint your sign
- redesign your business cards.

Do all the little things you don't have time to do when things are busy. You will feel good about yourself and you will be getting ready for the coming growth cycle.

Growth

The martial arts business is cyclical, growing and shrinking with the movements of popular perception, media attention and fads. Inevitably, a decline in any industry results in businesses closing or downsizing to survive. The consequence of a decline is a lack of supply when the demand returns. This stimulates growth for the remaining businesses.

Signs of Growth

Identifying a growth period is the first step to capitalizing on it. Your area is probably entering a growth period if:

- new schools are opening
- existing schools are adding classes/programs or locations
- new recreational classes are forming
- martial arts is getting a spurt of positive publicity
- local schools have increased their advertising

Capitalizing on Growth

A growth period is the time to invigorate your school. The greatest mistake school owners make when business is booming is to sit back and enjoy their good fortune. The schools who gain the most from a growth period are those who double their marketing efforts, double their advertising, and double their enthusiasm in teaching.

A growth period means that there are hundreds of potential students ready to sign-up for lessons, but it doesn't guarantee that they will join your school unless you do something extra to attract their attention.

Strategic Planning

The most important thing you can do when you see the indications of a coming growth cycle is to be prepared. Remember, during the downturn you used your spare time to improve yourself and your school.

This means you are one step ahead of other schools that were moping through the downturn, wasting energy on worrying about the future. Now that the growth cycle is upon you, it is time to put your improvements into place with a strategic plan.

First, plan your advertising and marketing strategy. Be prepared to invest in more advertising than you normally use, with a special offer to encourage potential students to choose your school over others. Tailor your offer to the growth segment of the market. Where is interest highest—children, adults, women? What type of classes are students looking for—self-defense, fitness, fun, stress-relief? Every growth cycle is fueled by a theme, usually created by the media (movies, TV, national advertising for a product like Taebo).

Bruce Lee popularized the use of nunchakus. The *Kung Fu* series made everyone want to learn the mysterious Eastern arts. The Ninja Turtles got kids interested in fancy moves. Van Damme caught the interest of young men who wanted to be tough fighters. Taebo launched the cardio craze. By identifying the fuel behind the fire, you can get inside potential students' heads and provide them with exactly what they are looking for.

Once you have an advertising and marketing strategy, prepare for the influx of students. This requires, enlarging your teaching and office staffs to meet increased demand.

Someone should be available to answer the telephone during business hours. Many people make an appointment with the first school they talk to. The more hours during the day you or your staff is available, the better chance you have of being the first appointment a potential student makes.

Secondly, have a staff member present at the school during class hours whose job is greeting visitors, signing up new students and providing information for drop-ins.

The third area that must be strong is your class structure. If you are not prepared for a growth spurt, you may find classes getting overcrowded. The ideal solution is to add one or two new classes for beginners. If this is not possible, add instructors to the current beginner classes to ensure that new students receive enough attention and personal instruction.

If you have advanced students in the beginner class, transfer them out before classes get crowded, or you might lose them as well as the newer students. A growth spurt is a good time to expand your instructor training program. If you become extremely pressed for space, you can set up satellite location classes taught by your assistants at a local gym or health club.

Managing Growth

There are some potential pitfalls that come with the exciting possibilities of expansion.

- **Too much expansion too soon.** Some instructors make the mistake of quickly moving to a larger location before they solidify the influx of new students. If a large group of students later drop out, it becomes difficult to pay the rent at a larger location.

- **Counting too heavily on marginal students.** Growth brings with it many marginal students, those who are more interested in learning their idea of what martial arts is rather than the reality of training. There is higher rate of dropouts in a growth period. Plan for this in your budgeting.

- **Quality suffers.** During a successful growth period, the quality of instruction can suffer. This is usually due to the fact that the head instructor can no longer teach all of the classes or he is too busy doing administrative tasks to pay enough attention to teaching. Practice delegating both teaching and administrative tasks before you absolutely have to so when the time comes to turn over more responsibilities to your staff they are fully prepared.

- **Complacency.** Success often breeds complacency. When your school is growing rapidly, the temptation to take it easy is strong. Many instructors fall into the trap of thinking they have "made it" and put the school on automatic pilot. This is the most dangerous pitfall.

Saturation

After a healthy growth period, inevitably there comes a time when there are more schools in a geographic area than the market can support. Supply exceeds demand leading to a predictable result: one or more schools close due to insufficient income.

There are several characteristics of a saturated market. The most obvious is heavy price competition. As the supply (number of schools/classes) begins to exceed the demand for lessons, at least one school deeply discounts their introductory program to combat the drop off in enrollments. Shortly after the first school cuts prices, other schools feel forced to follow their lead or lose new students.

This results in a heated round of advertising and discounting until the cost of advertising combined with the loss of income due to deep discounts puts one or more schools out of business. After this happens, supply is more in line with demand and the surviving schools can return to their regular marketing strategies.

There are two methods of surviving short-term price competition:

- Follow the leader and **discount** lessons. This works only if you succeed in bringing in plenty of new students who convert to lessons at regular price and if you have enough regular tuition income to cover the added advertising and discounting.

- Maintain your rates, but **offer more services** than the discounted schools. You can do this by offering unlimited classes, special classes, free use of equipment, open workout time, private lessons, personal training or some other extra as part of the regular lesson fee. While you have to work harder or give up some extra income, this strategy is more likely to result in enrolling students who stay until black belt.

In addition to surviving the outside competition of a saturated market, guard against the problems that saturation might bring into your classes. After a good growth period, your school may be overcrowded. Classes become large and there are more demands placed on your time by an increasingly large student body.

You may start feeling like you and your staff are stretched a little thin. Your teaching may suffer. If you can no longer teach every class, some students begin to feel like you no longer care about teaching or you are neglecting them. Others feel that classes are too large and they are not getting the attention they once did. Also, you may find that administrative tasks are beginning to cut into your teaching time or you are getting behind in your administrative duties.

You can prevent this by hiring more staff members or by limiting the number of new enrollments. If you can afford it, hiring additional staff is the best option.

The final problem faced during a saturation period is that students have more choices for lessons. If a school opens closer to their house, costs less, has a better family discount, offers weight machines, has a better variety of classes or looks like more fun, many people are eager to give it a try and compare it to your school.

During a saturation period, turnover increases and you may feel powerless to retain students who were marginally interested in classes. Carefully investigate your competitors to determine what aspects of their schools are more appealing and what you can do to compete with them. This may mean offering new classes, special seminars, new curriculum or additional services.

Everything you do to strengthen your school during a saturation period makes it more likely to be one of the schools left standing when the cycle is over.

Hosting a Tournament

Organizing a Successful Event

In this section . . .

243 Attributes of Success
247 Selecting the Right Size
253 Budgeting
258 Staffing
262 Master Timeline
265 Purchasing Supplies
268 The Entry Package
270 Post Event Reporting

A successful tournament is one that meets the expectations of competitors, coaches, spectators, officials and organizers. To organize a successful tournament, the tournament director must first clearly understand what these expectations are.

- Competitors expect a tournament to be run fairly, meaning the rules are applied consistently and accurately.

- Spectators like an exciting competition that is easy to observe, ongoing and has few injuries.

- Coaches expect their competitor to be matched against other competitors of a similar skill level and to be judged by competent officials.

- Officials expect to be treated with respect, clearly informed of the rules and allowed to apply their judgment without undue interference.

- The organizing committee expects cooperation and support from competitors, coaches and officials in running the tournament as efficiently as possible.

- Everyone expects the event to start on time, run efficiently and proceed without unnecessary delays.

Anyone who has been to a significant number of tournaments may have trouble recalling more than a few that fit this criteria. However, with careful planning and execution, a skilled tournament director can meet or exceed the expectations of all those involved.

First let's take a more specific look at the attributes of success:

1. Fair Judging

Fair judging is based on a clear set of rules. Before the tournament, the rules should be available to the competitors, coaches, and officials. If the rules will be modified in any way, everyone should be given sufficient notice in advance of the tournament day. Once the rules are established, the officials must apply them consistently in every ring throughout the day. If the referee in ring one is allowing contact to the head and the referee in ring three is disqualifying competitors for head contact, you will have myriad protests from both rings. The tournament director should monitor all rings and discreetly correct any inappropriate applications of the rules as soon as he sees them. The tournament director should also rotate officials frequently to prevent accusations of bias.

2. Clearly Written Rules

The tournament rules should be provided to everyone when they register for the competition. If you use the rules of a national governing body, competition circuit or sanctioning organization, state this in the information packet and be prepared to distribute copies of the rules to anyone unfamiliar with them. This prevents people from complaining about being disqualified for using the wrong amount of contact, wearing the wrong gear, using an illegal technique, etc. A clear set of rules also gives the officials a reference in the event of disputes or protests.

3. Punctuality

Punctuality is virtually impossible to achieve when working with hundreds or thousands of people, but is possible to approximate. There is nothing to prevent a tournament from starting on time. The tournament director is responsible for kicking off the tournament and must make starting on time a number one priority. During the day, delays occur and extra time should be worked into the schedule to account for them. When you have a schedule that is programmed for uncertainties, you can give the appearance of punctuality to the spectators and competitors. If nothing goes wrong, you will be ahead of schedule!

4. Disciplined Execution of the Tournament Plan

As the old maxim says, "Plan your work and work your plan." The first part is easy, because we have weeks to plan the tournament. However, when the day arrives there are dozens of distractions and temptations to pull the plan off course. Resist the urge to make major last minute changes and stick to your plan with reasonable discipline. Of course adaptation is necessary. Consider the impact of a change, positive or negative, before you implement it.

5. Adequate Safety/Medical Supervision

Martial arts tournaments include contact events that have the potential for injury. Even light or non-contact sparring results in accidental injuries. To reduce injuries, ensure that safety gear is used by all competitors, referees strictly enforce the contact rules, competitors are equally matched and respect is shown to the judges and other competitors. If an injury occurs, professional medical care should be administered at once. The safety of the competitors comes above all other rules and protocol.

6. Efficient Registration and Weigh-in

The goal of the registration process is to register as many people in advance as possible. On the competition day, set up a large, clearly marked registration area and a supervised weigh-in for all sparring competitors. The registration must be completed before the competition can begin.

7. Qualified Staff

Every tournament needs a qualified staff to run the event. Everything from judging the events to preparing lunch is planned and assigned to a staff member in advance. Staff members can be students, instructors and parents who are reliable and able to carry out the functions of their job.

8. Spectator Control

One of the major failings of tournaments is the inability of the staff to control the flow of spectators and other unauthorized persons on the competition floor. A large, well-trained contingent of security staff on the floor at all times can send spectators and inactive coaches and competitors to the spectator seats or holding areas. If this rule is enforced consistently, there are few complaints because everyone has a clear view of the floor from the spectator seating area.

9. Sportsmanship

Sportsmanship by the competitors, coaches and instructors is essential in maintaining control of the rings. Participants who do not exhibit self-control may be penalized or ejected from the tournament. Upholding the martial arts atmosphere is one of the primary goals of a successful tournament. Not only is it part of what we practice daily as martial artists, but self-control is a key trait spectators expect to see from martial artists.

10. Appropriate Division Sizes

The size of the divisions in a tournament depends on its level of competitiveness. A national level competition may have fifty or more people in a division and everyone shows up expecting such a competitive atmosphere. An interschool tournament, on the other hand, may have only four people in each division to ensure that everyone wins something. In making divisions, generally the smaller the tournament, the smaller the divisions are. Another common approach is to make the lower ranks and younger competitors' divisions less competitive while the adult black belts are the largest and most competitive divisions. Remember, success is about meeting people's expectations.

11. Exciting Competition

Don't forget about the spectators. Design the competition to be fast paced with something exciting happening at all times. Don't expect the spectators to sit through six rings of white and yellow belts. Always have a black belt division featured in at least one ring so spectators have an exciting focal point.

12. Leadership

Most importantly, the tournament director must provide strong leadership to pull together all of the elements of the tournament and give it an aura of excitement, fulfillment and success.

Selecting the Right Size

Interschool, intraschool, local or national

See also . . .
Budgeting . . . . page 253
Staffing . . . . page 258

There are basically five classes of tournaments to choose from: interschool, intraschool, open local, national, and international. Most first time tournament hosts begin with an interschool or intraschool tournament to test out their system with minimal risk. You may choose to start out larger or to progress to larger tournaments, so let's look at the function and preparation needed for each type.

Interschool Tournament

An interschool tournament is one in which only the students of one school participate. It is generally small (50-100 competitors) and is a great place for everyone to try out competition for the first time, including the tournament director and staff. An interschool tournament provides a number of advantages from the viewpoint of the instructor:

1. Every division and pairing can be controlled by the instructor.

2. It is ideal for first time competitors, noncompetitive students and students afraid of competition because the competitors know each other and know what to expect in advance.

3. The instructor can create the type of atmosphere he wants his students to experience.

4. Non-competing students can participate as volunteer staff members.

5. Higher rank students can learn to judge in an educational atmosphere.

6. Rules can be tailored to the students' needs.

7. Information can be easily distributed through regular school channels.

For the instructor and students, an interschool tournament can be a morale booster and a way of bringing students and their families together. It does, however, have a number of drawbacks:

1. There is little challenge for highly competitive or talented students.

2. The divisions are small and some students may not have opponents.

3. Being only open to school members, the school reputation does not grow.

4. The income from the tournament is small and may not meet expenses.

5. Schools with few high-ranking students do not have enough judges.

Based on these factors, an interschool tournament is best suited for a medium to large size school that is interested in boosting student morale and providing a low-risk competition experience for all students.

Intraschool Tournament

An intraschool tournament is one in which an instructor invites a few schools with whom he is affiliated such as branch schools or friends' schools. It is open only to members of invited schools. It is larger than the interschool tournament (100-150 competitors) and somewhat more complicated to organize. Let's look at the advantages and disadvantages of an intraschool tournament over an interschool tournament:

Advantages:

1. More variety and quantity of competitors allowing for bigger and better divisions.

2. More and better-qualified officials (instructors from other schools).

3. More volunteers to help in organizing and executing the tournament.

4. More income to meet expenses and enhance the tournament quality.

5. Higher degree of competitiveness among experienced competitors.

6. Potential for team competition among schools.

7. Control over philosophies of schools who enter and therefore over the tournament atmosphere.

Disadvantages:

1. Need for uniform rules that all schools agree to.

2. Potential for over-competitiveness or "clique-ishness" among individual schools.

3. Less control over level of competition and therefore more risk to first time competitors.

4. Possible bias on the part of judges for their own school or students.

5. More work in distributing and collecting registration information.

6. More work in coordinating volunteers among schools.

Based on this analysis, the intraschool tournament is recommended for instructors who are experienced at organizing and managing people. Distributing and collecting the information, managing the officials, organizing the volunteers and pleasing the competitors is more difficult when other schools are involved. Additionally, if you fail the first time out, instructors are reluctant to participate in the future, potentially damaging your school reputation.

On the other hand, an intraschool tournament can be beneficial to a group of cooperating instructors who have small clubs or part time schools and would not be able to mount a tournament on their own. The intraschool tournament, while more work than the interschool tournament, can be an excellent choice for the small school or club.

Open Local Tournament

An open local tournament is one in which all schools in a certain area are invited to participate. Depending on the instructor's contacts, the area can be a city, state or region of the country. He may also choose a single style tournament (based on the rules of a single martial art system) or a multi-style tournament based on the rules of a competition circuit. Whatever the format, an open local tournament is a large undertaking and the tournament director should plan to set aside at least six months for organizing and preparing the competition. Let's look at the advantages and disadvantages:

Advantages:

1. A great deal of publicity for the host school.

2. A moderate to high level of competition.

3. The potential for the host to profit financially or to raise money for charity or school events.

4. Many judges and volunteers to assist in running the event.

5. A wide variety of competitors to fill all divisions sufficiently.

6. Prestige for the host school and its students.

Disadvantages:

1. Significant investment of time and resources by the tournament director.

2. Little control over type or quality of competitors.

3. Potential inconsistencies in judging quality/application of rules.

4. Potential for unruly competitors, spectators, coaches.

5. Wide margin of error in planning and executing tournament events.

6. Great deal of energy required to manage all participants smoothly.

The open local tournament should only be undertaken after several years of experience with smaller competitions. The ability to organize and mobilize the hundreds of people involved in such an event is not something that can be learned in books or through theories. Experience is the primary weapon of the tournament director.

Open National or International Tournament

An open national or international tournament is a major undertaking that can consume up to two years of planning and preparation and requires the dedicated efforts of hundreds of staff and volunteers. National and international tournaments can draw anywhere from 500 to 5,000 competitors depending on the type and scope of the competition. These large tournaments are generally hosted by professional organizing committees and with good reason. The potential benefit from a well-run national tournament is limitless and the damage from a poorly run national tournament can be a career ender. Mounting a national or international tournament is recommended for those tournament directors who have at least ten years experience (1-2 tournaments a year) in organizing and hosting competitions.

Now that we have looked at the potential benefits and pitfalls of each type of tournament, use the work sheet at right to estimate the size of your tournament.

Tournament Size Work sheet

1. How many competitors do I anticipate having?

2. Will I invite competitors from my school(s)? Neighboring schools? Association schools? All schools in my region?

3. Competitors must be members of my association? A sanctioning body? A tournament circuit?

4. The tournament will be held at my school? A community site? A college gym?

5. How many volunteers can I recruit to help out?

6. How many qualified officials will I need? Can I recruit this many?

7. How many staff members/officials can I manage comfortably?

8. Which schools/instructors can I count on to support my tournament?

9. What size tournament will most benefit my school?

10. What size tournament will most benefit my community reputation?

11. What level of competition are my students ready to compete in?

12. How often will I hold my tournament?

13. What are the goals of my tournament?

14. To whom will the tournament proceeds go?

15. For how many years will I continue to host the tournament?

16. What is my past experience in tournament management?

The Benefits of Keeping your Tournament Small

While it's exciting and prestigious to host a tournament with thousands of competitors, sometimes it can be more beneficial to host a small tournament with an emphasis on sportsmanship and participation over winning. Some of the benefits of an intraschool or interschool tournament include:

- **Motivating students,** especially those who might want to compete but are afraid to enter a large, competitive tournament. A smaller tournament with a welcoming atmosphere can motivate a whole new group of students to think of themselves as competitors and increase the intensity of their training.

- Creating **competitive opportunities** for youngsters just like they have in baseball, soccer and swimming. Some kids lose interest in martial arts because it lacks the competitive element of other sports they enjoy. The chance to compete with others their age is a powerful motivation for coming to class.

251

- Attracting **new students** through pre-tournament publicity and advertising. There are many opportunities to promote your school such as putting a free lesson coupon on the back of spectator tickets, giving a demonstration during the opening ceremonies or black belt finals, and handing out fliers on the day of the tournament.

- Involving **parents and family members** as committee members and volunteers. At least half of the jobs that need to be staffed, including registration, setup, security and hospitality, are perfect opportunities for family members to get involved and feel like a part of their children's or spouse's martial arts activities.

In addition to these benefits, a smaller tournament can allow you to keep costs down. The biggest cost of a tournament is site rental and staffing. Hosting the tournament in your school eliminates this cost entirely. There are a number of benefits and drawbacks to using your school as the tournament site:

Benefits of Hosting at Your School

- Spectators who may be potential students are exposed to the school atmosphere and get a low-pressure chance to look around, see your art in action and talk with students and parents.

- Divisions can be scheduled throughout the day, allowing students to arrive only for their division and limiting the amount of time spent waiting to compete.

- Equipment and mats/rings are on hand and setup, eliminating transportation worries.

- Potential students can be signed up at a registration table at the tournament. Offer a "new student" special that is available only to members who sign up during the tournament.

Drawbacks of hosting at your school

- There is high spectator traffic, which might put a strain on your facilities (parking, bathrooms, mats, waiting area) depending on the size of your school.

- Most schools have a lack of spectator seating.

- A tournament held at an outside site is seen as more prestigious and can draw additional spectators from the site (college, community center).

Getting Started

Before you begin planning, assess your financial readiness for hosting a tournament. An event such as this requires the director to put up a significant amount of money in advance and wait several weeks or even months for his expenses to be covered.

At right is a list of budgetary considerations for different size tournaments beginning with the smallest and adding on extra expenses for larger size competitions. On the following pages are detailed instructors for completing the work sheet. Use this as a work sheet to figure your potential budget.

Budgeting

Staying within your means

See also . . .
Selecting the Right Size . . . . page 247

Interschool tournament budget (basic)

Awards _____

Photocopies _____

Food _____

Supplies _____

Stopwatches _____

Scale _____

Site rental _____

Personnel fees _____

Insurance _____

Demonstration supplies _____

Table/chair rental _____

Tickets _____

Medical personnel _____

Intraschool tournament budget

Postage _____

Incentives _____

Registration materials _____

Instructor awards _____

Open tournament budget

Posters _____

Lodging for officials _____

Advertising _____

Transportation for officials _____

Sanction fee _____

Program book _____

Mats/rings _____

Scoring Equipment _____

Total estimated budget _____

Total funds available _____

Sponsorship needed _____

Completing the Budget Work Sheet

The following is a step-by-step guide to completing the budget work sheet on the preceding page:

1. **Awards**: Awards can be trophies, medals, ribbons, plaques, or certificates. Figure $3.00 to $10.00 each for trophies or medals depending on the quality and quantity ordered. For certificates and ribbons, budget about $.50 to $1.00 each. Plaques for special awards (student of the year, outstanding competitor, etc.) can get expensive if the engraving is extensive. Look for companies that include free engraving in the plaque price. In either case, budget at least $20.00 and up to $50.00 or more each. For a small tournament, plan on 1 to 2 awards per person and for a large tournament figure .5 to 1 award per person. Shop around and compare prices.

2. **Photocopies**: All of the division papers, tournament information, registration forms, administration papers and scoring papers will have to be photocopied. If you get copies made in bulk, budget about $10.00 to $15.00 per 100 copies. Plan ahead and copy everything at once to save money.

3. **Food**: In addition to food you might sell at the tournament site, you must provide food (breakfast/lunch/dinner banquet) for the officials and staff members. For breakfast, budget about $5.00 per person and for lunch about $7.00 per person. Supplying meals makes it easier to get volunteers to help out all day.

4. **Supplies**: There are myriad miscellaneous supplies needed to run a tournament including tape for the rings, pens/pencils, scratch paper, scoring implements (flags/scoreboards/etc), office supplies, clip boards, and so forth. Plan to spend about $300.00 for supplies for the first tournament and about $100.00 thereafter, since many items are reusable from year to year.

5. **Stopwatches**: You need a stopwatch for each ring's timekeeper. Good, basic stopwatches cost anywhere from $15.00 to $40.00. Keep extra batteries on hand on the tournament day. Watch batteries are somewhat expensive (from $5.00 to $10.00 each).

6. **Scale**: A scale to weigh-in competitors may be necessary depending on your rules. A digital scale is best since it is not open to subjective interpretation. An institutional, digital scale costs at least $100.00 but is well worth the expense to head off arguments about a competitor's correct weight on the tournament day. If you are hosting the event at a college gym, the college should have a certified scale on hand for wrestling events.

7. **Site rental**: Depending on where you hold the tournament, you may have to pay a rental fee. A community center, health club or high school gym can be rented for $100.00 to $500.00 a day. A college gym or field house starts at $800.00 and may run as high as $2000.00 or more. If you can hold the competition in your school, you do not have a rental fee.

8. **Personnel fees**: If you hold a tournament at an outside facility, budget for supervisory personnel such as a janitor, security guard, and/or faculty supervisor. Check with the site for the range of these fees, but plan on at least $200.00.

9. **Insurance**: Liability insurance is a necessity and required by the site provider. For basic tournament coverage, expect to pay $1.50 to $3.00 per competitor.

10. **Demonstration supplies**: If you are putting on a demonstration, include the cost of any supplies you may need such as boards, bricks and special uniforms.

11. **Tables/chairs**: Rent enough tables and chairs for the administration and judging personnel. Plan on about 10 tables and 60 chairs for a medium size tournament. If you are lucky, the site provider will have chairs and tables you can use, saving the rental cost. If not, figure about $8.00 to $10.00 a table and up to a few dollars each per chair.

12. **Tickets**: Purchase a roll of tickets for spectators or have them printed at a copy shop. You should not have to spend more than $25.00. A less costly option is to stamp everyone's hand after they pay. In this case you need a stamp pad and rubber stamps.

13. **Medical personnel**: Every tournament should have at least one and preferably two or more medical personnel (EMT, paramedic, licensed trainer, nurse) on site. Larger tournaments should have a medical professional for every one or two rings. Depending on the level of training and experience of the medical staff, budget $100.00 to $500.00 for the day. Also plan to provide or pay for ice packs, bandages, tape and other consumable supplies that injured competitors use.

14. **Postage**: Once you begin inviting other schools, you have to mail the information to them and therefore must include postage costs in your estimate. Total postage cost per school ranges from $4.00 to $10.00 depending on the size of your package.

15. **Incentives**: When inviting other schools, incentives are useful in increasing participation. Incentives can be prizes for the most supporting schools, t-shirts for early registrants, accommodations for instructors or whatever you think may increase participation at your event. This budget varies with the size of the tournament but should not exceed 10% of the gross receipts.

16. **Registration materials**: Every competitor should receive a card or paper with his or her division information when he or she registers/checks-in on the tournament day. Budget about $20.00 per 100 competitors.

17. **Instructor awards**: Giving instructor appreciation awards to all attending instructors is a nice way to show your gratitude to supporting schools. Budget $20.00 to $50.00 per school.

18. **Posters**: Posters are an excellent way to advertise a large tournament. Post them in your neighborhood and provide some to each invited school. Depending on the complexity

of your poster (i.e. 1 color, 2 color, 4 color) the cost varies. Budget $100.00 to $1,000.00 for posters.

19. **Lodging for officials**: If you are hosting a large tournament, the attending officials should be provided with lodging for at least one night. Book a block of rooms at local hotel and budget $35.00 to $150.00 per official, depending on the quality of the hotel. (Note: The better the quality of the hotel, the better quality officials you will attract and maintain over the years.)

20. **Advertising**: Open tournaments require advertising to spread the word and attract the maximum number of competitors. Budget up to $500.00 for a local tournament and up to $5,000.00 for a national tournament.

21. **Transportation for officials**: If you have many officials flying to your tournament, you have to provide transportation from the airport and to and from the tournament site. If you have enough volunteers, they can provide this service or you can hire a transportation service. This budget varies widely by region.

22. **Sanction fee**: If you want to be sanctioned by an organization or competition circuit, there is a fee. The fee entitles you to use the organization's rules, invite their members, and sometimes be advertised/rated by the organization. Sanctioning also provides credibility and a built-in market of competitors who are familiar with the organization. Sanctioning runs from $200.00 to several thousand dollars depending on the organization and the size of the tournament.

23. **Program book**: A program book is a means to provide spectators with information about the tournament and raise money through selling advertisements. Ideally the program book breaks even or raises money before the tournament, so do not budget it as an expense per se. You may be able to use it to offset your expenses in the sponsorship column at the bottom of the worksheet.

24. **Mats/Rings**: Some styles require specialized mats or rings for the competition. You may be able to rent this equipment from a sanctioning body or another tournament promoter or invest in your own. Pricing can vary from a few hundred dollars into the thousands depending on the number of rings run.

25. **Scoring equipment**: Some styles use electronic or computerized scoring equipment. Again this can be rented from a sanctioning body or an independent company and the pricing can vary greatly.

26. **Totals**: Add up the total estimates. On many lines you may have range of figures (such as $100 - $150). If this is often the case, add up the lower numbers and higher numbers in two different sets to determine a minimum and maximum cost. Subtract your total available funds from your minimum estimate. If you have money left over, you can afford to spend more in areas that require it. If come up with a negative number, you need sponsorship, either through the program book or through private funding by a local company. Another

possibility for raising money is renting space at the site (for example, in the lobby) to vendors of food, martial arts supplies, etc. Each company pays a fee to set up a table and sell their goods and you both make money, while the competitors and spectators benefit from the variety of goods available.

See also . . .
Master Timeline . . . . page 262
Purchasing Supplies . . . . page 265

A successful tournament committee is made up of nine committee heads plus the tournament director and the tournament coordinator. Each committee performs a specific function and works independently, reporting directly to the director or coordinator. The following summary lists the key functions of each committee. The master timeline pinpoints the functions in more depth.

1. Setup Committee

The setup committee is responsible for procuring and handling the physical elements of the tournament. It develops a site plan, purchases or rents necessities, transports them to the site and physically sets up and cleans up on the tournament day. If possible, the setup committee secures use of the site one day prior to the tournament for setting up rings, posting signs, testing the PA system and getting the major elements in place. The setup committee consists of one chairperson who manages the budget and purchases items and five to thirty members who carry out the deployment and clean up phases. The setup committee budget consists of items 1, 4, 5, 7, 11, 24 and 25 from the master budget.

2. Registration Committee

The registration committee consists of the registration chairperson and five to twenty members. Their responsibility includes mailing/distributing registration packets, checking registrations as they are received, developing divisions, making pairings for sparring, administering weigh-in and registration on the tournament day and confirming competitors' weights. After the tournament, the committee chair files a report to the director detailing the type and number of divisions, the number of competitors, and any problems encountered, including protests. The registration committee is responsible for numbers 6, 14 and 16 on the master budget.

3. Security Committee

The security committee is responsible for maintaining the tournament atmosphere. Security teams should be posted at the entrances to monitor traffic flow and check credentials and tickets, in the registration area to monitor traffic flow, and on the tournament floor to clear spectators and nonparticipating competitors. There should also be a roving security team, headed by the chairperson, that can move about the site (competition floor, lobby, lockers, warm-up area, registration area, etc.) looking for unexpected problems and solving them as they arise. In addition to the chairperson, the security team has a minimum of two security personnel for every one hundred people at the tournament site.

4. Officials Committee

The officials committee is responsible for lining up referees, judges and time/score keepers to officiate and run the event. Each ring requires two scorekeepers and four to six officials to run smoothly. Scorekeepers are students or parents who volunteer. Officials are those trained and certified by the sanctioning organization, or at least trained by the tournament director, in the rules to be used. A meeting on the morning of the tournament is not enough to produce well-trained officials. Recruitment and training should begin at least three months prior to the event. If officials travel from out of state, the committee arranges accommodations and transportation. This committee is responsible for master budget items 17, 19 and 21.

5. Publicity Committee

The function of the publicity committee is to promote the tournament to the community at large and to potential competitors. These are two distinctly separate functions and are approached as such. To the general community, the tournament is promoted as an exciting spectator event by selling advance tickets, getting publicity in local newspapers, creating press releases and making posters to hang in local establishments. For competitors, the tournament is promoted for its competitive value by distributing posters, advertising in martial arts publications and creating word of mouth excitement on the tournament circuit or in participating schools. The publicity committee is made up of a chairperson and two subcommittees (community publicity and competitor publicity) of three to ten people each. The publicity committee is also responsible for coordinating with the registration committee on advance registration packets and with the tournament director to plan and promote the demonstration if there will be one. This committee is responsible for master budget items 10, 15, 18, 20 and 23.

6. Hospitality Committee

The hospitality committee is responsible for preparing meals, credentials and other amenities for the staff and officials. If the tournament committee is providing meals, including an after-tournament party, the hospitality committee is responsible for procuring food or services and overseeing the setup, service and cleanup of meals. If it is a small tournament, the committee members may do the actual serving and if it is a large tournament, an outside vendor should be contracted. In either case, the committee chairperson is responsible for making accurate guest estimates and planning suitable meals. The committee also prepares credentials for officials and staff members for identification and access to the competition floor. The hospitality committee is primarily responsible for master budget item 3 and should communicate with the officials committee to develop a coordinated plan. The size of this committee depends on the size of the tournament and the complexity of the hospitality plans.

7. Medical Committee

The medical committee chairperson is ideally someone with experience in sports medicine or a medical professional who understands the requirements for supplies and personnel. The chairperson is responsible for contracting medical services (EMT, paramedic, nurse or licensed trainer), briefing the medical personnel on what types of injuries are most likely to occur, providing liaison services on the tournament day (passing out medical report forms, calling for additional assistance, following up on injured competitors), completing accident/incident reports for all injuries and purchasing necessary medical supplies. The committee consists of the chairperson and medical personnel. This committee is responsible for master budget item number 13.

8. Organizing Committee

The organizing committee is divided into two functions: pre-tournament organization and tournament day management. The committee is headed by the tournament coordinator and the organizing committee chairperson who work as co-chairs. The pre-tournament organization consists of launching and overseeing all committees, monitoring budgets, monitoring the timeline progress, replacing or relieving personnel as necessary, authorizing expenses, and confirming that all committees are efficiently performing their functions. During the week prior to the tournament, the organizing committee might do a "dry run" of some or all aspects of the event with the committee chairs. This is especially helpful if many of the committee chairs are new to running a tournament.

On the tournament day, the organizing committee oversees the general flow of the tournament and deals with the minor problems that arise throughout the day. They also coordinate personnel shifts and committee interaction. The organizing committee is made up of two co-chairs and a small group of knowledgeable, experienced personnel who can oversee the myriad details of the tournament from beginning to end. The organizing committee is specifically responsible for master budget items 2, 8, 9, and 22 as well as overall budget management.

9. Sales Committee

The sales committee is responsible for selling tickets, t-shirts, food, gear, uniforms, program books, etc. The chairperson assigns subcommittee chairs to head each division such as tickets, food, and merchandise. In addition to overseeing the selling of items on the tournament day, the chairs are responsible for procuring and/or producing their subcommittee's goods. This includes accurately calculating how much of a given product will sell and setting prices. The chairperson is responsible for master budget items 3 and 12. Each subcommittee should consist of four to six people who transport the goods to the site, setup, sell the goods at the site and clean up afterwards. Commonly, chairpersons contract with outside vendors like martial arts supply stores and local restaurants to provide these services.

10. Tournament Director

The tournament director is responsible for choosing schools to invite, setting the rules and format of the tournament, rallying support for the competition, personally inviting dignitaries, selecting committee chairpersons, selecting staff/officials for awards, giving overall direction to the committees, reviewing reports from the committees, directing the tournament on the competition day and reviewing summary reports after the tournament. The tournament director should not get bogged down in minute details. That is the job of the organizing committee and the director should delegate this work as it arises.

Before the tournament, each chairperson prepares an action plan based on the master timeline and master budget, stating exactly what the committee will do, when it will do it and how much it will cost. At regular intervals, the chairperson presents interim reports based on this plan to the tournament director. The reports indicate whether the committee is on target, what changes have been made and any problems the director should be aware of. After the competition, each committee prepares a summary report correlating their action plan with the results and flagging any suggestions for subsequent tournaments.

Based on this organizational plan, a small tournament staff consists of about eighty people including officials. A large staff can easily run into the hundreds. With a staff of more than 200, it is necessary to add additional layers of administration such as an assistant tournament director, assistant coordinator and assistant committee chairpersons.

What follows is a timeline for key events that take place from the initial decision to host a tournament to the reports submitted after the event. Each event is listed with its time of occurrence, the committee responsible for its execution and the size of tournament for which it is necessary.

Master timeline abbreviations key:

Committee name abbreviations:
Setup: SU
Registration: RE
Security: SC
Officials OF
Publicity: PB
Hospitality: HP
Medical: MD
Organizing: OR
Sales: SA
Tournament Director: TD

Tournament size abbreviations.
Interschool: IS
Instraschool: AS
Open local: OL
Open national: ON
All sizes: ALL
**tournament size indicates the minimum size at which this event is required.
e.g. IS indicates interschool and larger, OL indicates open local and larger

*Tim*e is the amount of time prior to the tournament that the event takes place.
e.g. 6 months indicates the event occurs 6 months prior to the tournament date.

Event	Time	Committee	Tournament
Select date	9 months	TD	IS
Select size	9 months	TD	IS
Select place	9 months	TD	IS
Choose name	9 months	TD	IS
Select/make rules	9 months	TD	IS
Select competitors	9 months	TD	IS
Choose committee chairs	7 months	TD	IS
Prep action plans	7 months	ALL	IS
Form committees	6 months	ALL	IS
Apply for sanction	6 months	OR	AS
Apply for insurance	6 months	OR	IS
Reserve hotels rooms	6 months	OF	OL
Arrange transportation	6 months	OF	ON
Compile mailing list	5 months	RG	OL
Solicit sponsorship	5 months	PB	OL
Recruit volunteers	3 months	ALL	IS
Make entry package	3 months	RG	AS
Design posters	3 months	PB	OL
Order awards	3 months	SU	IS
Order posters	3 months	PB	OL
Advertise	3 months	PB	OL
Print entry packages	3 months	RG	IS
Arrange meals	3 months	HP	IS
Contract vendors	3 months	HP	AS
Contract medical person.	3 months	MD	IS
Purchase supplies	3 months	ALL	IS
Mail entry packages	2.5 months	RG	IS
Print administrative forms	2 months	ALL	IS
Print officiating forms	2 months	OR	IS
Recruit officials	2 months	OF	IS
Rent chairs/tables	2 months	SU	IS
Invite dignitaries	2 months	TD	OL
Send news releases	6 weeks	PB	OL
Setup registration process	6 weeks	RG	IS
Print program	6 weeks	PB	OL
Follow up to invitees	4 weeks	RG	OL
Make credentials	3 weeks	HP	AS
Assign staff jobs	3 weeks	ALL	IS
Purchase merchandise	3 weeks	SA	IS
Train volunteers	2 weeks	ALL	IS
Train officials	2 weeks	ALL	IS
Make divisions/pairings	1 week	RG	IS
Purchase food	1 week	HP	IS

Event	Time	Committee	Tournament
Confirm arrangements	1 week	ALL	IS
Pack equipment	1 week	ALL	IS
Setup site	Tourn. Day	SU	IS
Cleanup site	Tourn. Day	SU	IS

Additional Events that will take place at my tournament:

Event	Time	Committee

See also . . .
Budgeting . . . . page 253
Staffing . . . . page 258

Below is a committee-by-committee break down of what types of supplies may be needed. Evaluate each item in terms of your tournament size and style. Make lists of what you have and what each committee needs to purchase, borrow or rent.   Input these items into your master budget.

1. Setup committee supplies:

√ poster paper
√ ring tape (1" -2" width in colors)
√ chairs
√ tables
√ table clothes
√ pens/pencils/markers
√ clipboards
√ microphone/sound system
√ national anthem(s) on tape or CD
√ stopwatches
√ scoring implements (flags, score boards, dry erase board with markers)
√ trophies or awards
√ mats and/or rings
√ electronic scoring equipment

2. Registration committee supplies:

√ entry forms
√ entry packages
√ postage
√ office supplies
√ scale
√ contestant credentials

3. Security committee supplies:

√ credentials

4. Officials committee supplies:

√ credentials
√ officiating forms
√ rulebooks

5. Publicity committee supplies:

√   posters
√   advertisements
√   demo supplies (boards/bricks, etc.)
√   press releases

6. Hospitality committee supplies:

√ food/beverages
√ utensils/plates/cups/napkins
√ food vouchers for staff/officials

7. Medical committee supplies:

√ ice
√ bandages/gauze (various sizes)
√ medical tape (various widths)
√ professional medical kit (supplied by medical staff)
√ accident/insurance forms

8. Organizing committee supplies:

√ administrative supplies
√ computer and supplies

9. Sales committee supplies:

√ tickets
√ merchandise
√ lock box
√ change (coins and small bills)
√ calculator
√ receipt book

Supplies to purchase:

_____

_____

_____

_____

_____

_____

_____

_____

_____

_____

_____

_____

_____

Supplies to rent:

_____

_____

_____

_____

_____

_____

_____

_____

_____

_____

_____

_____

_____

The Entry Package

Getting the word out

See also . . .
Master Timeline . . . . page 262

In the early stages of planning a tournament, the tournament director, the registration committee and the publicity committee work together to develop an entry package consisting of some or all of the following:

1. A **cover letter** addressed to invited schools describing the goals of the tournament, the type of competition and the general information that instructors need to make the decision whether to attend or not. The letter is signed by the tournament director and perhaps the tournament coordinator.

2. An **information sheet** listing the details of the tournament such as:
- date
- place
- time schedule
- type of rules (highlights and/or system used)
- divisions (an approximate breakdown)
- events (sparring, breaking, form, team, etc.)
- gear requirements
- types of forms/breaking materials/etc. allowed
- entry fees
- deadlines
- spectator fees
- coaching fees
- video pass fees
- an information phone number
- an information web site address
- your mailing address
- any other information competitors or instructors should know

Keep the information sheet as brief as possible while including the vital information necessary for instructors and competitors. Group information by topic and use bold type to highlight key ideas.

3. At least two copies of the **competitor registration form** for the instructor to copy and distribute. The form contains places for the entrant to indicate his/her name, address, age, belt, weight, phone number, events entered, and fee enclosed. There should also be a waiver to be signed by the competitor and a parent for minors. Don't forget to include a phone number for questions and the deadline and address for returning the form.

4. A **coach registration form** for instructors and black belts who will be coaching their competitors. Include places for the coaches' name, school, rank, and fees enclosed.

5. An **official registration form** for all instructors and black belts who volunteer to officiate.

6. **Directions** to the tournament site from all possible points (i.e. north, south, east and west).

7. **Housing information** for out of state attendees. Provide at least two choices of hotels.

8. **Posters** to advertise the tournament at each invitee's school.

Post Event Reporting

Creating a permanent record

After the tournament, each committee prepares a post-event report detailing their participation in planning and executing the event. A sample report format follows. Depending on the committee, a report runs one to five pages.

Post Event Recognition

After the tournament, don't forget to reward and recognize those who made it possible. The most common way of recognizing a job well done is throwing a post tournament party. This can be as simple as ordering in pizza or as elaborate as renting a restaurant or club. How you do it is not as important as the underlying sentiment. Let your staff members, volunteers, officials and competitors know how much you appreciate their efforts and what a great success the event was thanks to their effort.

Committee Name _____

Chairperson _____

Committee formed on _____

 Number of members at start _____ at finish _____

Names of Committee members:

Meeting record:

Date   Subject   Action taken

Budget Summary:

Expense   Projected   Actual   Difference

Instructor Survival

Coping with Challenges

In this section . . .

273 Motivation

275 Managing Change

277 Defusing Anger

280 Preventing Burnout

283 Limited Training Time

285 Controlling Nervousness

287 Instructor Assessment

Every instructor, no matter how experienced, has had a day when few or even no students showed up for class.

It is easy to be motivated when you have a school full of eager students, but how can an instructor maintain his or her motivation when classes are small? If you appear to be disappointed at the small class size, students will sense this and be affected negatively:

Maintain a Positive Attitude

The key is to keep a positive attitude and take advantage of the benefits of a small class.

Most students view a small class as a chance to get more personal attention from their instructor. Forget about the students who did not show up and focus on making the attending people stronger. They are dedicated students who will become leaders in your school. Once you have a core group of enthusiastic students, their excitement is contagious.

With this in mind, build on the dedication of the students who are present. Resolve to teach them better than you have ever taught before.

Focus on Personal Instruction

For small classes, focus on individual skills such as:

1. Individual strategy
2. Personal style
3. Individual strengths and weaknesses
4. Theory behind the movements
5. Developing specialties
6. Addressing concerns/questions

Be Flexible in Planning

There are many activities to fulfill these objectives:

1. Select a movement or group of movements and analyze each student individually. Give practice time then check their progress.

2. Allow students to engage in free sparring/combat and analyze individual strategy, strengths, weakness, styles.

3. Teach complex movements that require your attention to develop correctly and cannot normally be taught in large groups.

4. Teach the underlying theory of movements or forms to help students increase their depth and interest in the art.

5. Ask the students what they feel they need more work on and spend time to make them feel more secure in that area.

6. Teach at least one special or advanced skill. Remind the students that dedication and consistency pay off.

Above all, make them feel that their training is worthwhile and they are an important part of your school.

Change is the nature of life, but it can be difficult to accept, especially in an atmosphere like a martial arts school where students are seeking security and consistency. However, as an open-minded instructor, you may often find it necessary to implement changes in your school administration, curriculum and policies. Implementing a change does not have to be upsetting to the balance of your school, if you take steps to manage the impact of the change. Let's look at a few ways to manage change in a school environment.

Make Changes Gradual

If you need to make a major change in your school, plan it as a series of gradual steps.

Example: You are changing the school affiliation to a federation that requires major changes in your curriculum. If you announce that as of Jan. 15th, everyone has to learn new forms and forget about the old forms, many advanced students may move to a school that uses the forms they have spent years learning rather than invest months in learning a new curriculum.

Instead, gradually introduce the new forms in addition to the old forms. Until everyone is familiar with the new requirements, keep both sets of forms and practice both in class. Once students have adjusted to the new forms, phase out the old forms, if necessary.

Clearly Identify the Change

When making a policy change, such as a new school rule, clearly identify what the change involves so that students do not start rumors or spread misinformation.

Example: Everyone is now required to wear headgear in sparring because your new insurance company requires it. Post a notice on the bulletin board and make announcements in class. If students can purchase the head gear at the school, include the price in the notice. Set a specific date for the new rule to go into effect, preferably a few weeks in the future. Explain the benefits of the new rule: safety, a reduction in injuries, less fear of sparring. Without an explanation, students tend to make up their own—perhaps a negative one.

Accentuate the Positive

When implementing a change, emphasize the benefits that students reap from the change. Never assume students see the benefits to a change even if you think they are obvious.

Example: If the new curriculum is more challenging or has a greater variety of movements, explain why.

Ask for Input

Students and parents are more likely to accept a change if they feel that they have some input. Even if you don't use everyone's suggestions, people feel better about a change when they participate in it.

Example: Before changing the class schedule, hand out a survey to gather feedback on the days and times students prefer to attend class.

Make One Change at a Time

There is a strong temptation to implement a group of changes at once, assuming one big transition is easier to make than a series of smaller changes. However, the opposite is true. Most people are better able to cope with one small change at a time than with a major overhaul. Too much change, whether good or bad, can be emotionally overwhelming. By planning changes in advance, you avoid overburdening your students.

Take Charge of Changes

When you implement a change, don't let it get out of hand. Create an action plan to control the implementation of the change and stick to it. If you find that the change is having a negative effect, adjust your plan while maintaining your original intent. Remember, there is always some resistance to change and you may lose a few students in the initial stages. But if your decision is sound, you will eventually see your school grow as a result of the change.

Defusing Anger

Successful customer service

See also . . .
Dealing with Aggression . . . . page 105
Managing Parents . . . . page 160

No matter how friendly, accommodating and just plain nice you are, you can't please everyone all of the time. Dealing with angry people is difficult, especially when they are students who may quit if the situation is not resolved to their satisfaction.

There are a few keys to dealing with anger. The first is to not avoid angry clients. Each person who becomes angry with your school has something to teach you. Even if you think there is no basis for the anger, try to see the other person's point of view. What can you learn or improve? What made them so angry? How can you prevent it from happening again? By expressing their anger, the student or parent is asking you to find a solution.

There are seven steps to defusing anger and solving a problem. Properly followed, they create a win-win situation out of what otherwise might be a disaster.

1. Thank the person for bringing the problem to your attention.

The first step is to thank the person for telling you what made them angry. By doing so, you acknowledge your desire to listen and solve the problem rather than getting defensive and arguing about it. Many people calm down once you acknowledge their anger. Try to create a team atmosphere, letting the other person know that you are on their side.

Example: "Mrs. Smith, I appreciate you letting me know that Johnny feels I ignore him in class. He's such a good student and I don't want him to feel left out. "

"Dissatisfied customers are more likely to tell others about their experience than satisfied customers."

2. Let the person express their anger.

Listen carefully and let the person express their feelings. Try not to interrupt or cut them short, even though you feel the urge to challenge their facts or feelings. After a brief "venting" session in which the person has the chance to blow off steam it is much easier to communicate rationally. Of course, this does not mean allowing him to become verbally abusive or use foul language.

3. Apologize.

Once the person has had a chance to express his anger, apologize for the inconvenience or frustration he is experiencing. This does not necessarily mean apologizing for what went wrong, particularly if you think you may not have done anything wrong.

Example: "Mrs. Smith, I'm very sorry that you've been having a problem with our billing company and I'd like to get all the details so we can work out a solution."

4. Ask questions.

Once you have established that you believe there is a problem and you want to help solve it, ask questions to clarify the facts and give you the information necessary to create a solution. Sometimes when people are angry they have a tendency to focus on how they feel about what happened rather than on what actually happened.

Example: Ask open-ended questions like "Tell me about what happened after you picked Johnny up? Or "What type of error do you think the billing company made?" To collect the details. Avoid "yes or no" questions that might prevent them from explaining the situation fully.

5. Paraphrase.

Once you have a grasp of the situation, paraphrase it to see if you correctly understand what the person is saying. To paraphrase, sum up the problem in one or two simple sentences and rephrase it as a question. Avoid using accusational language when you paraphrase.

Example: "So what you saying Mrs. Smith is that you thought Susie passed her test and are disappointed that she has to make up the sparring portion next week?"

6. Fix the problem promptly.

In most cases, as the instructor and school owner you should have the power and tools necessary to fix the problem.

Example: "Mrs. Smith, from today I'll make a special effort to compliment Johnny at least once in every class so he does not feel ignored."

If you cannot fix the problem, let the person know exactly what you can do. *Example:* "Mrs. Smith, I don't know exactly what happened with the billing company, but as soon as we finish talking, I will make a call to the customer service manager to resolve the situation. As soon as I have an answer, I will call you at home."

If you have made a serious error, you may need to do more than resolve the problem. You may need to make a "peace offering", a small gift or token of apology. Your gift should be something of immediate value. A guest pass, gift certificate or a number of free lessons is not as effective as a t-shirt or uniform.

Example: "Mrs. Smith, I'm very sorry you had to miss work to come down here and resolve this. It was obviously my office manager's fault that your check was not forwarded to the billing company. As a token of apology, I would like to give Susie a new gear bag."

7. Follow up.

After you have agreed on a solution, follow up to make sure that the solution was carried out (if someone other than yourself is in charge of resolving the problem) and that the customer is happy with the way things turned out.

Example: "Mrs. Smith, I'm calling to make sure that the billing company contacted you to confirm that they received your check and that your account is up to date. I've spoken to my office manager to be sure that all payments dropped off in the office are sent in the same day."

It is a fact that dissatisfied customers share their experience with friends much more often than satisfied customers do. By actively working to resolve customer dissatisfaction, you not only keep more students longer, you enhance your reputation in the community. When you go out of your way to solve a problem for a customer, the customer's loyalty goes up immeasurably.

After about ten years of teaching, instructor burnout becomes a real danger. The daily demands of teaching combined with the stress of running a business can create career-ending burnout. There are simple everyday things you can do to prevent burnout.

1. Set the right priorities.

Know what you want out of your career as an instructor and identify what you have to do to achieve those goals. Focus on a few priorities. Once you have met those goals, reassess your priorities and set new goals. When setting goals, balance personal priorities such as your family and hobbies with professional goals.

2. Identify your strengths and weaknesses.

Recognize that you cannot do everything well and choose the areas that are most important to you as well as those in which you have the most potential to excel. Then, identify your weaknesses so you know what jobs to delegate. Delegating your weaknesses gives you more energy to focus on excelling at your strengths

3. Develop skill in dealing with people.

Teaching requires constant interaction with people: students, parents, staff and the public. If you are skilled at interacting with people this aspect of teaching is enjoyable. If you have difficulty in social situations, the personal interaction is tiring and you may begin to feel burned out. Develop your "people" skills by joining local business groups like the chamber of commerce or the toastmasters. Attend networking meetings and "practice" meeting people in a low-pressure environment. Read books about dealing with the public then practice what you learn at least once each day. Not everyone is born a "people" person, but everyone can learn to enjoy the social aspect of teaching.

4. Choose the right staff.

In the daily grind of running a school, your staff can be a an asset or a drain on your resources. Hiring the right staff allows you to confidently delegate tasks you find difficult or boring to those who do them well. Micro-managing your staff drains your energies and distracts you from your job. Hire dependable people but always be prepared to admit when a new employee isn't working out.

5. Delegate responsibility.

If you have hired the right staff, it should be easy to delegate authority to instructors and office staff. As your school grows, you can no longer do everything yourself. If you have difficulty delegating, start with routine areas like hiring a cleaning company or someone to do the billing. As you become comfortable with delegation, assign more important tasks like teaching or running the school while you are away. Through delegation, you can free yourself to maintain a fresh outlook on teaching.

6. Get, use and communicate information.

Feeling stagnant or cut off from innovation can lead to burnout. It is essential to continue learning new things: new skills, new ways of teaching, new business strategies. When you are open to learning, you will be excited about teaching and sharing new knowledge with your students.

7. Motivate yourself and others.

Motivation does not just happen. Many instructors spend a great deal of effort to motivate their students, but they forget to motivate themselves. You can stay motivated by setting goals and rewarding yourself when you reach them. Take a proactive approach to motivation.

8. Plan and involve others in planning.

When you plan classes in advance, you are more excited about teaching, because you are fully prepared. Creating lesson plans forces you to think about classes in advance, to organize curriculum and to keep classes varied. Looking at your class plan on paper, you can readily spot problems with repetition, inconsistent curriculum and time management. Involve your assistant instructors in planning and insist that they turn in lesson plans for each class they teach.

9. Maintain a philosophical center.

If you have been teaching for even a short period of time, you probably have a teaching philosophy—an idea or concept that guides your teaching. It may be to help youngsters stay on the right course, to teach women to protect themselves, to produce champions. Whatever your guiding principles, keep them close to your heart and nourish them. They give you the strength to continue on in difficult times.

10. Keep the doors open.

Maintain an open attitude about life. Keep an open mind about new ideas. Keep the lines of communication open with your students and staff. Never close the door on a student when they quit. Always leave an opening for them to return to class. By keeping your mind open, you will not miss opportunities to grow and change.

11. Take risks.

Taking managed risks is essential to owning a business. If you stick to a safe course, you will soon find your world has narrowed and you are getting bored with running your school. Taking risks can include doing a little extra for a student who may not reap the benefits of your efforts, accepting a child who needs a great deal of attention, trying out new curriculum or teaching methods or developing new ways of doing business.

Not all risks pay off and you must calculate the worst possible outcome of every risk. If you cannot tolerate the worst possible outcome, that risk is not for you.

12. Make decisions.

A significant cause of burnout is indecisiveness. If you are faced with a choice, but cannot decide which course to take, that indecision nags at you. Until you make a decision, you feel restless and anxious. Some people avoid making important decisions because they are afraid to make the wrong choice and suffer the consequences. By not making a decision, they feel that they can put off the problem indefinitely. In reality, the problem grows larger and more intimidating and they find themselves no closer to a resolution, but still controlled by the situation. Avoiding decisions takes far more energy than making them.

Limited Training Time

Teaching as a full time job

See also . . .
Preventing Burnout . . . . page 280

One of the most difficult parts of the transition from student to instructor is the sudden reduction in time available for training. Many students imagine that instructors have all day to train because they teach only in the evening. The reality is that many instructors teach in the evening and work a regular job during the day. Full time instructors teach in the evening and use the daytime hours to keep up with the school business and their personal lives. Either way, most instructors cannot find as much time as they would like to maintain their training. Unfortunately, this often leads to a decrease in their conditioning, leaving them vulnerable to injury. When time for training is scarce, try these strategies to maintain your conditioning and prevent common injuries:

1. Avoid giving impromptu demonstrations in class if you have not fully warmed up.

Many nights you will be tempted to show the class a difficult or strenuous technique without warming up, especially if one of your assistants warmed up the class. Often, you feel fine during the demonstration only to find your back, legs, hips or shoulders ache the next day. If you plan to demonstrate a skill in class, be prepared. If you are not prepared, ask a senior ranking student or assistant instructor to show it instead.

2. Schedule regular training sessions.

Whether you practice alone, with one of your black belts or as part of instructor training, schedule your own personal

"Full time instructors may be more vulnerable to injury."

283

class just like you do for your students. The best time for this is probably after you finish teaching, since you are already in the training mindset. This training time gives you the chance to work out problems that occurred in class or develop new skills to teach. You don't need to spend a lot of time—thirty minutes four times a week is plenty if you do it regularly.

3. Crosstrain.

To avoid burnout, use other physical activities to maintain your general fitness level. Any sport or pastime you enjoy is suitable especially sports like running, swimming, weight training, tennis, racquetball, and aerobics. If you are getting all of your physical workouts from martial arts, you may find yourself burning out sooner than expected.

4. Keep your art in perspective.

As an instructor, you can no longer hope to be an Olympic class athlete. You have made a commitment to your students to devote your time and energies to teaching, not your personal training. If you want to be an Olympian, stick to training and put off your teaching career a few years. If you want to teach, accept the fact that your personal training might suffer a bit. Once you get over your "student mind" and move into your "instructor mind," balancing training and teaching is easier.

Controlling Nervousness

Successful public speaking

Public speaking is an important part of teaching. Whether explaining a new skill in class, giving a demonstration at the mall or making a speech at an elementary school, an instructor is called upon daily to speak in front of groups. Feeling comfortable in these situations makes your job easier and leads to success in your community.

One of the largest barriers to successful public speaking is overcoming the nervousness we feel when faced with presenting ideas to a crowd. There are several common ways nervousness can impede your performance:

Nervous Energy

Some people's nervousness manifests itself as an irresistible urge to keep moving. Whether it's pacing or making excessive hand gestures, this habit is distracting to the audience. A solution is to physically anchor yourself. To cure pacing, practice leaning lightly against a podium or desk when speaking. If hand gestures are a problem, try holding a notebook or target in your hands while speaking.

Drawing a Blank

Some people draw an absolute blank when faced with a crowd. The simplest solution is to bring notes for your presentation. Small note cards or an outline on the back of a business card can control the sense of helplessness that sometimes occurs in front of a crowd. If appropriate, make an outline on an easel for the crowd to follow along or pass out handouts as a guide. If you really draw a blank in the middle of your presentation, stop to take questions, break into discussion groups, take a water break or give students time to practice until you relax and reorient yourself. Whatever you do, don't panic.

Butterflies

Butterflies in the stomach, excessive sweating, dry mouth, the need to go to the bathroom frequently and other physical unpleasantness are all common side effects of nervousness. While these are more difficult to control, and sometimes involuntary, you can take positive steps toward managing your responses. When you feel a physical symptom coming on, practice a relaxation technique like deep breathing, meditation, stretching, sipping some water or exercising lightly.

General Speaking Tips

1. Practice visualization: visualize the key points of your presentation.

2. Familiarize yourself with the environment ahead of time. Practice in the presentation environment if possible.

3. Know the audience (age, gender, level of education, etc.)

4. Interact with the audience before speaking by shaking hands, passing out handouts or chatting.

5. Breathe deeply or meditate just before beginning.

6. Anchor yourself mentally and physically with the use of props, notes, charts or handouts.

7. Make eye contact with the audience.

8. Use natural gestures and a relaxed but confident posture.

9. Be in touch with the audience and adjust what you prepared to meet the needs of situation.

10. Speak slower and louder than normal so the back of the room can hear you.

11. Use notes as a guide, but don't read your presentation verbatim.

12. Be positive no matter what happens.

As an instructor, you almost certainly require students to evaluate their skills through promotion testing or competition, but how often do you evaluate your teaching skills? Do you have a consistent method of checking your progress as an instructor?

As you read each question, record your thoughts in writing. Note what areas you are doing well in and what areas need improvement. Then make an action plan to start improving today. Repeat the written evaluation every three months. Next time you review the questions, look for improvements you have made based on the steps of your action plan as well as areas where you may be falling behind.

1. What is the current skill level of my students compared to accepted standards?

This question requires you to step back and look critically at your students' skills versus other students at their level. Your comparison can be students you have observed at competitions, your instructor's students or a curriculum video. Ask yourself how your students measure up to the standards for each belt rank. Can the majority perform all of the required techniques for their rank? Can many of them perform at a better than average level? Do you have a system in place to assist lagging students?

If you find that your students are much better than other students at the same rank, you may be waiting too long to promote them. If they are below average, you may be promoting too fast or neglecting basic skills.

2. What areas do students need to improve?

This is a tough question, because often the areas your students are weak in are the areas you are weak in as well. Your answer to Question One should have given you a good idea of overall strengths and weaknesses. If your students are weak at advanced self-defense because you never learned advanced techniques from your instructor, attend a seminar or purchase some videotapes to fill in the holes in your curriculum. It's never too late to enhance your curriculum and you will see a boost in student retention.

3. Do I assess my students' performance regularly against consistent standards?

Keep a log for each student that includes his or her training records, promotions, serious injuries or absences, awards, competition records and notes on his or her performance. Create a simple fill-in-the-blanks log sheet for each student and collect them in a three ring binder. Or use a computer note card or database program to keep your notes electronically. Each day, take a few minutes to record notes about any student that stands out in your mind: injuries, setbacks, accomplishments and potential problems. After each promotion test, make a more detailed entry noting improvements and goals for the next rank. By reading over your student log, you may find trends in your school that you would not have otherwise recognized: a rash of injuries, overall improvement in performance, or a deficiency in certain skills.

4. Do I reinforce effective practice habits?

Giving students time to practice skills and teaching them how to practice correctly is as important as teaching new skills. Do your students understand the importance of practicing both new and basic skills? Do you give practice time in class to monitor the way they practice? Always reinforce the adage "Perfect Practice makes Perfect Performance."

5. Do I allow for individual differences within the curriculum structure?

While every instructor should have standards at each rank and a structured curriculum to teach from, it is important to allow for individual deviation. Some students are unable to meet a particular requirement due to limitations they have no power over. In this case, are you flexible enough to require the student to do his best while still allowing him to progress in rank? Develop a consistent policy regarding exceptions to the curriculum.

6. Do students have clear short and long-term goals?

Everyone should know what skills are required for advancement to the next rank. They should also know what long-term skills to work on for their level. Some skills take many months or even years to develop and students should be aware of the timeline for these complex skills is. Ambiguous goals result in frustration. Students may expect too much from themselves and give up too soon. If you find a large number of students dropping out at blue belt for example, you may be introducing long-term skills at that level, but not clearly identifying them as long-term goals. New blue belt students become intimidated by their perceived expectations and quit.

7. Is the class atmosphere more competitive or cooperative?

Every class tends toward a cooperative atmosphere in which people work in teams to help each other learn or a competitive atmosphere in which students see others as friendly (or not so friendly) rivals who drive each other to improve. Both atmospheres can work under the guidance of a skilled instructor, however a balance of the two works best for most schools. Cooperative atmospheres develop students who value the social or recreational aspect of training. Competitive atmospheres work best for younger students interested in advanced skill development and tournament competition.

How you choose to develop your class structure, standards or curriculum is not as important as the objectives you set. If the strategies you choose for running your school are bringing you closer to your objectives, you are on the right track. If you have not yet developed objectives, use the questions above to get started today.

Building Leadership

The Future of Your School

In this section . . .

291 Building Leadership
293 Staffing
298 Selecting Instructors
302 Outreach Programs
309 Branch Schools

Staff Rewards

Money isn't the only thing that staff members are looking for. Non-monetary job rewards include:

1. Recognition
2. Increased responsibility
3. Supervisory duties
4. Promotion
5. Positive atmosphere
6. Advanced training
7. Flexible work hours

Building Leadership

The future of your school

See also . . .
Staffing . . . . page 293
Outreach Programs . . . . page 302

Today's students are tomorrow's instructors and assistant instructors. Unless you take the time now to select and develop the leaders in your school, you will not have quality instructors two or three years from now. Identifying and building strong leaders should be one of the primary long term goals of your teaching. To promote leadership in the classroom, look for ways to implement the following strategies:

Recognize the different qualities of leadership present in different personalities.

Some people are good at group leadership while others excel at one-on-one development. Some students possess good demonstration skills while others are better at explaining new ideas. Identify strengths and weaknesses in potential leaders to build a varied group of future instructors.

Provide opportunities for leadership early and often.

Start with simple leadership skills like helping out new students with specific skills or holding a target for group practice. Progress to self-directed skills like leading warm-ups and assisting lower belts with new skills. Help the student progress slowly and provide plenty of feedback.

Give your classroom leaders a clear understanding of their role.

Their function is not to replace you, but to assist you in fulfilling your role as an instructor. Encourage assistant instructors and leadership team members to develop their own personal strengths, abilities and communication style rather than simply imitating other instructors.

Never expect more from your assistants than they are able to give.

Placing burdensome expectations on your assistants causes frustration and disappointment for both of you. Select leaders whose personalities match the task you need completed.

Create incentives and rewards for students who take on leadership roles.

Leaders often give up the camaraderie of fellow students when they step into a position of responsibility. Provide them with special privileges or rewards to encourage their continued enthusiasm.

Sometimes willingness is more important than talent.

Some less talented students are very willing to help out whenever they can. Give them a small role and look for their strong points. Everyone can contribute in some way. It's up to you to discover how.

Staff Retention

The top five reasons staff members quit:

1. Feeling unappreciated.
Feedback and recognition are the two best methods for making hard working employees feel appreciated.

2. Poor compensation.
Poor can mean too little, unequal or stagnant.

3. Lack of training or tools.
Employees need the right knowledge and equipment to do their jobs confidently.

4. Lack of opportunity for advancement.
No one wants to do the same job forever.

5. Unmatched skill set.
If the employee is a poor match for the job, both he and the school suffer.

Staffing

Hiring the right people

See also...
Selecting Instructors . . . . page 298
Branch Schools . . . . page 309

Most new school owners start out running their school and teaching entirely by themselves. More often than not, this is out of necessity. Without a large group of students, new school owners cannot afford to hire staff and may not have experienced students to draw on for assistants.

As the school grows, it is increasingly difficult for one person to manage the day-to-day chores of the business in addition to teaching. Before you start to feel overwhelmed by the business side of the school or find yourself putting off chores because you are too tired, recruit staff members to help you out.

Why Hire?

The first question to consider before hiring someone to help you out is "What jobs can I turn over to someone else?" There are three reasons to turn over duties to a staff member:

1) The staff member can do a better job than you because they have special knowledge or training.

2) A staff member can be trained to do the job because it does not require specialized knowledge.

3) You no longer have time for this job because you are busy with more important/urgent work and you can train someone to do it as well as you do.

Once have determined why you need to hire someone, begin looking for suitable candidates. Obviously, if you are looking for someone to take over a duty you are not good at (maybe sales, accounting or marketing) you need to hire someone with previous experience. If you are looking for someone to do a more trainable job like telephone answering, record keeping or cleaning up, search for a reliable person who learns quickly.

Staff Positions

There are a wide variety of jobs in a school. As your school grows, you can increasingly delegate areas of work that you were able to do yourself when you started out. The primary job you will always have, even after hiring staff members is that of head instructor. The head instructor is the captain of the ship, the quarterback. It is not a job you can easily turn over to an employee without losing the direction and overall mission of your school.

Head Instructor

The head instructor is responsible for:

- designing and implementing the curriculum

- scheduling and conducting promotions

- overseeing seminars, tournaments and other events

- training staff and instructors

- running the teaching side of the business

Since the head instructor is also the business owner, he or she normally has the final say in major decisions like renting space, hiring/firing employees, overseeing the finances and setting tuition rates. Many of these tasks may be undertaken with the consultation of the office manager if he or she is familiar with the day-to-day finances of the school.

Office Manager

The next major staff position is that of office manager. The office manager is responsible for:

- handling the clerical operation of the school

- tuition billing and collection

- scheduling classes

- answering the telephone

- greeting visitors

- providing information to interested visitors

- ordering supplies

- maintaining the school

In a large school, some of the office manager's duties may be taken over by the program director or delegated to a staff member in charge of the reception desk.

Program or Marketing Director

Unless your school is very large (over 200 students), the duties of the program or marketing director may be handled by the head instructor or office manager. A marketing director is in charge of:

- developing advertising and special offers

- placing ads

- tracking ad results

- developing community relations programs (seminars, speeches, demonstrations, etc.)

- promoting products and in-school programs to students

- designing brochures, stationery, logos, in-school newsletters and other branding tools

- managing public relations

This position requires prior professional experience. If you cannot afford to hire a professional, many advertising agencies will create template ads and other materials to adapt and use on an ongoing basis. Martial arts marketing associations also offer "canned" ads and advertising materials, however you run the risk of having the exact same ad as your competitor down the street if he or she belongs to the same association. This can be confusing for potential students, not to mention embarrassing for your school image.

If you cannot afford any outside help at all in this area, the last option is to find advertisements that you like and collect them in an idea file. When you run a newspaper ad, show the newspaper sales rep what type of ideas you like and provide them with some suitable photos. They are usually happy to make up an ad to your specifications.

Instructors

If you have more than three classes a day, it is helpful to have assistant instructors help teach classes. When you start out you may not have any black belts who are qualified to teach. If this is the case, select a few dedicated students and teach them how to warm-up the class as well as how to lead class if you need to step out for a few moments.

As they approach black belt, begin a more formal instructor training program that meets at least once a week to develop assistant instructors capable of teaching classes, giving private lessons or intro lessons and taking over for you when you are away. Ongoing training is essential for developing qualified instructors. This task must be done by the head instructor so all instructors in the school are teaching a consistent curriculum.

Fitness Instructor

If your school offers aerobics, cardio kickboxing, weights, yoga or other exercise programs, you need one or more staff members who specialize in these programs. The only way to grow fitness programs is to have a specialist leading them and devoting their full time energy to keeping the fitness students happy. By adding a fitness instructor, you can also offer one-on-one consultations to students who want to supplement their training, to parents/family members who want to get in shape and to competitors who need specialized conditioning routines.

As the school grows, expect to hire about one full time staff member (or a combination of part time staff members) per fifty students/members. And plan for attrition because at least one in ten staff members will not work out. Whether they quit or you let them go, an open position is a strain on the daily operation of the school. Having a strong leadership team from which you can readily draw additional staff members is a necessity.

Communication

With a staff of three or more, communication becomes increasingly important. As the head instructor and business owner, one of your central responsibilities is to facilitate communication. A few steps you can take to keep everyone informed and on the same page:

1. **Put it in writing.** Document everything that is expected of staff including curriculum, enrollment and tuition policies, employee benefits, job descriptions and office procedures from answering the telephone to handling an emergency.

2. **Use meetings effectively.** Know what you want out of a meeting and invite only the necessary staff members. One weekly staffwide meeting is plenty of time to communicate general information. More frequent small group meetings or one-on-one discussions are more effective for discussing specific action plans. At the staffwide meeting, you

might brainstorm ideas for developing a new introductory program, soliciting information from the instructors, program director and office manager. But implementing an idea is best done in a focused setting, for example, an instructor's meeting to discuss the introductory curriculum, a front office meeting to discuss how the program will be presented to prospects and a one-on-one meeting with the marketing director to review ads. By holding focused meetings, more gets done in less time.

3. **Practice.** When sharing new information with staff members, ask them to practice implementing what you have taught them so you can check the accuracy of your communication and their understanding. By using role-playing or watching a few run-throughs of a task, you reinforce new information and give staff members a chance to ask questions or detect unforeseen problems.

4. **Document.** Keeping accurate documentation allows staff members to access necessary records and cuts down needless exchanges and interruptions in the daily workflow. Documentation like sales reports, student records, marketing campaigns, daily receipts and sales goals also give you permanent record of the school's progress as the months and years pass. Whether the marketing director is looking for a one-week snapshot of income or the office manager needs an annual comparison of expenses to budget, they should be able to find it in minutes if you have a consistent system of documentation in place.

Communication

Effective communication is specific and fact-based:

Ineffective: Return all calls promptly

Effective: Return all calls within one hour of arriving at the office.

◆

Ineffective: Dress neatly.

Effective: Wear your school logo polo shirt with khakis or jogging suit pants.

◆

Ineffective: Be polite to visitors.

Effective: Greet every visitor with "Welcome to Smith's Martial Arts. How can I help you?"

Selecting Instructors

Your most important staff members

See also . . .
Building Leadership . . . . page 291
Staffing . . . . page 293

One of the most difficult tasks an instructor of a growing school faces is providing enough quality instruction time to each student on a daily basis. Once a school grows beyond fifty or so students, you have to begin turning over some teaching duties to a group of capable and enthusiastic assistants.

Finding the right combination of skill and willingness can be daunting. Often, skilled students are more interested in their own practice than in teaching others. You can require them to assist, but they may do more harm than good if their heart isn't in it. On the other hand, what about students who are more than willing to help out, but are lacking in technical skills? Can you trust their helpfulness to make up for their lack of knowledge?

How can you tell in advance if a student will make a good assistant? What qualities are necessary beyond sound technical knowledge and a willingness to help others?

Evaluation Scale for Instructors

A good strategy is to evaluate each candidate with a simple scoring system. Rate each candidate on a scale of 1-10 (10 is perfect, 8 is above average, 5 is average and 3 or lower is unacceptable) for each attribute listed below. Strong candidates score 84 or higher. Candidates with good potential, but needing guidance score between 70 and 83. Candidates scoring between 50 and 69 may be enrolled in an instructor-training program, but not allowed to teach just yet. Candidates scoring below 50 should be ruled out.

1. Ability to follow directions

Surprisingly, the most important quality in an assistant instructor is the ability to understand and follow directions with regard to what and how to teach. Assistant instructors in your school are seen by students as an extension of you and must be able to stick to the teaching style and curriculum you have designed and implemented. Students who want to impose their own style on others do not fit well into an assistant instructor program. They are better off teaching in outside programs. This is not to say that assistants must be clones of the head instructor, but they should be able to teach within the curriculum guidelines of the school.

2. Physical fitness and skill level

An assistant instructor is a role model for lower ranks and should have the physical condition and skill level to accurately demonstrate the skills he is teaching.

3. Ability to communicate

Good communication skills allow an assistant to give students useful feedback as well as to interpret what concerns students might have. Many students are too shy or intimidated to ask the question they really have in mind, so good communication skills help assistants draw relationships between what the student says and what he means.

4. Technical knowledge

As with skill level, every assistant should have a solid technical understanding of the movements she is teaching. Bear in mind that doing a movement well and knowing how to perform the movement well are two different things. Assistant instructors should be able to verbalize the key points of a movement and troubleshoot common errors.

5. Organizational skills

Each assistant instructor should be able to organize a practice session or class in a logical and safe manner. Assistants should also be able to keep track of the days and times they are expected to teach and manage their time accordingly.

6. Reliability

Assistant instructors must be reliable enough to show up regularly and give you plenty of notice if they will be absent.

7. Maturity

Regardless of age, assistants should be mature enough to take their teaching responsibility seriously and not abuse their position.

8. Enthusiasm

As a role model, each assistant should project an air of genuine enthusiasm for their teaching as well as their training. Their excitement, or lack of it, is contagious.

9. Discretion

Instructors are often privileged with knowledge or confidences that should not be shared with other students. If a student privately asks an assistant for advice or assistance, he should be able to trust the assistant to keep the matter confidential.

10. Trustworthiness

Assistants are entrusted with the head instructor's authority should not abuse this trust.

Instructor Competence

Once instructor selection is complete, a long supervised training period is required. There are three levels of instructor competence. Instructor training should be geared toward guiding instructors from one level to next over the long term.

1. Mastery of skills

The most fundamental level of teaching is the transmission of skills through conventional procedures. This is the minimum competence level required for teaching and is the main criteria for evaluating beginning instructors. All instructors begin their teaching careers with a focus on skill mastery and transmission but some never move beyond this stage. Instructors at the first level of competence require supervision by a more experienced instructor.

2. Problem Solving

The next stage of instructor competence is the ability to strategically solve both teaching challenges and student deficiencies. In this stage, an instructor begins to move away from conventional teaching methods to develop his own strategies. It is also during this stage, that an instructor's teaching style emerges. While direct supervision is not necessary, a mentor is helpful in solving particularly difficult problems.

3. Interpretation

The highest level of instructor competence is characterized by interpretation, application and innovation of skills. This stage goes beyond problem solving, which is often a reaction to daily challenges, and moves into a proactive approach to curriculum development and teaching methods. Most styles refer to instructors at this level as masters.

Outreach Programs

Serving the community

See also ...
Staffing .... page 293
Branch Schools .... page 309

An outreach program is any program in which you are teaching martial arts in your community. This includes classes held at:

- YMCA/YWCA

- Health club

- Day care

- Summer camp

- College campus

- Town recreation program

- Hospital or long-term care facility

- Corporate offices

- Boys'/Girls'club

The classes might be ongoing or limited in scope, depending on the scheduling policies of the host organization. They might be specialized, such as women's self-defense for rape victims, or the exact same classes you are teaching in your school. Whatever form an outreach program takes, it can be highly beneficial to your school.

The Benefits

1. Full time or part time

Do you have a "day job" that pays well and has great benefits? You don't have to give it up to teach martial arts. Is your town too small to support a commercial school? With an outreach program, you can teach just two or three nights a week.

2. Eliminate overhead

When your classes are hosted by another organization, you eliminate the major expenses that schools face including rent, insurance, advertising and utilities. Most host organizations advertise your classes, collect fees, cover insurance and give you a place to conduct class. Whether you get a set fee per class, per student or per session or an hourly salary, you don't have to worry about making a profit.

3. Low/no maintenance

The host facility bears the responsibility for upkeep and maintenance so you don't have to clean bathrooms and restock paper towels after a night of teaching.

4. Built in clientele

If your host facility is a fitness or educational organization, they already have a broad base of interested clients to advertise classes to. Programs like health clubs, YMCA's and corporate fitness centers allow you to build up a large enrollment very quickly.

5. Time off

Many outreach programs run in sessions, meaning you teach ten weeks then get three weeks off before the next session starts. A rolling schedule prevents burnout and keeps classes fresh.

6. Quality facility

Fitness centers, colleges and many public schools have lockers, showers and other facilities available for students to use. Often these are accommodations you would not be able to afford in your own school.

7. Perks

Teaching in a health club or fitness center often gains you access to the rest of the facilities, including the weight room, cardio equipment and pool for your own training.

8. No staff required

The host facility performs all of the tasks that you or an office manager would normally have to take care of including billing, answering the telephone, enrolling students and answering program-related questions.

9. High traffic, High visibility

Drop-ins and referrals are much higher in an established host facility because there is a great deal of foot traffic on a regular basis.

Getting Started

The first step toward establishing an outreach program is researching your options. Start with students and their parents, if you have them. Someone might know of a facility looking for a martial arts program or open to the idea of starting one. In addition to internal contacts, look at your community. Commercial facilities can be found in the yellow pages, civic organizations through the chamber of commerce and town run programs through the local town hall or recreation department.

When you narrow down your options to two or three potential facilities, contact the program or marketing director of each. This is the person who is in charge of creating new classes or arranging the rental of the facility. Keep your initial contact short and to the point. If the program director expresses an interest, suggest a longer meeting and offer to present a formal proposal either before or at that meeting.

A formal proposal includes:

1. **A statement of intent.** What are you teaching and why? How will it benefit the facility and the community at large? Why are you uniquely qualified to teach the class?

2. **A proposed schedule and class description.** Look at the facility's program guide if they have one and create your class description based on the descriptions in the guide. You may also choose to include a little background information about the art or style you teach.

3. **Your credentials.** A professional resume and a copy of your instructor certification.

4. **Back-up material.** Articles about you/your school and one or two letters of recommendation.

Limit your proposal to no more than ten pages. Gear it to impress but not overwhelm the program director.

Program Structure

Once your proposal is accepted, there are a number of details to be worked out with the host facility before you begin teaching:

1. Schedule

If the facility hosts many fitness classes in a limited number of rooms, you may have to negotiate for a prime spot on the schedule or for a suitable workout area. Don't forget to ask to see the room you are assigned to teach in. It doesn't do you much good to get a prime six o'clock class time in a room that is only big enough for ten students.

2. Equipment

Do you need mats or special flooring? Make the facility aware of this up front. Some rooms are better suited to martial arts training than others.

3. Employment

Are you an employee or an independent contractor? Ask if you have a choice and investigate the benefits and drawbacks of each.

4. Payment

Is payment on an hourly, per student, per class or per term basis? Do you receive payment in full and remit a fee per student? Do you have any costs to bear, such as rent, insurance, co-op advertising or use fees? Calculate how fees impact your income before agreeing to a payment arrangement. A big ticket item like insurance can quickly eat away at your profit.

5. Advertising

How much is done, when and who is responsible for developing class descriptions, photos and special offers?

Negotiating

Starting a new program requires negotiating with landlords, suppliers, program directors and governing boards. By understanding simple negotiation techniques, you can save hundreds or thousands of dollars a year.

1. Ask for ten to twenty percent more than you expect. *Example:* Offer $8.00 per square foot when you expect to pay $10.00.

2. Ask what items are negotiable or what the other party can give you in return for doing business with them.

3. If you have competing offers, mention them.

4. Describe past service issues or problems you've had in the past if applicable.

5. Cite market conditions (i.e. average price per square foot for rental space).

6. Negotiate non-monetary items like payment terms, length of contract, delivery schedule, equipment service and customer service in exchange for paying more. *Example:* Offer to meet the landlord's rent offer if he agrees to supply and service a dumpster and do interior maintenance.

Do students have to be members of the host facility or organization? Is there a fee to be included in fliers, newspaper ads and brochures?

6. Merchandising

Are you allowed to sell uniforms and other merchandise on site?

7. Term

What is the term of your agreement? Some facilities prefer to test out a new program for a ten or twelve week term then renew if enrollment is strong.

8. Expansion

Are there opportunities for you to expand into additional time slots as the classes grow? Can you establish an advanced class with a rank prerequisite?

9. Student Management

Can you decline students who you do not feel are qualified for or beneficial to the program? (*Example:* children with severe discipline problems)

10. Cancellation

Under what terms can you or the host facility cancel the arrangement? How much notice is required? Will you have access to contact information for students if you decide to hold classes elsewhere?

Making it a Success

There are two key elements to success in an outreach program: your relationship with your students and your relationship with the host facility.

The relationship with your students is much like that of any other instructor. The key difference is that you are not always the final authority on matters like billing, advertising or scheduling. It may be necessary from time to time for you to intervene with the staff of the host facility on behalf of a student. If a student is having difficulty with the host facility and brings the problem to your attention, do your best to help them solve it if possible. If a student becomes frustrated by an administrative problem, they might quit instead of going through the hassle of resolving it.

When dealing with outreach program students, you may need to be more flexible than with a traditional school program. Outreach program students tend to be more recreational in their attitudes, often signing up for a course to try something new or to keep a friend company. Use a little bit softer approach for beginner students, with an emphasis on fun and education over rigid discipline. As students become more committed to learning, increase the seriousness of the class demeanor.

Communicating with parents can be a challenge in an outreach program, because you may never see the parent at the facility. To overcome this problem and make parents aware of the benefits of the class, send home a newsletter at least once a month. If a child is having a problem in class, telephone the parent and, if possible, arrange a conference.

Dealing with the host facility is an ongoing challenge. There may be restrictions on the type of equipment you can use, the range of techniques allowed, the amount of noise the class can make and whether uniforms are worn. Be flexible in your requirements and try to work within the structure of the facility while maintaining your standards. And be aware that other programs may infringe on yours. If your class is taught in an open area, traffic,

Staff Conflicts

Staffing conflicts can affect students negatively in unseen ways.

Example: Jill, the receptionist and Joan the office manager are having a conflict over record keeping issues. A student asks Jill whether a tuition payment was received.

Jill pages Joan, who responds that Jill would have that information if she kept better records. Joan says she doesn't have time to look up the information for Jill and Jill is forced to put the student off until a later time.

Staffing conflicts confuse students who expect staff members to work together for the good of the school. Pinpoint and try to resolve interoffice conflicts at the earliest opportunity.

noise and observers can become a distraction. Adapt your teaching style to create a high-energy class that keeps students' attention focused on the lesson, not on the surroundings.

When working with a large organization, communication can be difficult, especially if you are dealing with one person for billing, another for advertising and another for payroll. Try to establish a single point of contact from the beginning. Make friends with your contact person and stay in touch at least weekly. Bring concerns to their attention before they become sore spots. By sharing information and keeping the lines of communication open, you create an atmosphere of trust and respect between yourself and the host facility. Remember, both you and the host facility want the same thing: a successful class filled with happy students.

What the Future Holds

A successful outreach program can lead to programs at other facilities or even to a commercial school. Whether you choose to pursue expansion or stick with your original outreach program, teaching at a host facility can be a fulfilling way to pursue your interest in martial arts.

As a service business, a martial arts school is limited in size by insurmountable factors like time and geography. Although you may be the greatest teacher in your state, you are unlikely to draw students from more than fifteen or twenty miles away. And although you could teach ten hours a day, there are a limited number of prime time slots available. Most parents prefer to bring their children between the close of school and dinner time. Most adults are limited to a couple of hours after work in which to pursue their training.

Once you fill the classes in these prime time slots, it is difficult to expand further. If you accept too many students into each class, lessons become crowded. If you make classes shorter to squeeze in an extra class a day, students no longer feel they are getting their money's worth. You could schedule more classes during the day or later at night, but attendance will not live up to the numbers in prime time classes.

Solutions

There are two solutions for overcoming this plateau in the growth of your school. The most obvious solution is to move to a larger space and hold two or three classes concurrently in different workout areas. This allows you to teach an unlimited number of people at any time, particularly after school and in the evening when most people prefer to attend class. This solution has its own limitation eventually—there are a limited number of potential students in any given geographic area and once you reach them, the school's growth slows significantly.

The second solution to a growth plateau is opening a second location far enough away from your current school to tap a new market.

Pros and Cons

Before deciding to open a second location, consider some of the potential benefits and pitfalls:

Benefits

- **Lower costs, greater profit.** Having two or more schools allows you to take advantage of the economy of scale when purchasing everything from paper towels to advertising.

- **Increased event income.** Tournaments, seminars and promotion tests benefit from a larger student pool.

- **Marketing clout.** When multiple locations pool resources they can buy more and more expensive advertising, including television ads.

- **Higher name recognition.** Multiple schools make an impression and build consumer confidence.

- **Increased enrollment.** Referrals and enrollments go up when people have more geographic options for attending lessons.

- **More options.** Multiple locations mean more staff members, giving you greater flexibility in developing benefits packages and employee retention tools.

Pitfalls

- **Increased responsibility.** A second school does not run itself, even if it has a competent staff and excellent instructors. Double the students means double the problems.

- **Increased risk exposure.** The risk of an injury or accident that endangers the future of the school increases as the student count increases, especially when you delegate to less experienced staff members.

- **Decreased teaching time.** With the addition of a second location, you spend less time teaching and more time doing administrative and management tasks.

- **Danger of spreading staff too thin.** If you do not have an adequate staff in place, you and your staff can quickly burnout trying to run two schools.

- **Possibility of cannibalizing the market.** Depending on how close the two schools are, they may compete for market share.

- **Longer workdays.** Commuting between schools, even if it's just for meetings, can become exhausting.

- **Loss of control.** A second school requires a tremendous amount of delegation. If you are a hands-on person, this is a stressful way to work.

Most of the above pitfalls can be avoided with advance planning and a reliable staff. However, there are times when expansion is definitely not recommended. If your school has been open less than one year, has a small student count, is lacking reliable staff members or has not been profitable for at least eighteen months, do not make plans to open a second location. Your time is better spent improving the core school before expanding.

Determining the Right Size

If you have a profitable, well-run school and ample staff members, an expansion can be beneficial in many ways. The first task in opening a branch school is choosing the right type of school to start with. The most conservative approach is to open a branch in a recreation facility like a health club or gym or to set up a program in a recreation program like the YMCA or Parks and Recreation. If this is your first branch school, a small outreach program with little overhead gives you the chance to build up a student base before you have to rent space and take on the expenses of running a commercial school.

If you are confident in your ability to get a new school going in a relatively short time, you may choose to open a commercial school right from the start by renting space in a shopping center or stand alone building. Whichever option you choose, there are a number of other decisions to consider before opening.

Choosing a Location

When you opened your first school, location was probably a given. Most instructors open in their hometown or a neighboring town they know well. Choosing the town for your second location involves a number of factors to consider.

A branch school should be close enough to the current school so it is convenient for you to travel to. It should also be close enough to take advantage of joint advertising. However, it shouldn't be so close that it competes with the first school.

If you are in a major city, you may be able to open a branch school on the opposite side of the city. If you are in a suburb or a small town, look at least one or two towns away. When considering another town, choose one that is geographically separated from your current school. This may mean having one school "east of the river" and one school "west of the river" or having one school in a suburb north of a major city and a branch school in a suburb south of the city.

Employee Rewards

Employee rewards don't have to be expensive to be motivating. Consider the following under $25 rewards:

1. Thank You note or postcard

2. Recognition in the school newsletter or on the bulletin board

3. Pizza party

4. Movie tickets

5. Gift certificate to the school pro shop

6. An afternoon or evening off with pay

7. Bouquet of balloons, flowers or cookies

8. Lunch for two

9. Favorite movie or DVD

10. Tournament or seminar entry fee

The Teaching Staff

Once you select the location and type of school, consider who will teach. If your current school is at its maximum capacity, it may be impossible for you to teach at the new school. Even if you only taught part time at the new school, you would have to sacrifice some of the classes at the main school.

Ideally, you need one reliable instructor who can take on the bulk of the teaching duties at the new branch or who can relieve you of some of the teaching duties at the main school. You also need assistant instructors who can help out at both schools.

Unfortunately, dividing your time between two schools can have more drawbacks than benefits. For example, if you stop teaching two nights a week at your main school, attendance on those nights may drop off. On the other hand, if you don't teach at least some classes at the new school, you may not be able to get it off the ground.

There are a couple of ways to minimize the impact of changing your teaching schedule. The first is to implement a system of assistant instructors far in advance of the expansion. Gradually implement a system where assistants take on greater portions of the class schedule so that students get used to the idea of someone other than the head instructor teaching every class.

The other option is to train a high-ranking black belt to become the head instructor at the branch school, leaving you free to focus on your main school and perhaps on opening additional branches. If you train your new instructor well, you can invest a minimum amount of time in the new school—giving promotion tests, seminars, higher belt classes—and still maintain the size of your original school.

Maximizing the Benefits

There are a number of ways a branch school can benefit your base school. The most important benefit lies in cost cutting. By combining advertising for the two schools, you reach a larger audience at a lower cost per school.

And by purchasing goods and services for both schools, you can take advantage of discounts on everything from cleaning services to office supplies.

The most significant benefit of adding branch schools is the value of name recognition. With two or more locations, the public perceives you as a successful business and your school's name is readily recognized in your community.

Index

A

accident rate 98
accuracy 62
ADD 79–102
ADHD 83–85, 87–102
advanced skills 132–143, 207
advertising 170, 203, 210, 216, 220, 223–241, 256, 295, 305, 310, 312
aerobics 296
aggression 105–107
agility 47, 51
anger 105, 277–289
applications 35, 66–71
assistant instructors 291–313
atmosphere 76, 200, 289
attendance 231–232
Attention Deficit Disorder 79–102
Attention Deficit/Hyperactivity Disorder 83–85, 87–102
awards 254

B

basic movements 20, 22, 26
behavior contract 110
behavior problems 87–91, 93
black belt 154–164
black belt club 123, 208
boredom 148
branch schools 309
break even point 228
brochures 200, 207, 220, 295
budgeting 233, 253
bulletin board 216
burnout 280–289
business management 158

C

cardio kickboxing 123, 296
change 275
charity 204, 216
children 73–115, 135, 160–164
class discussions 40
class structure 126–128, 239, 289
classified ad 207

coach 243, 269
communication 198–199, 278–289, 296–299, 307–308
competition 11, 160, 211
competition team 208
competition training 123
competitors 243, 269
complex movements 274
complex skills 79, 119, 132–135
conditioning 13, 13–42, 45–71, 132
confidence 52, 162
contact 54, 60–64, 107, 152
cool down 128
coordination 104, 116, 118
coupon books 225
credentials 304
credibility 168
credit cards 209
Criterion Referenced Grading 141
criticism 93
crosstraining 284
crying 108–115
curriculum 146, 157, 287–288, 294–296
customer service 203

D

decisions 282
dehydration 65
delegation 281
demonstration 204–205, 221, 235, 2 255, 283
demonstration team 123, 208
design 201
developmental stages 116–119
discipline 147, 162
discount 208, 215, 240
discretion 300
distance 51
documentation 297
doorknob hangers 214, 225
drawing 206
dress code 215
drills 11–42

E

electronic fund transfers 209
email newsletter 198
endurance 46, 48, 62
entry package 268
environment 76
equipment 305
evaluation 143
event announcements 172, 177, 180–
        181, 186
expenses 228–232, 235–241, 303, 310

F

family 77
FAQ 198
fear 59–61
feature story 172, 182, 187
feedback 88, 90, 93, 101, 143
financing 209
fitness instructor 296
flexibility 45–46
flyers 225
form
forms 34, 66–69

G

games 11–42, 98–102, 117
gift certificates 208
giving instructions
        73, 76, 80, 88, 92, 100, 102
goals 114, 130, 232, 288
grappling 24
gross motor skills 116

H

handout 212
head instructor 294
heat exhaustion 64
heavy bag drills 27
Human interest stories 172, 182–184, 193
hyperactivity 81–85

I

image 200–201, 203
incentives 221–222, 255, 292
incidental learning 125
independent contractor 305
information package 209, 216
injury prevention 53–71, 148–151
insight 75
instructor assessment 287
instructor training 123, 155
insurance 255
intensity 123, 126–143
intentional learning 125
internet 171, 197–201
interschool tournament 247, 253
interval training 48–49
interviews 172, 182, 190
intraschool tournament 248, 253

J

judging 243

K

kick-a-thon 204

L

leadership 291–300
leadership team 208
learning 74–78
learning disability 102–104
learning problem 102
line drills 18
location 219, 311
logo 201

M

magazines 170, 177, 187, 188, 206
maintenance 303
market development 217
market penetration 217
market share 217, 310
marketing 203–241, 217, 235, 310
marketing director 295
marketing strategy 238

medals 254
medical personnel 255, 260
meetings 296
memberships 214
mental health 138
merchandising 199, 203, 213, 306, 235
mini-classes 128
modality-related disorders 104
money back guarantee 209
motivation 130, 132, 135, 154, 273, 281

N

national tournament 250
negative consequences 96, 101, 106
negative reinforcement 94
negotiation 305
nervousness 285–289
newsletter 207, 212
newspaper 170, 178, 180–185, 225
newspaper column 206
niche 205
non-compliant children 91
Norm Referenced Grading 141

O

objectives 125
Observational Learning 129–130
obstacle course 14
office manager 294–295
officials 243, 259, 269
open classes 123–124
open tournament 249, 253
outreach program 168, 302–313
overcorrection 95
overtraining 56–71
overuse injuries 56–71

P

panic disorder 109
paraphrase 278
parents 77, 108–115, 160–164, 204, 212–213, 307
payment schedule 149, 208, 209
performance assessment 140
personality conflict 146–147
physical punishment 105
planning 274, 281

policy change 146
positive language 89
positive reinforcement 92
post event report 172, 180, 186–187
power 62
practice 288
praise 93, 101, 106, 117
press release 173–179, 205
price 220
priorities 280
private lessons 216
product development 218
product display 204
product diversification 218
products 205
program director 295
promotion 197, 203, 220, 223
promotion testing 142, 215
public relations 235, 295
public speaking 285–289
publicity 167–173, 186, 203, 221, 226, 259
punishment 92, 96

Q

query letter 188–189

R

races 14
radio 171, 190, 208, 225
rank 122
referrals 199, 204, 206, 208
reflexes 50
registration 245, 255, 258, 269
Reinforcement 92
reinforcement 74, 95, 130
relaxation 52, 113
release form 177
reprints 186
respect 136
retention 129, 145, 151, 154, 156, 293
review 134
rewards 88, 93, 94, 117, 132, 291, 292, 312
risk 282, 310
Ritalin 86
rituals 109

role models 133
role-playing 99, 114, 116
rolling falls 30
rules 118

S

safety 11, 54, 152, 212, 214
safety gear 152
sample 90
schedule 121–143, 294, 304–305
school rules 214, 275
search engine 197
self-defense 31–33, 50–52
self-defense seminar 205
self-discipline 97, 137
self-evaluation 140
self-expression 137
seminars 208, 221, 235, 295
separation anxiety 108–112
sexual harassment policy 152
shadow sparring 36
shaping 130
short attention span 79–80, 98–101
shyness 113–115
simulated performance 140
site rental 254
slogan 201
social anxiety 113
social environment 158
sparring 36–42, 59–63, 66–68, 274
speed 48–52
staff 232, 238, 240, 245, 261, 281, 291–313
stance 22
standards 287
statement of intent 304
strategic planning 238
strength 46
stretching 19
student log 288
student objectives 125
student questionnaire 211, 276
suggestion box 211
summer training 64–65
synchronization 51

T

target drills 23, 26, 28, 29
teaching new skills 129–131
teaching opportunities 155
teaching philosophy 282
telephone 194, 213, 216
television 177, 191–193, 208, 212, 225
testimonials 205
testing 140, 142–143, 160
testing requirements 142, 152
time-out 95
timeline 262
timing 50–52
tournaments 243–271
tournament committee 258–271
tournament director 261, 268
trial lesson 206, 220–221
trophies 254
tuition billing 294
tuition rates 228

V

video tapes 21, 133–35
visualization 39, 114

W

waiting room 161, 204
warm-up 13, 45, 54, 128
weapons 69–71, 123
website 197–201
weigh-in 245
White House Conference on Education 136
women 151–153
work sample testing 140

Y

yoga 123, 296

Also Available from Turtle Press:

Fighting Science
Guide to Martial Arts Injury Care and Prevention
Solo Training
Fighter's Fact Book
Conceptual Self-defense
Martial Arts After 40
Warrior Speed
The Martial Arts Training Diary
The Martial Arts Training Diary for Kids
Teaching Martial Arts
Combat Strategy
The Art of Harmony
A Guide to Rape Awareness and Prevention
Total MindBody Training
1,001 Ways to Motivate Yourself and Others
Ultimate Fitness through Martial Arts
Weight Training for Martial Artists
A Part of the Ribbon: A Time Travel Adventure
Herding the Ox
Neng Da: Super Punches
Taekwondo Kyorugi: Olympic Style Sparring
Martial Arts for Women
Parents' Guide to Martial Arts
Strike Like Lightning: Meditations on Nature
Everyday Warriors

For more information:
Turtle Press
PO Box 290206
Wethersfield CT 06129-0206
1-800-778-8785
e-mail: sales@turtlepress.com

http://www.turtlepress.com